MISS JULIE AND OTHER PLAYS

BY AUGUST STRINDBERG

TRANSLATED BY
EDITH AND WARNER OLAND
AND EDWIN BJÖRKMAN

A Digireads.com Book
Digireads.com Publishing

Miss Julie and Other Plays
By August Strindberg
Translated by Edith and Warner Oland and Edwin Björkman
ISBN: 1-4209-3844-4

Please visit *www.digireads.com*

CONTENTS

THE FATHER

CHARACTERS

A CAPTAIN OF CAVALRY
LAURA, his wife
BERTHA, their daughter
DOCTOR ÖSTERMARK
THE PASTOR
THE NURSE
NÖJD
AN ORDERLY

ACT I.

[*The sitting room at the Captain's. There is a door a little to the right at the back. In the middle of the room, a large, round table strewn with newspapers and magazines. To right a leather-covered sofa and table. In the right-hand corner a private door. At left there is a door leading to the inner room and a desk with a clock on it. Gamebags, guns and other arms hang on the walls. Army coats hang near door at back. On the large table stands a lighted lamp.*]

CAPTAIN [*rings, an orderly comes in.*]
ORDERLY. Yes, Captain.
CAPTAIN. Is Nöjd out there?
ORDERLY. He is waiting for orders in the kitchen.
CAPTAIN. In the kitchen again, is he? Send him in at once.
ORDERLY. Yes, Captain. [*Goes.*]
PASTOR. What's the matter now?
CAPTAIN. Oh the rascal has been cutting up with the servant-girl again; he's certainly a bad lot.
PASTOR. Why, Nöjd got into the same trouble year before last, didn't he?
CAPTAIN. Yes, you remember? Won't you be good enough to give him a friendly talking to and perhaps you can make some impression on him. I've sworn at him and flogged him, too, but it hasn't had the least effect.
PASTOR. And so you want me to preach to him? What effect do you suppose the word of God will have on a rough trooper?
CAPTAIN. Well, it certainly has no effect on me.
PASTOR. I know that well enough.
CAPTAIN. Try it on *him*, anyway.

[*Nöjd comes in.*]

CAPTAIN. What have you been up to now, Nöjd?
NÖJD. God save you, Captain, but I couldn't talk about it with the Pastor here.
PASTOR. Don't be afraid of me, my boy.

CAPTAIN. You had better confess or you know what will happen.

NÖJD. Well, you see it was like this; we were at a dance at Gabriel's, and then—then Ludwig said—

CAPTAIN. What has Ludwig got to do with it? Stick to the truth.

NÖJD. Yes, and Emma said "Let's go into the barn—"

CAPTAIN.—Oh, so it was Emma who led you astray, was it?

NÖJD. Well, not far from it. You know that unless the girl is willing nothing ever happens.

CAPTAIN. Never mind all that: Are you the father of the child or not?

NÖJD. Who knows?

CAPTAIN. What's that? Don't you know?

NÖJD. Why no—that is, you can never be sure.

CAPTAIN. Weren't you the only one?

NÖJD. Yes, that time, but you can't be sure for all that.

CAPTAIN. Are you trying to put the blame on Ludwig? Is that what you are up to?

NÖJD. Well, you see it isn't easy to know who is to blame.

CAPTAIN. Yes, but you told Emma you would marry her.

NÖJD. Oh, a fellow's always got to say that—

CAPTAIN [to Pastor.] This is terrible, isn't it?

PASTOR. It's the old story over again. See here, Nöjd, you surely ought to know whether you are the father or not?

NÖJD. Well, of course I was mixed up with the girl—but you know yourself, Pastor, that it needn't amount to anything for all that.

PASTOR. Look here, my lad, we are talking about you now. Surely you won't leave the girl alone with the child. I suppose we can't compel you to marry her, but you should provide for the child—that you shall do!

NÖJD. Well, then, so must Ludwig, too.

CAPTAIN. Then the case must go to the courts. I cannot ferret out the truth of all this, nor is it to my liking. So now be off.

PASTOR. One moment, Nöjd. H'm—don't you think it dishonorable to leave a girl destitute like that with her child? Don't you think so? Don't you see that such conduct— — —h'm— —h'm— — —

NÖJD. Yes, if I only knew for sure that I was father of the child, but you can't be sure of that, Pastor, and I don't see much fun slaving all your life for another man's child. Surely you, Pastor, and the Captain can understand for yourselves.

CAPTAIN. Be off.

NÖJD. God save you, Captain.

[*Goes.*]

CAPTAIN. But keep out of the kitchen, you rascal! [*To Pastor.*] Now, why didn't you get after him?

PASTOR. What do you mean?

CAPTAIN. Why, you only sat and mumbled something or other.

PASTOR. To tell the truth I really don't know what to say. It is a pity about the girl, yes, and a pity about the lad, too. For think if he were not the father. The girl can nurse the child for four months at the orphanage, and then it will be permanently provided for, but it will be different for him. The girl can get a good place afterwards in some respectable family, but the lad's future may be ruined if he is dismissed from the regiment.

CAPTAIN. Upon my soul I should like to be in the magistrate's shoes and judge this case. The lad is probably not innocent, one can't be sure, but we do know that the girl is guilty, if there is any guilt in the matter.

PASTOR. Well, well, I judge no one. But what were we talking about when this stupid business interrupted us? It was about Bertha and her confirmation, wasn't it?

CAPTAIN. Yes, but it was certainly not in particular about her confirmation but about her whole welfare. This house is full of women who all want to have their say about my child. My mother-in-law wants to make a Spiritualist of her. Laura wants her to be an artist; the governess wants her to be a Methodist, old Margret a Baptist, and the servant-girls want her to join the Salvation Army! It won't do to try to make a soul in patches like that. I, who have the chief right to try to form her character, am constantly opposed in my efforts. And that's why I have decided to send her away from home.

PASTOR. You have too many women trying to run this house.

CAPTAIN. You're right! It's like going into a cage full of tigers, and if I didn't hold a red-hot iron under their noses they would tear me to pieces any moment. And you laugh, you rascal! Wasn't it enough that I married your sister, without your palming off your old stepmother on me?

PASTOR. But, good heavens, one can't have stepmothers in one's own house!

CAPTAIN. No, you think it is better to have mothers-in-law in some one else's house!

PASTOR. Oh well, we all have some burden in life.

CAPTAIN. But mine is certainly too heavy. I have my old nurse into the bargain, who treats me as if I ought still to wear a bib. She is a good old soul, to be sure, and she must not be dragged into such talk.

PASTOR. You must keep a tight rein on the women folks. You let them run things too much.

CAPTAIN. Now will you please inform me how I'm to keep order among the women folk?

PASTOR. Laura was brought up with a firm hand, but although she is my own sister, I must admit she *was* pretty troublesome.

CAPTAIN. Laura certainly has her faults, but with her it isn't so serious.

PASTOR. Oh, speak out—I know her.

CAPTAIN. She was brought up with romantic ideas, and it has been hard for her to find herself, but she is my wife—

PASTOR And because she is your wife she is the best of wives? No, my dear fellow, it is she who really wears on you most.

CAPTAIN. Well, anyway, the whole house is topsy-turvy. Laura won't let Bertha leave her, and I can't allow her to remain in this bedlam.

PASTOR. Oh, so Laura won't? Well, then, I'm afraid you are in for trouble. When she was a child if she set her mind on anything she used to play dead dog till she got it, and then likely as not she would give it back, explaining that it wasn't the thing she wanted, but having her own way.

CAPTAIN. So she was like that even then? H'm—she really gets into such a passion sometimes that I am anxious about her and afraid she is ill.

PASTOR. But what do you want to do with Bertha that is so unpardonable? Can't you compromise?

CAPTAIN. You mustn't think I want to make a prodigy of her or an image of myself. I don't want to be it procurer for my daughter and educate her exclusively for matrimony, for then if she were left unmarried she might have bitter days. On the other hand, I don't want to influence her toward a career that requires a long course of training which would be entirely thrown away if she should marry.

PASTOR. What do you want, then?

CAPTAIN. I want her to be it teacher. If she remains unmarried she will be able to support herself, and at any rate she wouldn't be any worse off than the poor schoolmasters who have to share their salaries with a family. If she marries she can use her knowledge in the education of her children. Am I right?

PASTOR. Quite right. But, on the other hand, hasn't she shown such talent for painting that it would be a great pity to crush it?

CAPTAIN. No! I have shown her sketches to an eminent painter, and he says they are only the kind of thing that can be learned at schools. But then a young fop came here in the summer who, of course, understands the matter much better, and he declared that she had colossal genius, and so that settled it to Laura's satisfaction.

PASTOR. Was he quite taken with Bertha?

CAPTAIN. That goes without saying.

PASTOR. Then God help you, old man, for in that case I see no hope. This is pretty bad—and, of course, Laura has her supporters—in there?

CAPTAIN. Yes, you may be sure of that; the whole house is already up in arms, and, between ourselves, it is not exactly a noble conflict that is being waged from that quarter.

PASTOR. Don't you think I know that?

CAPTAIN. You do?

PASTOR. I do.

CAPTAIN. But the worst of it is, it strikes me that Bertha's future is being decided from spiteful motives. They hint that men better be careful, because women can do this or that now-a-days. All day long, incessantly, it is a conflict between man and woman. Are you going? No, stay for supper. I have no special inducements to offer, but do stay. You know I am expecting the new doctor. Have you seen him?

PASTOR. I caught a glimpse of him as I came along. He looked pleasant, and reliable.

CAPTAIN. That's good. Do you think it possible he may become my ally?

PASTOR. Who can tell? It depends on how much he has been among women.

CAPTAIN. But won't you really stay?

PASTOR. No thanks, my dear fellow; I promised to be home for supper, and the wife gets uneasy if I am late.

CAPTAIN. Uneasy? Angry, you mean. Well, as you will. Let me help you with your coat.

PASTOR. It's certainly pretty cold tonight. Thanks. You must take care of your health, Adolf, you seem rather nervous.

CAPTAIN. Nervous?

PASTOR. Yes, you are not, really very well.

CAPTAIN. Has Laura put that into your head? She has treated me for the last twenty years as if I were at the point of death.

PASTOR. Laura? No, but you make me uneasy about you. Take care of yourself—that's my advice! Good-bye, old man; but didn't you want to talk about the confirmation?

CAPTAIN. Not at all! I assure you that matter will have to take its course in the ordinary

way at the cost of the clerical conscience for I am neither a believer nor a martyr.
PASTOR. Good-bye. Love to Laura.

[*Goes.*]
[*The Captain opens his desk and seats himself at it. Takes up account books.*]

CAPTAIN [*Figuring.*] Thirty-four—nine, forty-three—seven, eight, fifty-six—
LAURA [*Coming in from inner room.*] Will you be kind enough—
CAPTAIN. Just a moment! Sixty-six—seventy-one, eighty-four, eighty-nine, ninety-two, a hundred. What is it?
LAURA. Am I disturbing you?
CAPTAIN. Not at all. Housekeeping money, I suppose?
LAURA. Yes, housekeeping money.
CAPTAIN. Put the accounts down there and I will go over them.
LAURA. The accounts?
CAPTAIN. Yes.
LAURA. Am I to keep accounts now?
CAPTAIN. Of course you are to keep accounts. Our affairs are in a precarious condition, and in case of a liquidation, accounts are necessary, or one is liable to punishment for being careless.
LAURA. It's not my fault that our affairs are in a precarious condition.
CAPTAIN. That is exactly what the accounts will decide.
LAURA. It's not my fault that our tenant doesn't pay.
CAPTAIN. Who recommended this tenant so warmly? You! Why did you recommend a—good-for-nothing, we'll call him?
LAURA. But why did you rent to this good-for-nothing?
CAPTAIN. Because I was not allowed to eat in peace, nor sleep in peace, nor work in peace, till you women got that man here. You wanted him so that your brother might be rid of him, your mother wanted him because I didn't want him, the governess wanted him because he reads his Bible, and old Margret because she had known his grandmother from childhood. That's why he was taken, and if he hadn't been taken, I'd be in a madhouse by now or lying in my grave. However, here is the housekeeping money and your pin money. You may give me the accounts later.
LAURA [*Curtsies.*] Thanks so much. Do you too keep an account of what you spend besides the housekeeping money?
CAPTAIN. That doesn't concern you.
LAURA. No, that's true—just as little as my child's education concerns me. Have the gentlemen come to a decision after this evening's conference?
CAPTAIN. I had already come to a decision, and therefore it only remained for me to talk it over with the one friend I and the family have in common. Bertha is to go to boarding school in town, and starts in a fortnight.
LAURA. To which boarding school, if I may venture to ask?
CAPTAIN. Professor Säfberg's.
LAURA. That free thinker!
CAPTAIN. According to the law, children are to be brought up in their father's faith.
LAURA. And the mother has no voice in the matter?
CAPTAIN. None whatever. She has sold her birthright by a legal transaction, and

forfeited her rights in return for the man's responsibility of caring for her and her children.

LAURA. That is to say she has no rights concerning her child.

CAPTAIN. No, none at all. When once one has sold one's goods, one cannot have them back and still keep the money.

LAURA. But if both father and mother should agree?

CAPTAIN. Do you think that could ever happen? I want her to live in town, you want her to stay at home. The arithmetical result would be that she remain at the railway station midway between train and home. This is a knot that cannot be untied, you see.

LAURA. Then it must be broken. What did Nöjd want here?

CAPTAIN. That is an official secret.

LAURA. Which the whole kitchen knows!

CAPTAIN. Good, then you must know it.

LAURA. I do know it.

CAPTAIN. And have your judgment ready-made?

LAURA. My judgment is the judgment of the law.

CAPTAIN. But it is not written in the law who the child's father is.

LAURA. No, but one usually knows that.

CAPTAIN. Wise minds claim that one can never know.

LAURA. That's strange. Can't one ever know who the father of a child is?

CAPTAIN. No; so they claim.

LAURA. How extraordinary! How can the father have such control over the children then?

CAPTAIN. He has control only when he has assumed the responsibilities of the child, or has had them forced upon him. But in wedlock, of course, there is no doubt about the fatherhood.

LAURA. There are no doubts then?

CAPTAIN. Well, I should hope not.

LAURA. But if the wife has been unfaithful?

CAPTAIN. That's another matter. Was there anything else you wanted to say?

LAURA. Nothing.

CAPTAIN. Then I shall go up to my room, and perhaps you will be kind enough to let me know when the doctor arrives.

[*Closes desk and rises*]

LAURA. Certainly.

[*Captain goes through the primate door right.*]

CAPTAIN. As soon as he comes. For I don't want to seem rude to him, you understand.

[*Goes.*]

LAURA. I understand.

[*Looks at the money she holds in her hands.*]

MOTHER-IN-LAW'S VOICE [*Within.*] Laura!

LAURA. Yes.

MOTHER-IN-LAW'S VOICE. Is my tea ready?

LAURA [*In doorway to inner room*]. In just a moment.

[*Laura goes toward hall door at back as the orderly opens it.*]

ORDERLY. Doctor Östermark.

DOCTOR. Madam!

LAURA [*Advances and offers her hand*]. Welcome, Doctor—you are heartily welcome. The Captain is out, but he will be back soon.

DOCTOR. I hope you will excuse my coming so late, but I have already been called upon to pay some professional visits.

LAURA. Sit down, won't you?

DOCTOR. Thank you.

LAURA. Yes, there is a great deal of illness in the neighborhood just now, but I hope it will agree with you here. For us country people living in such isolation it is of great value to find a doctor who is interested in his patients, and I hear so many nice things of you, Doctor, that I hope the pleasantest relations will exist between us.

DOCTOR. You are indeed kind, and I hope for your sake my visits to you will not often be caused by necessity. Your family is, I believe, as a rule in good health—

LAURA. Fortunately we have bear spared acute illnesses, but still things are not altogether as they should be.

DOCTOR. Indeed?

LAURA. Heaven knows, things are not as might be wished.

DOCTOR. Really, you alarm me.

LAURA. There are some circumstances in a family which through honor and conscience one is forced to conceal from the whole world—

DOCTOR. Excepting the doctor.

LAURA. Exactly. It is, therefore, my painful duty to tell you the whole truth immediately.

DOCTOR. Shouldn't we postpone this conference until I have had the honor of being introduced to the Captain?

LAURA. No! You must hear me before seeing him.

DOCTOR. It relates to him then?

LAURA. Yes, to him, my poor, dear husband.

DOCTOR. You alarm me, indeed, and believe me, I sympathize with your misfortune.

LAURA [*Taking out handkerchief*]. My husband's mind is affected. Now you know all, and may judge for yourself when you see him.

DOCTOR. What do you say? I have read the Captain's excellent treatises on mineralogy with admiration, and have found that they display a clear and powerful intellect.

LAURA. Really? How happy I should be if we should all prove to be mistaken.

DOCTOR. But of course it is possible that his mind might be affected in other directions.

LAURA. That is just what we fear, too. You see he has sometimes the most extraordinary ideas which, of course, one might expect in a learned man, if they did not have a disastrous effect on the welfare of his whole family. For instance, one of his whims is buying all kinds of things.

DOCTOR. That is serious; but what does he buy?

LAURA. Whole boxes of books that he never reads.

DOCTOR. There is nothing strange about a scholar's buying books.

LAURA. You don't believe what I am saying?

DOCTOR. Well, Madam, I am convinced that you believe what you are saying.

LAURA. Tell me, is it reasonable to think that one can see what is happening on another planet by looking through a microscope?

DOCTOR. Does he say he can do that?

LAURA. Yes, that's what he says.

DOCTOR. Through a microscope?

LAURA. Through a microscope, yes.

DOCTOR. This is serious, if it is so.

LAURA. If it is so! Then you have no faith in me, Doctor, and here I sit confiding the family secret to—

DOCTOR. Indeed, Madam, I am honored by your confidence, but as a physician I must investigate and observe before giving an opinion. Has the Captain ever shown any symptoms of indecision or instability of will?

LAURA. Has he! We have been married twenty years, and he has never yet made a decision without changing his mind afterward.

DOCTOR. Is he obstinate?

LAURA. He always insists on having his own way, but once he has got it he drops the whole matter and asks me to decide.

DOCTOR. This is serious, and demands close observation. The will, you see, is the mainspring of the mind, and if it is affected the whole mind goes to pieces.

LAURA. God knows how I have taught myself to humor his wishes through all these long years of trial. Oh, if you knew what a life I have endured with him—if you only knew.

DOCTOR. Your misfortune touches me deeply, and I promise you to see what can be done. I pity you with all my heart, and I beg you to trust me completely. But after what I have heard I must ask you to avoid suggesting any ideas that might make a deep impression on the patient, for in a weak brain they develop rapidly and quickly turn to monomania or fixed ideas.

LAURA. You mean to avoid arousing suspicions?

DOCTOR. Exactly. One can make the insane believe anything, just because they are receptive to everything.

LAURA. Indeed? Then I understand. Yes—yes. [*A bell rings within.*] Excuse me, my mother wishes to speak to me. One moment— —Ah, here is Adolf.

[*Captain comes in through private door.*]

CAPTAIN. Oh, here already, Doctor? You are very welcome.

DOCTOR. Captain! It is a very great pleasure to me to make the acquaintance of so celebrated a man of science.

CAPTAIN. Oh, I beg of you. The duties of service do not allow me to make any very profound investigations, but I believe I am now really on the track of a discovery.

DOCTOR. Indeed?

CAPTAIN. You see, I have submitted meteoric stones to spectrum analysis, with the result that I have found carbon, that, is to say, a clear trace of organic life. What do you say to that?

DOCTOR. Can you see that with it microscope?

CAPTAIN. Lord, no—with the spectroscope.

DOCTOR. The spectroscope! Pardon. Then you will soon be able to tell us what is happening on Jupiter.

CAPTAIN. Not what is happening, but what has happened. If only the confounded booksellers in Paris would send me the books; but I believe all the booksellers in the universe have conspired against me. Think of it, for the last two months not a single one has ever answered my communications, neither letters nor abusive telegrams. I shall go mad over it, and I can't imagine what's the matter.

DOCTOR. Oh, I suppose it's the usual carelessness; you mustn't let it vex you so.

CAPTAIN. But the devil of it is I shall not get my treatise done in time, and I know they are working along the same lines in Berlin. But we shouldn't be talking about this— but about you. If you care to live here we have rooms for you in the wing, or perhaps you would rather live in the old quarters?

DOCTOR. Just as you like.

CAPTAIN. No, as you like. Which is it to be?

DOCTOR. You must decide that, Captain.

CAPTAIN. No, it's not for me to decide. You must say which you prefer. I have no preference in the matter, none at all.

DOCTOR. Oh, but I really cannot decide.

CAPTAIN. For heaven's sake, Doctor, say which you prefer. I have no choice in the matter, no opinion, no wishes. Haven't you got character enough to know what you want? Answer me, or I shall be provoked.

DOCTOR. Well, if it rests with me, I prefer to live here.

CAPTAIN. Thank you—forgive me, Doctor, but nothing annoys me so touch as to see people undecided about anything. [*Nurse comes in.*] Oh, there you are, Margret. Do you happen to know whether the rooms in the wing are in order for the Doctor?

NURSE. Yes, sir, they are.

CAPTAIN. Very well. Then I won't detain you, Doctor; you must be tired. Good bye, and welcome once more. I shall see you tomorrow, I hope.

DOCTOR. Good evening, Captain.

CAPTAIN. I daresay that my wife explained conditions here to you a little, so that you have some idea how the land lies?

DOCTOR. Yes, your excellent wife has given me a few hints about this and that, such as were necessary to a stranger. Good evening, Captain.

CAPTAIN [*To Nurse*]. What do you want, you old dear? What is it?

NURSE. Now, little Master Adolf, just listen—

CAPTAIN. Yes, Margret, you are the only one I can listen to without having spasms.

NURSE. Now, listen, Mr. Adolf. Don't you think you should go half-way and come to an agreement with Mistress in this fuss over the child? Just think of a mother—

CAPTAIN. Think of a father, Margret.

NURSE. There, there, there. A father has something besides his child, but a mother has nothing but her child.

CAPTAIN. Just so, you old dear. She has only one burden, but I have three, and I have her burden too. Don't you think that I should hold a better position in the world than that of a poor soldier if I had not had her and her child?

NURSE. Well, that isn't what I wanted to talk about.

CAPTAIN. I can well believe that, for you wanted to make it appear that I am in the wrong.

NURSE. Don't you believe, Mr. Adolf, that I wish you well?

CAPTAIN. Yes, dear friend, I do believe it; but you don't know what is for my good. You see it isn't enough for me to have given the child life, I want to give her my soul, too.

NURSE. Such things I don't understand. But I do think that you ought to be able to agree.

CAPTAIN. You are not my friend, Margret.

NURSE. I? Oh, Lord, what are you saying, Mr. Adolf? Do you think I can forget that you were my child when you were little?

CAPTAIN. Well, you dear, have I forgotten it? You have been like a mother to me, and always have stood by me when I had everybody against me, but now, when I really need you, you desert me and go over to the enemy.

NURSE. The enemy!

CAPTAIN, Yes, the enemy! You know well enough how things are in this house! You have seen everything from the beginning.

NURSE. Indeed I have seen! But, God knows, why two people should torment the life out of each other; two people who are otherwise so good and wish all others well. Mistress is never like that to me or to others—

CAPTAIN. Only to me, I know it. But let me tell you, Margret, if you desert me now, you will do wrong. For now they have begun to weave a plot against me, and that doctor is not my friend.

NURSE. Oh, Mr. Adolf, you believe evil about everybody. But you see it's because you haven't the true faith; that's just what it is.

CAPTAIN. Yes, you and the Baptists have found the only true faith. You are indeed lucky!

NURSE. Anyway, I'm not unhappy like you, Mr. Adolf. Humble your heart and you will see that God will make you happy in your love for your neighbor.

CAPTAIN. It's a strange thing that you no sooner speak of God and love than your voice becomes hard and your eyes fill with hate. No, Margret, surely you have not the true faith.

NURSE. Yes, go on being proud and hard in your learning, but it won't amount to much when it comes to the test.

CAPTAIN. How mightily you talk, humble heart. I know very well that knowledge is of no use to you women.

NURSE. You ought to be ashamed of yourself. But in spite of everything old Margret cares most for her great big boy, and he will come back to the fold when it's stormy weather.

CAPTAIN. Margret! Forgive me, but believe me when I say that there is no one here who wishes me well but you. Help me, for I feel that something is going to happen here. What it is, I don't know, but something evil is on the way. [*Scream from within.*] What's that? Who's that screaming?

[*Berths enters from inner room.*]

BERTHA. Father! Father! Help me; save me.

CAPTAIN. My dear child, what is it? Speak!

BERTHA. Help me. She wants to hurt me.

CAPTAIN. Who wants to hurt you? Tell me! Speak!

BERTHA. Grandmother! But it's my fault for I deceived her.

CAPTAIN. Tell me more.

BERTHA. Yes, but you mustn't say anything about it. Promise me you won't.

CAPTAIN. Tell me what it is then.

[*Nurse goes.*]

BERTHA. In the evening she generally turns down the lamp and then she makes me sit at a table holding a pen over a piece of paper. And then she says that the spirits are to write.

CAPTAIN. What's all this—and you have never told me about it?

BERTHA. Forgive me, but I dared not, for Grandmother says the spirits take revenge if one talks about them. And then the pen writes, but I don't know whether I'm doing it or not. Sometimes it goes well, but sometimes it won't go at all, and when I am tired nothing comes, but she wants it to come just the same. And tonight I thought I was writing beautifully, but then grandmother said it was all from Stagnelius, and that I had deceived her, and then she got terribly angry.

CAPTAIN. Do you believe that there are spirits?

BERTHA. I don't know.

CAPTAIN. But I know that there are none.

BERTHA. But Grandmother says that you don't understand, Father, and that you do much worse things—you who can see to other planets.

CAPTAIN. Does she say that! Does she say that? What else does she say?

BERTHA. She says that you can't work witchery.

CAPTAIN. I never said that I could. You know what meteoric stones are,—stones that fall from other heavenly bodies. I can examine them and learn whether they contain the same elements as our world. That is all I can tell.

BERTHA. But Grandmother says that there are things that she can see which you cannot see.

CAPTAIN. Then she lies.

BERTHA. Grandmother doesn't tell lies.

CAPTAIN. Why doesn't she?

BERTHA. Then Mother tells lies too.

CAPTAIN. H'm!

BERTHA. And if you say that Mother lies, I can never believe in you again.

CAPTAIN. I have not said so; and so you must believe in me when I tell you that it is for your future good that you should leave home. Will you? Will you go to town and learn something useful?

BERTHA. Oh, yes, I should love to go to town, away from here, anywhere. If I can only see you sometimes—often. Oh, it is so gloomy and awful in there all the time, like a winter night, but when you come home Father, it is like a morning in spring when they take off the double windows.

CAPTAIN. My beloved child! My dear child!

BERTHA. But, Father, you'll be good to Mother, won't you? She cries so often.

CAPTAIN. H'm—then you want to go to town?

BERTHA. Yes, yes.

CAPTAIN. But if Mother doesn't want you to go?

BERTHA. But she must let me.

CAPTAIN. But if she won't?

BERTHA. Well, then, I don't know what will happen. But she must! She must!

CAPTAIN. Will you ask her?

BERTHA. You must ask her very nicely; she wouldn't pay any attention to my asking.

CAPTAIN. H'm! Now if you wish it, and I wish it, and she doesn't wish it, what shall we do then?

BERTHA. Oh, then it will all be in a tangle again! Why can't you both—

[*Laura comes in.*]

LAURA. Oh, so Bertha is here. Then perhaps we may have her own opinion as the question of her future has to be decided.

CAPTAIN. The child can hardly have any well-grounded opinion about what a young girl's life is likely to be, while we, on the contrary, can more easily estimate what it may be, as we have seen so many young girls grow up.

LAURA. But as we are of different opinions Bertha must be the one to decide.

CAPTAIN. No, I let no one usurp my rights, neither women nor children. Bertha, leave us.

[*Bertha goes out.*]

LAURA. You were afraid of hearing her opinion, because you thought it would be to my advantage.

CAPTAIN. I know that she wishes to go away from home, but I know also that you possess the power of changing her mind to suit your pleasure.

LAURA. Oh, am I really so powerful?

CAPTAIN. Yes, you have a fiendish power of getting your own way; but so has anyone who does not scruple about, the way it is accomplished. How did you get Doctor Norling away, for instance, and how did you get this new doctor here?

LAURA. Yes, how did I manage that?

CAPTAIN. You insulted the other one so much that he left, and made your brother recommend this fellow.

LAURA. Well, that was quite simple and legitimate. Is Bertha to leave home now?

CAPTAIN. Yes, she is to start in a fortnight.

LAURA. That is your decision?

CAPTAIN. Yes.

LAURA. Then I must try to prevent it.

CAPTAIN. You cannot.

LAURA. Can't I? Do you really think I would trust my daughter to wicked people to have her taught that everything her mother has implanted in her child is mere foolishness? Why, afterward, she would despise me all the rest of her life!

CAPTAIN. Do you think that a father should allow ignorant and conceited women to teach his daughter that he is a charlatan?

LAURA. It means less to the father.

CAPTAIN. Why so?

LAURA. Because the mother is closer to the child, as it has been discovered that no one can tell for a certainty who the father of a child is.

CAPTAIN. How does that apply to this case?

LAURA. You do not know whether you are Bertha's father or not.

CAPTAIN. I do not know?

LAURA. No; what no one knows, you surely cannot know.

CAPTAIN. Are you joking?

LAURA. No; I am only making use of your own teaching. For that matter, how do you know that I have not been unfaithful to you?

CAPTAIN. I believe you capable of almost anything, but not that, nor that you would talk about it if it were true.

LAURA. Suppose that I was prepared to bear anything, even to being despised and driven out, everything for the sake of being able to keep and control my child, and that I am truthful now when I declare that Bertha is my child, but not yours. Suppose—

CAPTAIN. Stop now!

LAURA. Just suppose this. In that case your power would be at an end.

CAPTAIN. When you had proved that I was not the father.

LAURA. That would not be difficult! Would you like me to do so?

CAPTAIN. Stop!

LAURA. Of course I should only need to declare the name of the real father, give all details of place and time. For instance—when was Bertha born? In the third year of our marriage.

CAPTAIN. Stop now, or else—

LAURA. Or else, what? Shall we stop now? Think carefully about all you do and decide, and whatever you do, don't make yourself ridiculous.

CAPTAIN. I consider all this most lamentable.

LAURA. Which makes you all the more ridiculous.

CAPTAIN. And you?

LAURA. Oh, we women are really too clever.

CAPTAIN. That's why one cannot contend with you.

LAURA. Then why provoke contests with a superior enemy?

CAPTAIN. Superior?

LAURA. Yes, it's queer, but I have never looked at a man without knowing myself to be his superior.

CAPTAIN. Then you shall be made to see your superior for once, so that you shall never forget it.

LAURA. That will be interesting.

NURSE [comes in]. Supper is served. Will you come in?

LAURA. Very well.

[Captain lingers; sits down with a magazine in an arm chair near table.]

LAURA. Aren't you coming in to supper?

CAPTAIN. No, thanks. I don't want anything.

LAURA. What, are you annoyed?

CAPTAIN. No, but I am not hungry.

LAURA. Come, or they will ask unnecessary questions—be good now. You won't? Stay there then.

[Goes.]

NURSE. Mr. Adolf! What is this all about?

CAPTAIN. I don't know what it is. Can you explain to me why you women treat an old man as if he were a child?

NURSE. I don't understand it, but it must be because all you men, great and small, are women's children, every man of you.

CAPTAIN. But no women are born of men. Yes, but I am Bertha's father. Tell me, Margret, don't you believe it? Don't you?

NURSE. Lord, how silly you are. Of course you are your own child's father. Come and eat now, and don't sit there and sulk. There, there, come now.

CAPTAIN. Get out, woman. To hell with the hags. *[Goes to private door.]* Svärd, Svärd!

[Orderly comes in.]

ORDERLY. Yes, Captain.

CAPTAIN. Hitch into the covered sleigh at once.

NURSE. Captain, listen to me.

CAPTAIN. Out, woman! At once!

[Orderly goes.]

NURSE. Good Lord, what's going to happen now.

[Captain puts on his cap and coat and prepares to go out.]

CAPTAIN. Don't expect me home before midnight.

[Goes.]

NURSE. Lord preserve us, whatever will be the end of this!

ACT II.

[The same scene as in previous act. A lighted lamp is on the table; it is night. The Doctor and Laura are discovered at rise of curtain.]

DOCTOR. From what I gathered during my conversation with him the case is not fully proved to me. In the first place you made a mistake in saying that he had arrived at these astonishing results about other heavenly bodies by means of a microscope. Now that I have learned that it was a spectroscope, he is not only cleared of any suspicion of insanity, but has rendered a great service to science.

LAURA. Yes, but I never said that.

DOCTOR. Madam, I made careful notes of our conversation, and I remember that I asked about this very point because I thought I had misunderstood you. One must be very careful in making such accusations when a certificate in lunacy is in question.

LAURA. A certificate in lunacy?

DOCTOR. Yes, you must surely know that an insane person loses both civil and family rights.

LAURA. No, I did not know that.

DOCTOR. There was another matter that seemed to me suspicious. He spoke of his communications to his booksellers not being answered. Permit me to ask if you, through motives of mistaken kindness, have intercepted them?

LAURA. Yes, I have. It was my duty to guard the interests of the family, and I could not let him ruin us all without some intervention.

DOCTOR. Pardon me, but I think you cannot have considered the consequences of such an act. If he discovers your secret interference in his affairs, he will have grounds for suspicions, and they will grow like an avalanche. And besides, in doing this you have thwarted his will and irritated him still more. You must have felt yourself how the mind rebels when one's deepest desires are thwarted and one's will is crossed.

LAURA. Haven't I felt that!

DOCTOR. Think, then, what he must have gone through.

LAURA [*Rising*]. It is midnight and he hasn't come home. Now we may fear the worst.

DOCTOR. But tell me what actually happened this evening after I left. I must know everything.

LAURA. He raved in the wildest way and had the strangest ideas. For instance, that he is not the father of his child.

DOCTOR. That is strange. How did such an idea come into his head?

LAURA. I really can't imagine, unless it was because he had to question one of the men about supporting a child, and when I tried to defend the girl, he grew excited and said no one could tell who was the father of a child. God knows I did everything to calm him, but now I believe there is no help for him.

[*Cries.*]

DOCTOR. But this cannot go on. Something must be done here without, of course, arousing his suspicions. Tell me, has the Captain ever had such delusions before?

LAURA. Six years ago things were in the same state, and then he, himself, confessed in his own letter to the doctor that he feared for his reason.

DOCTOR. Yes, yes, yes, this is a story that has deep roots and the sanctity of the family life—and so on—of course I cannot ask about everything, but must limit myself to appearances. What is done can't be undone, more's the pity, yet the remedy should be based upon all the past.—Where do you think he is now?

LAURA. I have no idea, he has such wild streaks.

DOCTOR. Would you like to have me stay until he returns? To avoid suspicion, I could say that I had come to see your mother who is not well.

LAURA. Yes, that will do very nicely. Don't leave us, Doctor; if you only knew how troubled I am! But wouldn't it be better to tell him outright what you think of his condition.

DOCTOR. We never do that unless the patient mentions the subject himself, and very seldom even then. It depends entirely on the case. But we mustn't sit here; perhaps I had better go into the next room; it will look more natural.

LAURA. Yes, that will be better, and Margret can sit here. She always waits up when he is out, and she is the only one who has any power over him. [*Goes to the door left*] Margret, Margret!

NURSE. Yes, Ma'am. Has the master come home?

LAURA. No; but you are to sit here and wait for him, and when he does come you are to say my mother is ill and that's why the doctor is here.

NURSE. Yes, yes. I'll see that everything is all right.

LAURA [*Opens the door to inner rooms*]. Will you come in here, Doctor?

DOCTOR. Thank you.

> [*Nurse seats herself at the table and takes up a hymn book and spectacles and reads.*]

NURSE. Ah, yes, ah yes!

> [*Reads half aloud*]

Ah woe is me, how sad a thing
Is life within this vale of tears,
Death's angel triumphs like a king,
And calls aloud to all the spheres—
    Vanity, all is vanity.
Yes, yes! Yes, yes!

> [*Reads again*]

All that on earth hath life and breath
To earth must fall before his spear,
And sorrow, saved alone from death,
Inscribes above the mighty bier.
    Vanity, all is vanity.
Yes, Yes.

BERTHA [*Comes in with a coffee-pot and some embroidery. She speaks in a low voice*]. Margret, may I sit with you? It is so frightfully lonely up there.

NURSE. For goodness sake, are you still up, Bertha?

BERTHA. You see I want to finish Father's Christmas present. And here's something that you'll like.

NURSE. But bless my soul, this won't do. You must be up in the morning, and it's after midnight now.

BERTHA. What does it matter? I don't dare sit up there alone. I believe the spirits are at work.

NURSE. You see, just what I've said. Mark my words, this house was not built on a lucky spot. What did you hear?

BERTHA. Think of it, I heard some one singing up in the attic!

NURSE. In the attic? At this hour?

BERTHA. Yes, it was such it sorrowful, melancholy song! I never heard anything like it. It sounded as if it came from the store-room, where the cradle stands, you know, to the left— — —

NURSE. Dear me, Dear me! And such a fearful night. It seems as if the chimneys would blow down. "Ah, what is then this earthly life, But grief, affliction and great strife? E'en when fairest it has seemed, Nought but pain it can be deemed." Ah, dear child, may God give us a good Christmas!

BERTHA. Margret, is it true that Father is ill?

NURSE. Yes, I'm afraid he is.

BERTHA. Then we can't keep Christmas eve? But how can he be up and around if he is Ill?

NURSE. You see, my child, the kind of illness he has doesn't keep him from being up. Hush, there's some one out in the hall. Go to bed now and take the coffee pot away or the master will be angry.

BERTHA [*Going out with tray*]. Good night, Margret.

NURSE. Good night, my child. God bless you.

[*Captain comes in, takes off his overcoat.*]

CAPTAIN. Are you still up? Go to bed.

NURSE. I was only waiting till— —

[*Captain lights a candle, opens his desk, sits down at it and takes letters and newspapers out of his pocket.*]

NURSE. Mr. Adolf.

CAPTAIN. What do you want?

NURSE. Old mistress is ill and the doctor is here.

CAPTAIN. Is it anything dangerous?

NURSE. No, I don't think so. Just a cold.

CAPTAIN [*Gets up*]. Margret, who was the father of your child?

NURSE. Oh, I've told you many and many a time; it was that scamp Johansson.

CAPTAIN. Are you sure that it was he?

NURSE. How childish you are; of course I'm sure when he was the only one.

CAPTAIN. Yes, but was he sure that he was the only one? No, he could not be, but you could be sure of it. There is a difference, you see.

NURSE. Well, I can't see any difference.

CAPTAIN. No, you cannot see it, but the difference exists, nevertheless. [*Turns over the pages of a photograph album which is on the table.*] Do you think Bertha looks like me?

NURSE. Of course! Why, you are as like as two peas.

CAPTAIN. Did Johansson confess that he was the father?

NURSE. He was forced to!

CAPTAIN. How terrible! Here is the Doctor. [*Doctor comes in.*] Good evening, Doctor. How is my mother-in-law?

DOCTOR. Oh, it's nothing serious; merely a slight sprain of the left ankle.

CAPTAIN. I thought Margret said it was a cold. There seem to be different opinions about the same case. Go to bed, Margret.

[*Nurse goes. A pause.*]

CAPTAIN. Sit down, Doctor.

DOCTOR [*Sits*]. Thanks.

CAPTAIN. Is it true that you obtain striped foals if you cross a zebra and a mare?

DOCTOR [*Astonished*]. Perfectly true.

CAPTAIN. Is it true that the foals continue to be striped if the breed is continued with a stallion?

DOCTOR. Yes, that is true, too.

CAPTAIN. That is to say, under certain conditions a stallion can be sire to striped foals or the opposite?

DOCTOR. Yes, so it seems.

CAPTAIN. Therefore an offspring's likeness to the father proves nothing?

DOCTOR. Well— — —

CAPTAIN. That is to say, paternity cannot be proven.

DOCTOR. H'm— —well— —

CAPTAIN. You are a widower, aren't you, and have had children?

DOCTOR. Ye-es.

CAPTAIN. Didn't you ever feel ridiculous as a. father? I know of nothing so ludicrous as to see a father leading his children by the hand around the streets, or to hear it father talk about his children. "My wife's children," he ought to say. Did you ever feel how false your position was? Weren't you ever afflicted with doubts, I won't say suspicions, for, as a gentleman, I assume that your wife was above suspicion.

DOCTOR. No, really, I never was; but, Captain, I believe Goethe says a man must take his children on good faith.

CAPTAIN. It's risky to take anything on good faith where a woman is concerned.

DOCTOR. Oh, there are so many kinds of women.

CAPTAIN. Modern investigations have pronounced that there is only one kind! Lately I have recalled two instances in my life that make me believe this. When I was young I was strong and, if I may boast, handsome. Once when I was making a trip on a steamer and sitting with a few friends in the saloon, the young stewardess came and flung herself down by me, burst into tears, and told us that her sweetheart was drowned. We sympathized with her, and I ordered some champagne. After the second glass I touched her foot; after the fourth her knee, and before morning I had consoled her.

DOCTOR. That was just a winter fly.

CAPTAIN. Now comes the second instance—and that was a real summer fly. I was at Lysekil. There was a young married woman stopping there with her children, but her husband was in town. She was religious, had extremely strict principles, preached morals to me, and was, I believe, entirely honorable. I lent her a book, two books, and when she was leaving, she returned them, strange to say! Three months later, in those very books I found her card with a declaration on it. It was innocent, as innocent its it declaration of love can be from a married woman to a strange man who never made any advances. Now comes the moral: Just don't have too much faith.

DOCTOR. Don't have too little faith either.

CAPTAIN. No, but just enough. But, you see, Doctor, that woman was so unconsciously dishonest that she talked to her husband about the fancy she had taken to me. That's what makes it dangerous, this very unconsciousness of their instinctive dishonesty. That is a mitigating circumstance, I admit, but it cannot nullify judgment, only soften it.

DOCTOR. Captain, your thoughts are taking a morbid turn, and you ought to control them.

CAPTAIN. You must not use the word morbid. Steam boilers, as you know, explode at it certain pressure, but the same pressure is not needed for all boiler explosions. You understand? However, you are here to watch me. If I were not a man I should have the right to make accusations or complaints, as they are so cleverly called, and perhaps I should be able to give you the whole diagnosis, and, what is more, the history of my disease. But unfortunately, I am a man, and there is nothing for me to do but, like a Roman, fold my arms across my breast and hold my breath till I die.

DOCTOR. Captain, if you are ill, it will not reflect upon your honor as a man to tell me all. In fact, I ought to hear the other side.

CAPTAIN. You have had enough in hearing the one, I imagine. Do you know when I heard Mrs. Alving eulogizing her dead husband, I thought to myself what a damned pity it was the fellow was dead. Do you suppose that he would have spoken if he had been alive? And do you suppose that if any of the dead husbands came back they would be believed? Good night, Doctor. You see that I am calm, and you can retire without fear.

DOCTOR. Good night, then, Captain. I'm afraid. I can be of no further use in this case.

CAPTAIN. Are we enemies?

DOCTOR. Far from it. But it is too bad we cannot be friends. Good night.

[*Goes. The Captain follows the Doctor to the door at back and then goes to the door at left and opens it slightly.*]

CAPTAIN. Come in, and we'll talk. I heard you out there listening. [*Laura, embarrassed. Captain sits at desk.*] It is late, but we must come to some decision. Sit down. [*Pause.*] I have been at the post office tonight to get my letters. From these it appears that you have been keeping back my mail, both coming and going. The consequence of which is that the loss of time has its good as destroyed the result I expected from my work.

LAURA. It was an act of kindness on my part, as you neglected the service for this other work.

CAPTAIN. It was hardly kindness, for you were quite sure that some day I should win more honor from that, than from the service; but you were particularly anxious that I should not win such honors, for fear your own insignificance would be emphasized by it. In consequence of all this I have intercepted letters addressed to you.

LAURA. That was a noble act.

CAPTAIN. You see, you have, as you might say, a high opinion of me. It appears from these letters that, for some time past you have been arraying my old friends against me by spreading reports about my mental condition. And you Dave succeeded in your efforts, for now not more than one person exists from the Colonel down to the cook, who believes that I am sane. Now these are the facts about my illness; my mind is sound, as you know, so that I can take care of my duties in the service as well its my responsibilities as a father; my feelings are more or less under my control, as my will has not been completely undermined; but you have gnawed and nibbled at it so that it will soon slip the cogs, and then the whole mechanism will slip and go to smash. I will not appeal to your feelings, for you have none; that is your strength; but I will appeal to your interests.

LAURA. Let me hear.

CAPTAIN. You have succeeded in arousing my suspicions to such an extent that my judgment is no longer clear, and my thoughts begin to wander. This is the approaching insanity that you are waiting for, which may come at any time now. So you are face to face with the question whether it is more to your interest that I should be sane or insane. Consider. If I go under I shall lose the service, and where will you be then? If I die, my life insurance will fall to you. But if I take my own life, you will get nothing. Consequently, it is to your interest that I should live out my life.

LAURA. Is this a trap?

CAPTAIN. To be sure. But it rests with you whether you will run around it or stick your head into it.

LAURA. You say that you will kill yourself! You won't do that!

CAPTAIN. Are you sure? Do you think a man can live when he has nothing and no one to live for?

LAURA. You surrender, then?

CAPTAIN. No, I offer peace.

LAURA. The conditions?

CAPTAIN. That I may keep my reason. Free me from my suspicions and I give up the conflict.

LAURA. What suspicions?

CAPTAIN. About Bertha's origin.

LAURA. Are there any doubts about that?

CAPTAIN. Yes, I have doubts, and you have awakened them.

LAURA. I?

CAPTAIN. Yes, you have dropped them like henbane in my ears, and circumstances have strengthened them. Free me from the uncertainty; tell me outright that it is true and I will forgive you beforehand.

LAURA. How can I acknowledge a sin that I have not committed?

CAPTAIN. What does it matter when you know that I shall not divulge it? Do you think a man would go and spread his own shame broadcast?

LAURA. If I say it isn't true, you won't be convinced; but if I say it is, then you will be convinced. You seem to hope it is true!

CAPTAIN. Yes, strangely enough; it must be, because the first supposition can't be proved; the latter can be.

LAURA. Have you tiny ground for your suspicions?

CAPTAIN. Yes, and no.

LAURA. I believe you want to prove me guilty, so that you can get rid of me and then have absolute control over the child. But you won't catch me in any such snare.

CAPTAIN. Do you think that I would want to be responsible for another man's child, if I were convinced of your guilt?

LAURA. No, I'm sure you wouldn't, and that's what makes me know you lied just now when you said that you would forgive me beforehand.

CAPTAIN. [Rises]. Laura, save me and my reason. You don't seem to understand what I say. If the child is not mine I have no control over her and don't want to have any, and that is precisely what you do want, isn't it? But perhaps you want even more—to have power over the child, but still have me to support you.

LAURA. Power, yes! What has this whole life and death struggle been for but power?

CAPTAIN. To me it has meant more. I do not believe in a hereafter; the child was my future life. That was my conception of immortality, and perhaps the only one that has any analogy in reality. If you take that away from me, you cut off my life.

LAURA. Why didn't we separate in time?

CAPTAIN. Because the child bound us together; but the link became a chain. And how did it happen; how? I have never thought about this, but now memories rise up accusingly, condemningly perhaps. We had been married two years, and had no children; you know why. I fell ill and lay at the point of death. During a conscious interval of the fever I heard voices out in the drawing-room. It was you and the lawyer talking about the fortune that I still possessed. He explained that you could inherit nothing because we had no children, and he asked you if you were expecting to become a mother. I did not hear your reply. I recovered and we had a child. Who is its father?

LAURA. You.

CAPTAIN. No, I am not. Here is a buried crime that begins to stench, and what a hellish crime! You women have been compassionate enough to free the black slaves, but you have kept the white ones. I have worked and slaved for you, your child, your mother, your servants; I have sacrificed promotion and career; I have endured torture, flagellation, sleeplessness, worry for your sake, until my hair has grown gray; and all that you might enjoy a life without care, and when you grew old, enjoy life over again in your child. I have borne everything without complaint, because I thought myself the father of your child. This is the commonest kind of theft, the most brutal slavery. I have had seventeen years of penal servitude and have been innocent. What can you give me in return for that?

LAURA. Now you are quite mad.

CAPTAIN. That is your hope!—And I see how you have labored to conceal your crime. I sympathized with you because I did not understand your grief. I have often lulled your evil conscience to rest when I thought I was driving away morbid thoughts. I have heard you cry out in your sleep and not wanted to listen. I remember now night before last—Bertha's birthday—it was between two and three in the morning, and I was sitting up reading; you shrieked, "Don't, don't!" as if someone were strangling you; I knocked on the wall—I didn't want to hear any more. I have had my suspicions for a long time but I did not dare to hear them confirmed. All this I have suffered for you. What will you do for me?

LAURA. What can I do? I will swear by God and all I hold sacred that you are Bertha's father.

CAPTAIN. What use is that when you have often said that a mother can and ought to commit any crime for her child? I implore you as a wounded man begs for a death blow, to tell me all. Don't you see I'm as helpless as a child? Don't you hear me complaining as to a mother? Won't you forget that I am a man, that I am a soldier who can tame men and beasts with a word? Like a sick man I only ask for compassion. I lay down the tokens of my power and implore you to have mercy on my life.

[*Laura approaches him and lays her hand on his brow.*]

LAURA. What! You are crying, man!

CAPTAIN. Yes, I am crying although I am a man. But has not a man eyes! Has not a man hands, limbs, senses, thoughts, passions? Is he not fed with the wine food, hurt by the same weapons, warmed and cooled by the same summer and winter as a woman? If you prick us do we not bleed? If you tickle us do we not laugh? And if you poison us, do we not die? Why shouldn't a man complain, a soldier weep? Because it is unmanly? Why is it unmanly?

LAURA. Weep then, my child, as if you were with your mother once more. Do you remember when I first came into your life, I was like a second mother? Your great strong body needed nerves; you were a giant child that had either come too early into the world, or perhaps was not wanted at all.

CAPTAIN. Yes, that's how it was. My father's and my mother's will was against my coming into the world, and consequently I was born without a will. I thought I was completing myself when you and I became one, and therefore you were allowed to rule, and I, the commander at the barracks and before the troops, became obedient to you, grew through you, looked up to you as to it more highly-gifted being, listened to you as if I had been your undeveloped child.

LAURA. Yes, that's the way it was, and therefore I loved you as my child. But you know, you must have seen, when the nature of your feelings changed and you appeared as my lover that I blushed, and your embraces were joy that was followed by a remorseful conscience as if my blood were ashamed. The mother became the mistress. Ugh!

CAPTAIN. I saw it, but I did not understand. I believed you despised me for my unmanliness, and I wanted to win you as a woman by being a man.

LAURA. Yes, but there was the mistake. The mother was your friend, you see, but the woman was your enemy, and love between the sexes is strife. Do not think that I gave myself; I did not give, but I took—what I wanted. But you had one advantage. I felt that, and I wanted you to feel it.

CAPTAIN. You always had the advantage. You could hypnotize me when I was wide awake, so that I neither saw nor heard, but merely obeyed; you could give me a raw potato and make me imagine it was a peach; you could force me to admire your foolish caprices as though they were strokes of genius. You could have influenced me to crime, yes, even to mean, paltry deeds. Because you lacked intelligence, instead of carrying out my ideas you acted on your own judgment. But when at last I awoke, I realized that my honor had been corrupted and I wanted to blot out the memory by a great deed, an achievement, a discovery, or an honorable suicide. I wanted to go to war, but was not permitted. It was then that I threw myself into science. And now when I was about to reach out my hand to gather in its fruits, you chop off my arm. Now I am dishonored and can live no longer, for a man cannot live without honor.

LAURA. But a woman?

CAPTAIN. Yes, for she has her children, which he has not. But, like the rest of mankind, we lived our lives unconscious as children, full of imagination, ideals, and illusions, and then we awoke; it was all over. But we awoke with our feet on the pillow, and he who waked us was himself a sleep-walker. When women grow old and cease to be women, they get beards on their chins; I wonder what men get when they grow old and cease to be men. Those who crowed were no longer cocks but capons, and the pullets answered their call, so that when we thought the sun was about to rise we found ourselves in the bright moon light amid ruins, just as in the good old times. It had only been a little morning slumber with wild dreams, and there was no awakening.

LAURA. Do you know, you should have been a poet!

CAPTAIN. Who knows.

LAURA. Now I am sleepy, so if you have any more fantastic visions keep them till to-morrow.

CAPTAIN. First, a word more about realities. Do you hate me?

LAURA. Yes, sometimes, when you are a man.

CAPTAIN. This is like race hatred. If it is true that we are descended from monkeys, at least it must be from two separate species. We are certainly not like one another, are we?

LAURA. What do you mean to say by all this?

CAPTAIN. I feel that one of us must go under in this struggle.

LAURA. Which?

CAPTAIN. The weaker, of course.

LAURA. And the stronger will be in the right?

CAPTAIN. Always, since he has the power.

LAURA. Then I am in the right.

CAPTAIN. Have you the power already then?

LAURA. Yes, and a legal power with which I shall put you under the control of a guardian.

CAPTAIN. Under a guardian?

LAURA. And then I shall educate my child without listening to your fantastic notions.

CAPTAIN. And who will pay for the education when I am no longer here?

LAURA. Your pension will pay for it.

CAPTAIN [*Threateningly*]. How can you have me put under a guardian?

LAURA [*Takes out a letter*]. With this letter of which an attested copy is in the hands of the board of lunacy.

CAPTAIN. What letter?

LAURA [*Moving backward toward the door left*]. Yours! Your declaration to the doctor that you are insane. [*The Captain stares at her in silence.*] Now you have fulfilled your function as an unfortunately necessary father and breadwinner, you are not needed any longer and you must go. You must go, since you have realized that my intellect is as strong as my will, and since you will not stay and acknowledge it.

[*The Captain goes to the table, seizes the lighted lamp and hurls it at Laura, who disappears backward through the door.*]

CURTAIN DROP.

ACT III.

[*Same Scene. Another lamp on the table. The private door is barricaded with a chair.*]

LAURA [*to Nurse*]. Did he give you the keys?

NURSE. Give them to me, no! God help me, but I took them from the master's clothes that Nöjd had out to brush.

LAURA. Oh, Nöjd is on duty today?

NURSE. Yes, Nöjd.

LAURA. Give me the keys.

NURSE. Yes, but this seems like downright stealing. Do you hear him walking up there, Ma'am? Back and forth, back and forth.

LAURA. Is the door well barred?

NURSE. Oh, yes, it's barred well enough!

LAURA. Control your feelings, Margret. We must be calm if we are to be saved. [*Knock.*] Who is it?

NURSE [*Opens door to hall*]. It is Nöjd.

LAURA. Let him come in.

NÖJD [*Comes in*]. A message from the Colonel.

LAURA. Give it to me [*Reads*] Ah!—Nöjd, have you taken all the cartridges out of the guns and pouches?

NÖJD. Yes, Ma'am.

LAURA. Good, wait outside while I answer the Colonel's letter.

[*Nöjd goes. Laura writes.*]

NURSE. Listen. What in the world is he doing up there now?

LAURA. Be quiet while I write.

[*The sound of sawing is heard.*]

NURSE [*Half to herself*]. Oh, God have mercy on us all! Where will this end!

LAURA. Here, give this to Nöjd. And my mother must not know anything about all this. Do you hear?

[*Nurse goes out, Laura opens drawers in desk and takes out papers. The Pastor comes in, he takes a chair and sits near Laura by the desk.*]

PASTOR. Good evening, sister. I have been away all day, as you know, and only just got back. Terrible things have been happening here.

LAURA. Yes, brother, never have I gone through such a night and such a day.

PASTOR. I see that you are none the worse for it all.

LAURA. No, God be praised, but think what might have happened!

PASTOR. Tell me one thing, how did it begin? I have heard so many different versions.

LAURA. It began with his wild idea of not being Bertha's father, and ended with his throwing the lighted lamp in my face.

PASTOR. But this is dreadful! It is fully developed insanity. And what is to be done now?

LAURA. We must try to prevent further violence and the doctor has sent to the hospital for a straightjacket. In the meantime I have sent a message to the Colonel, and I am now trying to straighten out the affairs of the household, which he has carried on in a most reprehensible manner.

PASTOR. This is a deplorable story, but I have always expected something of the sort. Fire and powder must end in an explosion. What have you got in the drawer there?

LAURA [*Has pulled out a drawer in the desk*]. Look, he has hidden everything here.

PASTOR [*Looking into drawer*]. Good Heavens, here is your doll and here is your christening cap and Bertha's rattle; and your letters; and the locket. [*Wipes his eyes.*] After all he must have loved you very dearly, Laura. I never kept such things!

LAURA. I believe he used to love me, but time—time changes so many things.

PASTOR. What is that big paper? The receipt for a grave! Yes, better the grave than the lunatic asylum! Laura, tell me, are you blameless in all this?

LAURA. I? Why should I be to blame because a man goes out of his mind?

PASTOR. Well, well, I shan't say anything. After all, blood is thicker than water.

LAURA. What do you dare to intimate?

PASTOR [*Looking at her penetratingly*]. Now, listen!

LAURA. Yes?

PASTOR. You can hardly deny that it suits you pretty well to be able to educate your child as you wish?

LAURA. I don't understand.

PASTOR. How I admire you!

LAURA. Me? H'm!

PASTOR. And I am to become the guardian of that free-thinker! Do you know I have always looked on him as a weed in our garden.

[*Laura gives a short laugh, and then becomes suddenly serious.*]

LAURA. And you dare say that to me—his wife?

PASTOR. You are strong, Laura, incredibly strong. You are like a fox in a trap, you would rather gnaw off your own leg than let yourself be caught! Like a master thief—no accomplice, not even your own conscience. Look at yourself in the glass! You dare not!

LAURA. I never use a looking glass!

PASTOR. No, you dare not! Let me look at your hand. Not a tell-tale blood stain, not a trace of insidious poison! A little innocent murder that the law cannot reach, an unconscious crime—unconscious! What a splendid idea! Do you hear how he is working up there? Take care! If that man gets loose he will make short work of you.

LAURA. You talk so much, you must have a bad conscience. Accuse me if you can!

PASTOR. I cannot.

LAURA. You see! You cannot, and therefore I am innocent. You take care of your ward, and I will take care of mine! Here's the doctor.

[*Doctor comes in.*]

LAURA [*Rising*]. Good evening, Doctor. You at least will help me, won't you? But unfortunately there is not much that can be done. Do you hear how he is carrying on up there? Are you convinced now?

DOCTOR. I am convinced that an act of violence has been committed, but the question now is whether that act of violence can be considered an outbreak of passion or madness.

PASTOR. But apart from the actual outbreak, you must acknowledge that he has "fixed ideas."

DOCTOR. I think that your ideas, Pastor, are much more fixed.

PASTOR. My settled views about the highest things are—

DOCTOR. We'll leave settled views out of this. Madam, it rests with you to decide whether your husband is guilty to the extent of imprisonment and fine or should be put in an asylum! How do you class his behavior?

LAURA. I cannot answer that now.

DOCTOR. That is to say you have no decided opinion as to what will be most advantageous to the interests of the family? What do you say, Pastor?

PASTOR. Well, there will be a scandal in either case. It is not easy to say.

LAURA. But if he is only sentenced to a fine for violence, he will be able to repeat the violence.

DOCTOR. And if he is sent to prison he will soon be out again. Therefore we consider it most advantageous for all parties that he should be immediately treated as insane. Where is the nurse?

LAURA. Why?

DOCTOR. She must put the straightjacket on the patient when I have talked to him and given the order! But not before. I have—the—garment out here. [*Goes out into the hall rind returns with a large bundle.*] Please ask the nurse to come in here.

[*Laura rings.*]

PASTOR. Dreadful! Dreadful!

[*Nurse comes in.*]

DOCTOR [*Takes out the straightjacket*]. I want you to pay attention to this. We want you to slip this jacket on the Captain, from behind, you understand, when I find it necessary to prevent another outbreak of violence. You notice it has very long sleeves to prevent his moving and they are to be tied at the back. Here are two straps that go through buckles which are afterwards fastened to the arm of a chair or the sofa or whatever is convenient. Will you do it?

NURSE. No, Doctor, I can't do that; I can't.

LAURA. Why don't you do it yourself, Doctor?

DOCTOR. Because the patient distrusts me. You, Madam, would seem to be the one to do it, but I fear he distrusts even you.

[*Laura's face changes for an instant.*]

DOCTOR. Perhaps you, Pastor—

PASTOR. No, I must ask to be excused.

[*Nöjd comes in.*]

LAURA. Have you delivered the message already?

NÖJD. Yes, Madam.

DOCTOR. Oh, is it you, Nöjd? You know the circumstances here; you know that the Captain is out of his mind and you must help us to take care of him.

NÖJD. If there is anything I can do for the Captain, you may be sure I will do it.

DOCTOR. You must put this jacket on him—

NURSE. No, he shan't touch him. Nöjd might hurt him. I would rather do it myself, very, very gently. But Nöjd can wait outside and help me if necessary. He can do that.

[*There is loud knocking on the private door.*]

DOCTOR. There he is! Put the jacket under your shawl on the chair, and you must all go out for the time being and the Pastor and I will receive him, for that door will not hold out many minutes. Now go.

NURSE [*Going out left.*] The Lord help us!

> [*Laura locks desk, then goes out left. Nöjd goes out back. After a moment the private door is forced open, with such violence that the lock is broken and the chair is thrown into the middle of the room. The Captain comes in with a pile of books under his arm, which he puts on the table.*]

CAPTAIN. The whole thing is to be read here, in every book. So I wasn't out of my mind after all! Here it is in the Odyssey, book first, verse 215, page 6 of the Upsala translation. It is Telemachus speaking to Athene. "My mother indeed maintains that he, Odysseus, is my father, but I myself know it not, for no man yet hath known his own origin." And this suspicion is harbored by Telemachus about Penelope, the most virtuous of women! Beautiful, eh? And here we have the prophet Ezekiel: "The fool saith; behold here is my father, but who can tell whose loins engendered him." That's quite clear! And what have we here? The History of Russian Literature by Mersläkow. Alexander Puschkin, Russia's greatest poet, died of torture front the reports circulated about his wife's unfaithfulness rather than by the bullet in his breast, from a duel. On his death-bed he swore she was innocent. Ass, ass! How could he swear to it? You see, I read my books. Ah, Jonas, art you here? and the doctor, naturally. Have you heard what I answered when an English lady complained about Irishmen who used to throw lighted lamps in their wives' faces? "God, what women," I cried. "Women," she gasped. "Yes, of course," I answered. "When things go so far that a man, a man who loved and worshipped a woman, takes a lighted lamp and throws it in her face, then one may know."

PASTOR. Know what?

CAPTAIN. Nothing. One never knows anything. One only believes. Isn't that true, Jonas? One believes and then one is saved! Yes, to be sure. No, I know that one can be damned by his faith. I know that.

DOCTOR. Captain!

CAPTAIN. Silence! I don't want to talk to you; I won't listen to you repeating their chatter in there, like a telephone! In there! You know! Look here, Jonas; do you believe that you are the father of your children? I remember that you had a tutor in your house who had a handsome face, and the people gossiped about him.

PASTOR. Adolf, take care!

CAPTAIN. Grope under your toupee and feel if there are not two bumps there. By my soul, I believe he turns pale! Yes, yes, they will talk; but, good Lord, they talk so much. Still we are a lot of ridiculous dupes, we married men. Isn't that true, Doctor? How was it with your marriage bed? Didn't you have a lieutenant in the house, eh? Wait a moment and I will make a guess—his name was—[*whispers in the Doctor's ear*]. You see he turns pale, too! Don't be disturbed. She is dead and buried and what is done can't be undone. I knew him well, by the way, and he is now—look at me, Doctor—No, straight in my eyes—a major in the cavalry! By God, if I don't believe he has horns, too.

DOCTOR [*Tortured*]. Captain, won't you talk about something else?

CAPTAIN. Do you see? He immediately wants to talk of something else when I mention horns.

PASTOR. Do you know, Adolf, that you are insane?

CAPTAIN. Yes; I know that well enough. But if I only had the handling of your illustrious brains for awhile I'd soon have you shut up, too! I am mad, but how did I become so? That doesn't concern you, and it doesn't concern anyone. But you want to talk of something else now. [*Takes the photograph album from the table.*] Good Lord, that is my child! Mine? We can never know. Do you know what we would have to do to make sure? First, one should marry to get the respect of society, then be divorced soon after and become lovers, and finally adopt the children. Then one would at least be sure that they were one's adopted children. Isn't that right? But how can all that help us now? What can keep me now that you have taken my conception of immortality from me, what use is science and philosophy to me when I have nothing to live for, what can I do with life when I am dishonored? I grafted my right arm, half my brain, half my marrow on another trunk, for I believed they would knit themselves together and grow into a more perfect tree, and then someone came with a knife and cut below the graft, and now I am only half a tree. But the other half goes on growing with my arm and half my brain, while I wither and die, for they were the best parts I gave away. Now I want to die. Do with me as you will. I am no more.

[*Buries his head on his arms on table. The Doctor whispers to the Pastor, and they go out through the door left. Soon after Bertha comes in.*]

BERTRA [*Goes up to Captain*]. Are you ill, Father?

CAPTAIN [*Looks up dazed*]. I?

BERTHA. Do you know what you have done? Do you know that you threw the lamp at Mother?

CAPTAIN. Did I?

BERTHA. Yes, you did. Just think if she had been hurt.

CAPTAIN. What would that have mattered?

BERTHA. You are not my father when you talk like that.

CAPTAIN. What do you say? Am I not your father? How do you know that? Who told you that? And who is your father, then? Who?

BERTHA. Not you at any rate.

CAPTAIN. Still not I? Who, then? Who? You seem to be well informed. Who told you? That I should live to see my child come and tell me to my face that I am not her father! But don't you know that you disgrace your mother when you say that? Don't you know that it is to her shame if it is so?

BERTHA. Don't say anything bad about Mother; do you hear?

CAPTAIN. No; you hold together, every one of you, against me! and you have always done so.

BERTHA. Father!

CAPTAIN. Don't use that word again!

BERTHA. Father, father!

CAPTAIN [*Draws her to him*]. Bertha, dear, dear child, you are my child! Yes, Yes; it cannot be otherwise. It is so. The other was only sickly thoughts that come with the wind like pestilence and fever. Look at me that I may see my soul in your eyes!—

But I see her soul, too! You have two souls and you love me with one and hate me with the other. But you must only love me! You must have only one soul, or you will never have peace, nor I either. You must have only one mind, which is the child of my mind and one will, which is my will.

BERTHA. But I don't want to, I want to be myself.

CAPTAIN. You must not. You see, I am a cannibal, and I want to eat you. Your mother wanted to eat me, but she was not allowed to. I am Saturn who ate his children because it had been prophesied that they would eat him. To eat or be eaten! That is the question. If I do not eat you, you will eat me, and you have already shown your teeth! But don't be frightened my dear child; I won't harm you.

[*Goes and takes a revolver from the wall.*]

BERTHA [*Trying to escape*]. Help, Mother, help, he wants to kill me.

NURSE [*Comes in*]. Mr. Adolf, what is it?

CAPTAIN [*Examining revolver*]. Have you taken out the cartridges?

NURSE. Yes, I put them away when I was tidying up, but sit down and be quiet and I'll get them out again!

[*She takes the Captain by the arm and gets him into a chair, into which he sinks feebly. Then she takes out the straitjacket and goes behind the chair. Bertha slips out left.*]

NURSE. Mr. Adolf, do you remember when you were my dear little boy and I tucked you in at night and used to repeat: "God who holds his children dear" to you, and do you remember how I used to get up in the night and give you a drink, how I would light the candle and tell you stories when you had bad dreams and couldn't sleep? Do you remember all that?

CAPTAIN. Go on talking, Margret, it soothes my head so. Tell me some more.

NURSE. O yes, but you must listen then! Do you remember when you took the big kitchen knife and wanted to cut out boats with it, and how I came in and had to get the knife away by fooling you? You were just a little child who didn't understand, so I had to fool you, for you didn't know that it was for your own good. "Give me that snake," I said, "or it will bite you!" and then you let go of the knife. [*Takes the revolver out of the Captain's hand.*] And then when you had to be dressed and didn't want to, I had to coax you and say that you should have a coat of gold and be dressed like a prince. And then I took your little blouse that was just made of green wool and held it in front of you and said: "In with both arms," and then I said, "Now sit nice and still while I button it down the back," [*She puts the straightjacket on*] and then I said, "Get up now, and walk across the floor like a good boy so I can see how it fits." [*She leads him to the sofa.*] And then I said, "Now you must go to bed."

CAPTAIN. What did you say? Was I to go to bed when I was dressed—damnation! what have you done to me? [*Tries to get free.*] Ah! you cunning devil of a woman! Who would have thought you had so much wit. [*Lies down on sofa.*] Trapped, shorn, outwitted, and not to be able to die!

NURSE. Forgive me, Mr. Adolf, forgive me, but I wanted to keep you from killing your child.

CAPTAIN. Why didn't you let me? You say life is hell and death the kingdom of heaven, and children belong to heaven.

NURSE. How do you know what comes after death?

CAPTAIN. That is the only thing we do know, but of life we know nothing! Oh, if one had only known from the beginning.

NURSE. Mr. Adolf, humble your hard heart and cry to God for mercy; it is not yet too late. It was not too late for the thief on the cross, when the Saviour said, "Today shalt thou be with me in Paradise."

CAPTAIN. Are you croaking for a corpse already, you old crow?

[*Nurse takes a hymnbook out of her pocket.*]

CAPTAIN [*Calls*]. Nöjd, is Nöjd out there?

[*Nöjd comes in.*]

CAPTAIN. Throw this woman out! She wants to suffocate me with her hymn-book. Throw her out of the window, or up the chimney, or anywhere.

NÖJD. [*Looks at Nurse*]. Heaven help you, Captain, but I can't do that, I can't. If it were only six men, but a woman!

CAPTAIN. Can't you manage one woman, eh?

NÖJD. Of course I can,—but—well, you see, it's queer, but one never wants to lay hands on a woman.

CAPTAIN. Why not? Haven't they laid hands on me?

NÖJD. Yes, but I can't, Captain. It's just as if you asked me to strike the Pastor. It's second nature, like religion, I can't!

[*Laura comes in, she motions Nöjd to go.*]

CAPTAIN. Omphale, Omphale! Now you play with the club while Hercules spins your wool.

LAURA [*Goes to sofa*]. Adolf, look at me. Do you believe that I am your enemy?

CAPTAIN. Yes, I do. I believe that you are all my enemies! My mother was my enemy when she did not want to bring me into the world because I was to be born with pain, and she robbed me of my embryonic life of its nourishment, and made a weakling of me. My sister was my enemy when she taught me that I must be submissive to her. The first woman I embraced was my enemy, for she gave me ten years of illness in return for the love I gave her. My daughter became my enemy when she had to choose between me and you. And you, my wife, you have been my arch enemy, because you never let up on me till I lay here lifeless.

LAURA. I don't know that. I ever thought or even intended what you think I did. It may be that a dim desire to get rid of you as an obstacle lay at the bottom of it, and if you see any design in my behavior, it is possible that it existed, although I was unconscious of it. I have never thought how it all came about, but it is the result of the course you yourself laid out, and before God and my conscience I feel that I am innocent, even if I am not. Your existence has lain like a stone on my heart—lain so heavily that I tried to shake off the oppressive burden. This is the truth, and if I have unconsciously struck you down, I ask your forgiveness.

CAPTAIN. All that sounds plausible. But how does it help me? And whose fault is it?

Perhaps spiritual marriages! Formerly one married a wife, now, one enters into partnership with a business woman, or goes to live with a friend—and then one ruins the partner, and dishonors the friend!—What has become of love, healthy sensuous love? It died in the transformation. And what is the result of this love in shares, payable to the bearer without joint liability? Who is the bearer when the crash comes? Who is the fleshly father of the spiritual child?

LAURA. And as for your suspicions about the child, they are absolutely groundless.

CAPTAIN. That's just what makes it so horrible. If at least there were any grounds for them, it would be something to get hold of, to cling to. Now there are only shadows that hide themselves in the bushes, and stick out their heads and grin; it is like fighting with the air, or firing blank cartridges in a sham fight. A fatal reality would have called forth resistance, stirred life and soul to action; but now my thoughts dissolve into air, and my brain grinds a void until it is on fire.—Put a pillow under my head, and throw something over me, I am cold. I am terribly cold!

[*Laura takes her shawl and spreads it over him. Nurse goes to get a pillow.*]

LAURA. Give me your hand, friend.

CAPTAIN. My band! The hand that you have bound! Omphale! Omphale!—But I feel your shawl against my mouth; it is as warm and soft as your arm, and it smells of vanilla, like your hair when you were young! Laura, when you were young, and we walked in the birch woods, with the primroses and the thrushes—glorious, glorious! Think how beautiful life was, and what it is now. You didn't want to have it like this, nor did I, and yet it happened. Who then rules over life?

LAURA. God alone rules—

CAPTAIN. The God of strife then! Or the Goddess perhaps, nowadays.—Take away the cat that is lying on me! Take it away!

[*Nurse brings in a pillow and takes the shawl away.*]

CAPTAIN. Give me my army coat!—Throw it over me! [*Nurse gets the coat and puts it over him.*] Ah, my rough lion skin that, you wanted to take away from me! Omphale! Omphale! You cunning woman, champion of peace and contriver of man's disarmament. Wake, Hercules, before they take your club away from you! You would wile our armor from us too, and make believe that it is nothing but glittering finery. No, it was iron, let me tell you, before it ever glittered. In olden days the smith made the armor, now it is the needle woman. Omphale! Omphale! Rude strength has fallen before treacherous weakness. Out on you infernal woman, and damnation on your sex! [*He raises himself to spit but falls back on the sofa.*] What have you given me for a pillow, Margret? It is so hard, and so cold, so cold. Come and sit near me. There. May I put my head on your knee? So!—This is warm! Bend over me so that I can feel your breast! Oh, it is sweet to sleep against a woman's breast, a mother's, or a mistress's, but the mother's is sweetest.

LAURA. Would you like to see your child, Adolf?

CAPTAIN. My child? A man has no children, it is only woman who has children, and therefore the future is hers when we die childless. Oh, God, who holds his children dear!

NURSE. Listen, he is praying to God.

CAPTAIN. No, to you to put me to sleep, for I am tired, so tired. Good night, Margret, and blessed be you among women.

*[He raises himself, but falls with a cry on the nurse's lap. Laura goes to
left and calls the Doctor who comes in with the Pastor.]*

LAURA. Help us, Doctor, if it isn't too late. Look, he has stopped breathing.

DOCTOR [*Feels the Captain's pulse.*] It is a stroke.

PASTOR. Is he dead?

DOCTOR. No, he may yet cone back to life, but to what an awakening we cannot tell.

PASTOR. "First death, and then the judgment."

DOCTOR. No judgment, and no accusations, you who believe that a God shapes man's destiny must go to him about this.

NURSE. Ah, Pastor, with his last breath he prayed to God.

PASTOR [*To Laura*]. Is that true?

LAURA. It is.

DOCTOR. In that case, which I can understand as little as the cause of his illness, my skill is at an end. You try yours now, Pastor.

LAURA. Is that all you have to say at this death-bed, Doctor?

DOCTOR. That is all! I know no more. Let him speak who knows more.

[Bertha comes in from left and runs to her mother.]

BERTHA. Mother, Mother!

LAURA. My child, my own child!

PASTOR. Amen.

CURTAIN.

MISS JULIE

CHARACTERS
MISS JULIE, twenty-five years old
JEAN, a valet, thirty
KRISTIN, a cook, thirty-five
FARM SERVANTS

The action takes place on Saint John's night, the mid-summer festival surviving from pagan times.

[SCENE.—*A large kitchen. The ceiling and walls are partially covered by draperies and greens. The back wall slants upward from left side of scene. On back wall, left, are two shelves filled with copper kettles, iron casseroles and tin pans. The shelves are trimmed with fancy scalloped paper. To right of middle a large arched entrance with glass doors through which one sees a fountain with a statue of Cupid, syringa bushes in bloom and tall poplars. To left corner of scene a large stove with hood decorated with birch branches. To right, servants' dining table of white pine and a few chairs. On the cud of table stands a Japanese jar filled with syringa blossoms. The floor is strewn with juniper branches.*]
[*Near stove, an ice-box, sink and dish-table. A large old-fashioned bell, hangs over the door, to left of door a speaking tube.*]
[*Kristin stands at stork engaged in cooking something. She wears a light cotton dress and kitchen apron. Jean comes in wearing livery; he carries a large pair of riding-boots with spurs, which he puts on floor.*]

JEAN. Tonight Miss Julie is crazy again, perfectly crazy.
KRISTIN. So—you're back at last.
JEAN. I went to the station with the Count and coming back I went in to the barn and danced and then I discovered Miss Julie there leading the dance with the gamekeeper. When she spied me, she rushed right toward me and asked me to waltz, and then she waltzed so—never in my life have I seen anything like it! Ah—she is crazy tonight.
KRISTIN. She has always been. But never so much as in the last fortnight, since her engagement was broken off.
JEAN. Yes, what about that gossip? He seemed like a fine fellow although he wasn't rich! Ach! they have so much nonsense about them. [*Seats himself at table.*] It's queer about Miss Julie though—to prefer staying here at home among these people, eh, to going away with her father to visit her relatives, eh?
KRISTIN. She's probably shamefaced about breaking off with her intended.
JEAN. No doubt! but he was a likely sort just the same. Do you know, Kristin, how it happened? I saw it, although I didn't let on.
KRISTIN. No—did you see it?
JEAN. Yes, indeed, I did. They were out in the stable yard one evening and she was "training" him as she called it. Do you know what happened? She made him leap over her riding whip, the way you teach a dog to jump. He jumped it twice and got a lash each time; but the third time he snatched the whip from her hand and broke it

into pieces. And then he vanished!

KRISTIN. Was that the way it happened? No, you don't say so!

JEAN. Yes, that's the way the thing happened. But what have you got to give me that's good, Kristin?

KRISTIN. [*She takes things from the pans on stove and serves them to him.*] Oh, it's only a bit of kidney that I cut out of the veal steak for you.

JEAN [*Smelling the food*]. Splendid! My favorite delicacy. [*Feeling of plate*]. But you might have warmed the plate.

KRISTIN. You're fussier than the Count, when you get started.

[*Tweaks his hair.*]

JEAN. Don't pull my hair! You know how sensitive I am.

KRISTIN. Oh—there, there! you know I was only loving you.

[*Jean eats, and Kristin opens bottle of beer.*]

JEAN. Beer on midsummer night—thank you, no! I have something better than that myself. [*Takes bottle of wine from drawer of table.*] Yellow seal, how's that? Now give me a glass—a wine glass you understand, of course, when one drinks the genuine.

KRISTIN. [*Fetches a glass. Then goes to stove and puts on casserole.*] Heaven help the woman who gets you for her husband. Such a fuss budget!

JEAN. Oh, talk! You ought to be glad to get such a fine fellow as I am. And I don't think it's done you any harm because I'm considered your intended. [*Tastes wine.*] Excellent, very excellent! Just a little too cold. [*Warms glass with hands*]. We bought this at Dijon. It stood at four francs a liter in the bulk; then of course there was the duty besides. What are you cooking now that smells so infernally?

KRISTIN. Oh, it's some devil's mess that Miss Julie must have for Diana.

JEAN. Take care of your words, Kristin. But why should you stand there cooking for that damned dog on a holiday evening? Is it sick, eh?

KRISTIN. Yes, it's sick. Diana sneaked out with the gatekeeper's mongrels and now something is wrong. Miss Julie can't stand that.

JEAN. Miss Julie has a great deal of pride about some things—but not enough about others! Just like her mother in her lifetime; she thrived best in the kitchen or the stable, but she must always drive tandem—never one horse! She would go about with soiled cuffs but she had to have the Count's crest on her cuff buttons. And as for Miss Julie, she doesn't take much care of her appearance either. I should say she isn't refined. Why just now out there she pulled the forester from Anna's side and asked him to dance with her. We wouldn't do things that way. But when the highborn wish to unbend they become vulgar. Splendid she is though! Magnificent! Ah, such shoulders and—

KRISTIN. Oh, don't exaggerate. I've heard what Clara says who dresses her sometimes, I have.

JEAN. Ha! Clara—you women are always jealous of each other. I who've been out riding with her—!!! And such a dancer!

KRISTIN. Come now, Jean, don't you want to dance with me when I'm through?

JEAN. Of course I want to.

KRISTIN. That is a promise?

JEAN. Promise! When I say I will do a thing I do it! Thanks for the supper—it was excellent.

[*Pushes cork in the bottle with a bang. Miss Julie appears in doorway, speaking to someone outside.*]

JULIE. I'll be back soon, but don't let things wait for me.

[*Jean quickly puts bottle in table drawer and rises very respectfully.*]
[*Enter Miss Julie and goes to Kristin.*]

JULIE. Is it done?

[*Kristin indicating Jean's presence.*]

JEAN [*Gallantly*]. Have you secrets between you?

JULIE. [*Flipping handkerchief in his face*]. Curious, are you?

JEAN. How sweet that violet perfume is!

JULIE [*Coquettishly*]. Impudence! Do you appreciate perfumes too? Dance—that you can do splendidly. [*Jean looks towards the cooking store*]. Don't look. Away with you.

JEAN [*Inquisitive but polite*]. Is it some troll's dish that you are both concocting for midsummer night? Something to pierce the future with and evoke the face of your intended?

JULIE [*Sharply*]. To see him one must have sharp eyes. [*To Kristin*]. Put it into a bottle and cork it tight. Come now, Jean and dance a schottische with me.

[*Jean hesitates.*]

JEAN. I don't wish to be impolite to anyone but—this dance I promised to Kristin.

JULIE. Oh, she can have another—isn't that so, Kristin? Won't you lend Jean to me.

KRISTIN. It's not for me to say, if Miss Julie is so gracious it's not for me to say no. [*To Jean*]. Go you and be grateful for the honor.

JEAN. Well said—but not wishing any offense I wonder if it is prudent for Miss Julie to dance twice in succession with her servant, especially as people are never slow to find meaning in—

JULIE [*Breaking out*]. In what? What sort of meaning? What were you going to say?

JEAN [*Taken aback*]. Since Miss Julie does not understand I must speak plainly. It may look strange to prefer one of your—underlings—to others who covet the same honor—

JULIE. To prefer—what a thought! I, the lady of the house! I honor the people with my presence and now that I feel like dancing I want to have a partner who knows how to lead to avoid being ridiculous.

JEAN. As Miss Julie commands. I'm here to serve.

JULIE [*Mildly*]. You mustn't look upon that as a command. Tonight we are all in holiday spirits—full of gladness and rank is flung aside. So, give me your arm! Don't be alarmed, Kristin, I shall not take your sweetheart away from you.

[*Jean offers arm. They exit.*]

[PANTOMIME.—*Played as though the actress were really alone. Turns her back to the audience when necessary. Does not look out into the auditorium. Does not hurry as though fearing the audience might grow restless. Soft violin music from the distance, schottische time. Kristin hums with the music. She cleans the table; washes plate, wipes it and puts it in the china closet. Takes off her apron and then opens drawer of table and takes a small hand glass and strands it against a flower pot on table. Lights a candle and heats a hair pin with which she crimps her hair around her forehead. After that she goes to door at back and listens. Then she returns to table and sees the Countess' handkerchief, picks it up, smells of it, then smoothes it out and folds it. Enter Jean.*]

JEAN. She is crazy I tell you! To dance like that! And the people stand grinning at her behind the doors. What do you say to that, Kristin?

KRISTIN. Oh, didn't I say she's been acting queer lately? But isn't it my turn to dance now?

JEAN. You are not angry because I let myself be led by the forelock?

KRISTIN. No, not for such a little thing. That you know well enough. And I know my place too—

JEAN [*Puts arm around her waist*]. You're a pretty smart girl, Kristin, and you ought to make a good wife.

[*Enter Miss Julie.*]

JULIE [*Disagreeably surprised, but with forced gaiety*]. You're a charming cavalier to run away from your partner.

JEAN. On the contrary, Miss Julie, I have hastened to my neglected one as you see.

JULIE [*Changing subject*]. Do you know, you dance wonderfully well! But why are you in livery on a holiday night? Take it off immediately.

JEAN. Will you excuse me—my coat hangs there.

[*Goes R. and takes coat.*]

JULIE. Does it embarrass you to change your coat in my presence? Go to your room then—or else stay and I'll turn my back.

JEAN. With your permission, Miss Julie.

[*Exit Jean R. One sees his arm as he changes coat.*]

JULIE [*To Kristin*]. Is Jean your sweetheart, that he is so devoted?

KRISTIN. Sweetheart? Yes, may it please you. Sweetheart—that's what they call it.

JULIE. Call it?

KRISTIN. Oh Miss Julie has herself had a sweetheart and—

JULIE. Yes, we were engaged—

KRISTIN. But it came to nothing.

[*Enter Jean in black frock coat.*]

JULIE. Très gentil, Monsieur Jean, très gentil.

JEAN. Vous voulez plaisanter, Mademoiselle.

JULIE. Et vous voulez parler français? Where did you learn that?

JEAN. In Switzerland where I was butler in the largest hotel at Lucerne.

JULIE. Why, you look like a gentleman in your frock coat. Charmant!

[*Seats herself by table.*]

JEAN. You flatter me!

JULIE. Flatter! [*Picking him up on the word.*]

JEAN. My natural modesty forbids me to believe that you could mean these pleasant things that you say to a—such as I am—and therefore I allowed myself to fancy that you overrate or, as it is called, flatter.

JULIE. Where did you learn to use words like that? Have you frequented the theatres much?

JEAN. I have frequented many places, I have!

JULIE. But you were born here in this neighborhood?

JEAN. My father was a deputy under the public prosecutor, and I saw Miss Julie as a child—although she didn't see me!

JULIE. No, really?

JEAN. Yes, I remember one time in particular. But I mustn't talk about that.

JULIE. Oh yes, do, when was it?

JEAN. No really—not now, another time perhaps.

JULIE. "Another time" is a good for nothing. Is it so dreadful then?

JEAN. Not dreadful—but it goes against the grain. [*Turns and points to Kristin, who has fallen asleep in a chair near stove*]. Look at her.

JULIE. She'll make a charming wife! Does she snore too?

JEAN. No, but she talks in her sleep.

JULIE [*Cynically*]. How do you know that she talks in her sleep?

JEAN [*Boldly*]. I have heard her.

[*Pause and they look at each other.*]

JULIE. Why don't you sit down?

JEAN. I can't allow myself to do so in your presence.

JULIE. But if I command you?

JEAN. Then I obey.

JULIE. Sit down then. But wait—can't you get me something to drink first?

JEAN. I don't know what there is in the icebox. Nothing but beer, probably.

JULIE. Is beer nothing? My taste is so simple that I prefer it to wine.

[*Jean takes out beer and serves it on plate.*]

JEAN. Allow me.

JULIE. Won't you drink too?

JEAN. I am no friend to beer—but if Miss Julie commands.

JULIE [*Gaily*]. Commands! I should think as a polite cavalier you might join your lady.

JEAN. Looking at it in that way you are quite right. [*Opens another bottle of beer and fills glass.*]

JULIE. Give me a toast!

[*Jean hesitates.*]

JULIE [*Mockingly*]. Old as he is, I believe the man is bashful!

JEAN [*On his knee with mock gallantry, raises glass*]. A health to my lady of the house!

JULIE. Bravo! Now you must kiss my slipper. Then the thing is perfect.

[*Jean hesitates and then seizes her foot and kisses it lightly.*]

JULIE. Splendid! You should have been an actor.

JEAN [*Rising*]. But this mustn't go any further, Miss Julie. What if someone should come in and see us?

JULIE. What harm would that do?

JEAN. Simply that it would give them a chance to gossip. And if Miss Julie only knew how their tongues wagged just now—then—

JULIE. What did they say? Tell me. And sit down now.

JEAN [*Sitting*]. I don't wish to hurt you, but they used an expression—threw hints of a certain kind—but you are not a child, you can understand. When one sees a lady drinking alone with a man—let alone a servant—at night—then—

JULIE. Then what? And for that matter, we are not alone. Kristin is here.

JEAN. Sleeping! Yes.

JULIE. Then I shall wake her. [*Rises*]. Kristin, are you asleep?

KRISTIN. [*In her sleep*]. Bla—bla—bla—bla.

JULIE. Kristin! She certainly can sleep. [*Goes to Kristin.*]

KRISTIN. [*In her sleep*]. The Count's boots are polished—put on the coffee—soon—soon—soon. Oh—h-h-h—puh!

[*Breathes heavily. Julie takes her by the nose.*]

JULIE. Won't you wake up?

JEAN [*Sternly*]. Don't disturb the sleeping.

JULIE [*Sharply*]. What?

JEAN. Anyone who has stood over the hot stove all day long is tired when night comes. One should respect the weary.

JULIE. That's a kind thought—and I honor it. [*Offers her hand.*] Thanks for the suggestion. Come out with me now and pick some syringas.

[*Kristin has awakened and goes to her room, right, in a sort of sleep stupefied way.*]

JEAN. With Miss Julie?

JULIE. With me.

JEAN. But that wouldn't do—decidedly not.

JULIE. I don't understand you. Is it possible that you fancy that I—

JEAN. No—not I, but people.

JULIE. What? That I'm in love with my coachman?

JEAN. I am not presumptuous, but we have seen instances—and with the people nothing is sacred.

JULIE. I believe he is an aristocrat!

JEAN. Yes, I am.

JULIE. But I step down— —

JEAN. Don't step down, Miss Julie. Listen to me—no one would believe that you stepped down of your own accord; people always say that one falls down.

JULIE. I think better of the people than you do. Come—and try them—come!

[*Dares him with a look.*]

JEAN. Do you know that you are wonderful?

JULIE. Perhaps. But you are too. Everything is wonderful for that matter. Life, people— everything. Everything is wreckage, that drifts over the water until it sinks, sinks. I have the same dream every now and then and at this moment I am reminded of it. I find myself seated at the top of a high pillar and I see no possible way to get down. I grow dizzy when I look down, but down I must. But I'm not brave enough to throw myself; I cannot hold fast and I long to fall—but I don't fall. And yet I can find no rest or peace until I shall come down to earth; and if I came down to earth I would wish myself down in the ground. Have you ever felt like that?

JEAN. No, I dream that I'm lying in a dark wood under a tall tree and I would up—up to the top, where I can look far over the fair landscape, where the sun is shining. I climb—climb, to plunder the birds' nests up there where the golden eggs lie, but the tree trunk is so thick, so smooth, and the first limb is so high! But I know if I reached the first limb I should climb as though on a ladder, to the top. I haven't reached it yet, but I shall reach it, if only in the dream.

JULIE. Here I stand talking about dreams with you. Come now, just out in the park.

[*She offers her arm and they start.*]

JEAN. We should sleep on nine midsummer flowers tonight and then our dreams would come true.

[*She turns, Jean quickly holds a hand over his eye.*]

JULIE. What is it, something in your eye?

JEAN. Oh, it is nothing—just a speck. It will be all right in a moment.

JULIE. It was some dust from my sleeve that brushed against you. Now sit down and let me look for it. [*Pulls him into a chair, looks into his eye.*] Now sit still, perfectly still. [*Uses corner of her handkerchief in his eye. Strikes his hand.*] So—will you mind? I believe you are trembling, strong man that you are. [*Touching his arm.*] And such arms!

JEAN [*Warningly.*] Miss Julie!

JULIE. Yes, Monsieur Jean!

JEAN. Attention. Je ne suis qu' un homme!

JULIE. Will you sit Still! So, now it is gone! Kiss my hand and thank me!

[*Jean rises.*]

JEAN. Miss Julie, listen to me. Kristin has gone to bed now—will you listen to me—
JULIE. Kiss my hand first.
JEAN. Listen to me—
JULIE. Kiss my hand first.
JEAN. Yes, but blame yourself.
JULIE. For what?
JEAN. For what? Are you a child at twenty-five? Don't you know that it is dangerous to play with fire?
JULIE. Not for me. I am insured!
JEAN. No, you are not. But even if you are, there is inflammable material in the neighborhood.
JULIE. Might that be you?
JEAN. Yes, not because it is I, but because I'm a young man—
JULIE [*Scornfully*]. With a grand opportunity—what inconceivable presumption! A Don Juan perhaps! Or a Joseph! On my soul, I believe he is a Joseph!
JEAN. You do?
JULIE. Almost.

[*Jean rushes towards her and tries to take her in his arms to kiss her.*]

JULIE [*Gives him a box on the ear*]. Shame on you.
JEAN. Are you in earnest, or fooling?
JULIE. In earnest.
JEAN. Then you were in earnest a moment ago, too. You play too seriously with what is dangerous. Now I'm tired of playing and beg to be excused that I may go on with my work. The Count must have his boots in time, and it is long past midnight.

[*Jean picks up boots.*]

JULIE. Put those boots away.
JEAN. No, that is my work which it is my duty to do, but I was not hired to be your play thing and that I shall never be. I think too well of myself for that.
JULIE. You are proud.
JEAN. In some things—not in others.
JULIE. Were you ever in love?
JEAN. We do not use that word, but I have liked many girls. One time I was sick because I couldn't have the one I wanted—sick, you understand, like the princesses in the Arabian Nights who could not eat nor drink for love sickness.
JULIE. Who was she? [*Jean is silent.*] Who was she?
JEAN. That you could not make me tell.
JULIE. Not if I ask you as an equal, as a—friend? Who was she?
JEAN. It was you!

[*Julie seats herself.*]

JULIE. How extravagant!

JEAN. Yes, if you will, it was ridiculous. That was the story I hesitated to tell, but now I'm going to tell it. Do you know how people in high life look from the under world? No, of course you don't. They look like hawks and eagles whose backs one seldom sees, for they soar up above. I lived in a hovel provided by the state, with seven brothers and sisters and a pig; out on a barren stretch where nothing grew, not even a tree, but from the window I could see the Count's park walls with apple trees rising above them. That was the garden of paradise; and there stood many angry angels with flaming swords protecting it; but for all that I and other boys found the way to the tree of life—now you despise me.

JULIE. Oh, all boys steal apples.

JEAN. You say that, but you despise me all the same. No matter! One time I entered the garden of paradise—it was to weed the onion beds with my mother! Near the orchard stood a Turkish pavilion, shaded and overgrown with jessamine and honeysuckle. I didn't know what it was used for and I had never seen anything so beautiful. People passed in and out and one day—the door was left open. I sneaked in and beheld walls covered with pictures of kings and emperors and there were red-fringed curtains at the windows—now you understand what I mean—I—[*Breaks off a spray of syringes and puts it to her nostrils.*] I had never been in the castle and how my thoughts leaped—and there they returned ever after. Little by little the longing came over me to experience for once the pleasure of—enfin, I sneaked in and was bewildered. But then I heard someone coming—there was only one exit for the great folk, but for me there was another, and I had to choose that. [*Julie who has taken the syringa lets it fall on table.*] Once out I started to run, scrambled through a raspberry hedge, rushed over a strawberry bed and came to a stop on the rose terrace. For there I saw a figure in a white dress and white slippers and stockings—it was you! I hid under a heap of weeds, under, you understand, where the thistles pricked me, and lay on the damp, rank earth. I gazed at you walking among the roses. And I thought if it is true that the thief on the cross could enter heaven and dwell among the angels it was strange that a pauper child on God's earth could not go into the castle park and play with the Countess' daughter.

JULIE [*Pensively*]. Do you believe that all poor children would have such thoughts under those conditions?

JEAN [*Hesitates, then in a positive voice*]. That all poor children—yes, of course, of course!

JULIE. It must be a terrible misfortune to be poor.

JEAN [*With deep pain and great chagrin*]. Oh, Miss Julie, a dog may lie on the couch of a Countess, a horse may be caressed by a lady's hand, but a servant—yes, yes, sometimes there is stuff enough in a man, whatever he be, to swing himself up in the world, but how often does that happen! But to return to the story, do you know what I did? I ran down to the mill dam and threw myself in with my clothes on—and was pulled out and got a thrashing. But the following Sunday when all the family went to visit my grandmother I contrived to stay at home; I scrubbed myself well, put on my best dollies, such its they were, and went to church so that I might see you. I saw you. Then I went home with my mind made up to put, an cud to myself. But I wanted to do it beautifully and without pain. Then I happened to remember that elderberry blossoms are poisonous. I knew where there was a big elderberry bush in full bloom and I stripped it of its riches and made a bed of it in the oat-bin. Have you ever noticed how smooth and glossy oats are? As soft as a woman's arm.—Well, I got in and let down the cover, fell asleep, and when I awoke I was very ill, but didn't die—as you see. What I wanted—I don't know. You were unattainable, but through the vision of you I was made to realize how hopeless it was to rise above the conditions of my birth.

JULIE. You tell it well! Were you ever at school?

JEAN. A little, but I have read a good deal and gone to the theatres. And besides, I have always heard the talk of fine folks and from them I have learned most.

JULIE. Do you listen then to what we are saying?

JEAN. Yes, indeed, I do. And I have heard much when I've been on the coachbox. One time I heard Miss Julie and a lady—

JULIE. Oh, what was it you heard?

JEAN. Hm! that's not so easy to tell. But I was astonished and could not understand where you had heard such things. Well, perhaps at bottom there's not so much difference between people and—people.

JULIE. Oh, shame! We don't behave as you do when we are engaged.

JEAN. [Eyeing her]. Are you sure of that? It isn't worthwhile to play the innocent with me.

JULIE. I gave my love to a rascal.

JEAN. That's what they always say afterward.

JULIE. Always?

JEAN. Always, I believe, as I have heard the expression many times before under the same circumstances.

JULIE. What circumstances?

JEAN. Those we've been talking about. The last time I— —

JULIE. Silence. I don't wish to hear any more.

JEAN. Well, then I beg to be excused so I may go to bed.

JULIE. Go to bed! On midsummer night?

JEAN. Yes, for dancing out there with that pack has not amused me.

JULIE. Then get the key for the boat and row me out over the lake. I want to see the sun rise.

JEAN. Is that prudent?

JULIE. One would think that, you were afraid of your reputation.

JEAN. Why not? I don't want to be made ridiculous. I am not willing to be driven out without references, now that I am going to settle down. And I feel I owe something to Kristin.

JULIE. Oh, so it's Kristin now—

JEAN. Yes, but you too. Take my advice, go up and go to bed.

JULIE. Shall I obey you?

JEAN. For once—for your own sake. I beg of you. Night is crawling along, sleepiness makes one irresponsible and the brain grows hot. Go to your room. In fact—if I hear rightly some of the people are coming for me. If they find us here—then you are lost.

[Chorus is heard approaching, singing.]

"There came two ladies out of the woods
Tridiridi-ralla tridiridi-ra.
One of them had wet her foot,
Tridiridi-ralla-la.

"They talked of a hundred dollars,
Tridiridi-ralla tridiridi-ra.
But neither had hardly a dollar,
Tridiridi-ralla-la.

"The mitten I'm going to send you,
Tridirichi-ralla tridiridi-ra.
For another I'm going to jilt you,
Tridiridi-ralla tridiridi-ra."

JULIE. I know the people and I love them and they respect me. Let them come, you shall see.

JEAN. No, Miss Julie, they don't love you. They take your food and spit upon your kindness, believe me. Listen to them, listen to what they're singing! No! Don't listen!

JULIE [*Listening*]. What are they singing?

JEAN. It's something suggestive, about you and me.

JULIE. Infamous! Oh horrible! And how cowardly!

JEAN. The pack is always cowardly. And in such a battle one can only run away.

JULIE. Run away? Where? We can't get out and we can't go to Kristin.

JEAN. Into my room then. Necessity knows no law. You can depend on me for I am your real, genuine, respectful friend.

JULIE. But think if they found you there.

JEAN. I will turn the key and if they try to break in I'll shoot. Come—come!

JULIE. [*Meaningly*]. You promise me—?

JEAN. I swear...

> [*She exits* R. *Jean follows her.*]
> [BALLET.—*The farm folk enter in holiday dress with flowers in their hats, a fiddler in the lead. They carry a keg of home-brewed beer and a smaller keg of gin, both decorated with greens which are placed on the table. They help themselves to glasses and drink. Then they sing and dance a country dance to the melody of "There came two ladies out of the woods." When that is over they go out, singing.*]
> [*Enter Julie alone, sees the havoc the visitors have made, clasps her hands, takes out powder box and powders her face. Enter Jean exuberant.*]

JEAN. There, you see, and you heard them. Do you think it's possible for us to remain here any longer?

JULIE. No, I don't. But what's to be done?

JEAN. Fly! Travel—far from here!

JULIE. Travel—yes—but where?

JEAN. To Switzerland—to the Italian lakes. You have never been there?

JULIE. No—is it beautiful there?

JEAN. Oh, an eternal summer! Oranges, trees, laurels—oh!

JULIE. But what shall we do there?

JEAN. I'll open a first-class hotel for first-class patrons.

JULIE. Hotel?

JEAN. That is life—you shall see! New faces constantly, different languages. Not a moment for boredom. Always something to do night and day—the bell ringing, the trains whistling, the omnibus coming and going and all the time the gold pieces rolling into the till—that is life!

JULIE. Yes, that is life. And I—?

JEAN. The mistress of the establishment—the ornament of the house. With your looks—and your manners—oh, it's a sure success! Colossal! You could sit like a queen in the office and set the slaves in action by touching an electric button. The guests line up before your throne and shyly lay their riches on your desk. You can't believe how people tremble when they get their bills—I can salt the bills and you can sweeten them with your most bewitching smile—ha, let us get away from here—[*Takes a time table from his pocket*] immediately—by the next train. We can be at Malmö at 6.30, Hamburg at 8.40 tomorrow morning, Frankfort the day after and at Como by the St. Gothard route in about—let me see, three days. Three days!

JULIE. All that is well enough, but Jean—you must give me courage. Take me in your arms and tell me that you love me.

JEAN [*Hesitatingly*]. I will—but I daren't—not again in this house. I love you of course—do you doubt that?

JULIE [*Shyly and with womanliness*]. You! Say thou to me! Between us there can be no more formality. Say thou.

JEAN. I can't—There must be formality between us—as long as we are in this house. There is the memory of the past—and there is the Count, your father. I have never known anyone else for whom I have such respect. I need only to see his gloves lying in a chair to feel my own insignificance. I have only to hear his bell to start like a nervous horse—and now as I see his boots standing there so stiff and proper I feel like bowing and scraping. [*Gives boots a kick*]. Superstitions and prejudices taught in childhood can't be uprooted in a moment. Let us go to a country that is it republic where they'll stand on their heads for my coachman's livery—on their heads shall they stand—but I shall not. I am not, born to bow and scrape, for there's stuff in me—character. If I only get hold of the first limb, you shall see me climb. I'm a coachman today, but next year I shall be a proprietor, in two years a gentleman of income; then for Roumania where I'll let them decorate me and can, mark you, *can* end a count!

JULIE. Beautiful, beautiful!

JEAN. Oh, in Roumania, one can buy a title cheap—and so you can be a countess just the same—my countess!

JULIE. What do I care for all that—which I now cast behind me. Say that you love me—else, what am I, without it?

JEAN. I'll say it a thousand times afterwards, but not here. Above all, let us have no sentimentality now or everything will fall through. We must look at this matter coldly like sensible people. [*Takes out a cigar and lights it.*] Now sit down there and

I'll sit here and we'll take it over as if nothing had happened.

JULIE [*Staggered*]. Oh, my God, have you no feeling?

JEAN. I? No one living has more feeling than I but I can restrain myself.

JULIE. A moment ago you could kiss my slipper and now—

JEAN [*Harshly*]. That was—then. Now we have other things to think about.

JULIE. Don't speak harshly to me.

JEAN. Not harshly, but wisely. One folly has been committed—commit no more. The Count may be here at any moment, and before he comes, our fate must be settled. How do my plans for the future strike you? Do you approve of them?

JULIE. They seem acceptable enough. But one question. For such a great undertaking a large capital is necessary, have you that?

JEAN [*Chewing his cigar*]. I? To be sure. I have my regular occupation, my unusual experience, my knowledge of different languages—that is capital that counts, I should say.

JULIE. But with all that you could not buy a railway ticket.

JEAN. That's true, and for that reason I'm looking for a backer who can furnish the funds.

JULIE. How can that be done at a moment's notice?

JEAN. That is for you to say, if you wish to be my companion.

JULIE. I can't—as I have nothing myself.

      [*A pause.*]

JEAN. Then the whole matter drops— —

JULIE. And— —

JEAN. Things remain as they are.

JULIE. Do you think I could remain under this roof after——Do you think I will allow the people to point at me in scorn, or that I can ever look my father in the face again? Never! Take me away from this humiliation and dishonor. Oh, what have I done! Oh, my God, what have I done!

      [*Weeping.*]

JEAN. So, you are beginning in that tune now. What have you done? The same as many before you.

JULIE. And now you despise me. I am falling! I am falling!

JEAN. Fall down to my level, I'll lift you up afterwards.

JULIE. What strange power drew me to you—the weak to the strong—the falling to the rising, or is this love! This—love! Do you know what love is?

JEAN. I? Yes! Do you think it's the first time?

JULIE. What language, what thoughts.

JEAN. I am what life has made me. Don't be nervous and play the high and mighty, for now we are on the same level. Look here, my little girl, let me offer you a glass of something extra fine.

      [*Opens drawer of table and takes out wine bottle, then fills two glasses that have been already used.*]

JULIE. Where did you get that wine?

JEAN. From the cellar.

JULIE. My father's Burgundy.

JEAN. What's the matter, isn't that good enough for the son-in-law?

JULIE. And I drink beer—I!

JEAN. That only goes to prove that your taste is poorer than mine.

JULIE. Thief!

JEAN. Do you intend to tattle?

JULIE. Oh ho! Accomplice to a house thief. Was I intoxicated—have I been walking in my sleep this night—midsummer night, the night for innocent play—

JEAN. Innocent, eh!

JULIE [*Pacing back and forth*]. Is there a being on earth so miserable as I.

JEAN. Why are you, after such a conquest. Think of Kristin in there, don't you think she has feelings too?

JULIE. I thought so a little while ago, but I don't any more. A servant is a servant.

JEAN. And a whore is a whore.

JULIE [*Falls on her knees with clasped hands*]. Oh, God in heaven, end my wretched life, save me from this mire into which I'm sinking—Oh save me, save me.

JEAN. I can't deny that it hurts me to see you like this.

JULIE. And you who wanted to die for me.

JEAN. In the oat-bin? Oh, that was only talk.

JULIE. That is to say—a lie!

JEAN [*Beginning to show sleepiness*]. Er—er almost. I believe I read something of the sort in a newspaper about a chimney-sweep who made a death bed for himself of syringa blossoms in a wood-bin—[*laughs*] because they were going to arrest him for non-support of his children.

JULIE. So you are such a—

JEAN. What better could I have hit on! One must always be romantic to capture a woman.

JULIE. Wretch! Now you have seen the eagle's back, and I suppose I am to be the first limb—

JEAN. And the limb is rotten—

JULIE [*Without seeming to hear*]. And I am to be the hotel's signboard—

JEAN. And I the hotel—

JULIE. And sit behind the desk and allure guests and overcharge them—

JEAN. Oh, that'll be my business.

JULIE. That a soul can be so degraded!

JEAN. Look to your own soul.

JULIE. Lackey! Servant! Stand up when I speak.

JEAN. Don't you dare to moralize to me. Lackey, eh! Do you think you have shown yourself finer than any maid-servant tonight?

JULIE [*Crushed*]. That is right, strike me, trample on me, I deserve nothing better. I have done wrong, but help me now. Help me out of this if there is any possible way.

JEAN [*Softens somewhat*]. I don't care to shirk my share of the blame, but do you think any one of my position would ever have dared to raise his eyes to you if you yourself had not invited it? Even now I am astonished—

JULIE. And proud.

JEAN. Why not? Although I must confess that the conquest was too easy to be exciting.

JULIE. Go on, strike me again—

JEAN [*Rising*]. No, forgive me, rather, for what I said. I do not strike the unarmed, least of all, a woman. But I can't deny that from a certain point of view it gives me satisfaction to know that it is the glitter of brass, not gold, that dazzles us from below, and that the eagle's back is grey like the rest of him. On the other hand, I'm sorry to have to realize that all that I have looked up to is not worthwhile, and it pains me to see you fallen lower than your cook as it pains me to see autumn blossoms whipped to pieces by the cold rain and transformed into—dirt!

JULIE. You speak as though you were already my superior.

JEAN. And so I am! For I can make you a countess and you could never make me a count.

JULIE. But I am born of a count, that you can never be.

JEAN. That is true, but I can be the father of counts—if—

JULIE. But you are a thief—that I am not.

JEAN. There are worse things than that, and for that matter when I serve in a house I regard myself as a member of the family, a child of the house as it were. And one doesn't consider it theft if children snoop a berry from full bushes. [*With renewed passion*]. Miss Julie, you are a glorious woman—too good for such as I. You have been the victim of an infatuation and you want to disguise this fault by fancying that you love me. But you do not—unless perhaps my outer self attracts you. And then your love is no better than mine. But I cannot be satisfied with that, and your real love I can never awaken.

JULIE. Are you sure of that?

JEAN. You mean that we could get along with such an arrangement? There's no doubt about my loving you—you are beautiful, you are elegant—[*Goes to her and takes her hand*] accomplished, lovable when you wish to be, and the flame that you awaken in man does not die easily. [*Puts arm around her.*] You are like hot wine with strong spices, and your lips—

[*Tries to kiss her. Julie pulls herself away slowly.*]

JULIE. Leave me—I'm not to be won this way.

JEAN. How then? Not with caresses and beautiful words? Not by thoughts for the future, to save humiliation? How then?

JULIE. How? I don't know. I don't know! I shrink from you as I would from a rat. But I cannot escape from you.

JEAN. Escape with me.

JULIE. Escape? Yes, we must escape.—But I'm so tired. Give me a glass of wine. [*Jean fills a glass with wine, Julie looks at her watch.*] We must talk it over first for we have still a little time left.

[*She empties the glass and puts it out for more.*]

JEAN. Don't drink too much. It will go to your head.

JULIE. What harm will that do?

JEAN. What harm? It's foolish to get intoxicated. But what did you want to say?

JULIE. We must go away, but we must talk first. That is, I must speak, for until now you have done all the talking. You have told me about your life—now I will tell you about mine, then we will know each other through and through before we start on our wandering together.

JEAN. One moment, pardon. Think well whether you won't regret having told your life's secrets.

JULIE. Aren't you my friend?

JEAN. Yes. Sometimes. But don't depend on me.

JULIE. You only say that. And for that matter I have no secrets. You see, my mother was not of noble birth. She was brought up with ideas of equality, woman's freedom and all that. She had very decided opinions against matrimony, and when my father courted her she declared that she would never be his wife—but she did so for all that. I came into the world against my mother's wishes, I discovered, and was brought up like a child of nature by my mother, and taught everything that a boy must know as well; I was to be an example of a woman being as good as a man—I was made to go about in boy's clothes and take care of the horses and harness and saddle and hunt, and all such things; in fact, all over the estate women servants were taught to do men's work, with the result that the property came near being ruined—and so we became the laughing stock of the countryside. At last my father must have awakened from his bewitched condition, for he revolted, and ran things according to his ideas. My mother became ill—what it was I don't know, but she often had cramps and acted queerly—sometimes hiding in the attic or the orchard, and would even be gone all night at times. Then came the big fire which of course you have heard about. The house, the stables—everything was burned, under circumstances that pointed strongly to an incendiary, for the misfortune happened the day after the quarterly insurance was due and the premiums sent in by father were strangely delayed by his messenger so that they arrived too late.

[*She fills a wine glass and drinks.*]

JEAN. Don't drink any more.

JULIE. Oh, what does it matter? My father was utterly at a loss to know where to get money to rebuild with. Then my mother suggested that he try to borrow from a man who had been her friend in her youth—a brick manufacturer here in the neighborhood. My father made the loan, but wasn't allowed to pay any interest, which surprised him. Then the house was rebuilt. [*Julie drinks again.*] Do you know who burned the house?

JEAN. Her ladyship, your mother?

JULIE. Do you know who the brick manufacturer was?

JEAN. Your mother's lover?

JULIE. Do you know whose money it was?

JEAN. Just a moment, that I don't know.

JULIE. It was my mother's.

JEAN. The Count's—that is to say, unless there was a contract.

JULIE. There was no contract. My mother had some money which she had not wished to have in my father's keeping and therefore, she had entrusted it to her friend's care.

JEAN. Who kept it.

JULIE. Quite right—he held on to it. All this came to my father's knowledge. He couldn't proceed against him, wasn't allowed to pay his wife's friend, and couldn't prove that it was his wife's money. That was my mother's revenge for his taking the reins of the establishment into his own hands. At that time he was ready to shoot himself. Gossip had it that he had tried and failed. Well, he lived it down—and my mother paid full penalty for her misdeed. Those were five terrible years for me, as you can fancy. I sympathized with my father, but I took my mother's part, for I didn't know the true circumstances. Through her I learned to distrust and hate men, and I swore to her never to be a man's slave.

JEAN. But you became engaged to the Lieutenant Governor.

JULIE. Just to make him my slave.

JEAN. But that he didn't care to be.

JULIE. He wanted to be, fast enough, but I grew tired of him.

JEAN. Yes—I noticed that—in the stable-yard!

JULIE. What do you mean?

JEAN. I saw how he broke the engagement.

JULIE. That's a lie. It was I who broke it. Did he say he broke it—the wretch!

JEAN. I don't believe that he was a wretch. You hate men, Miss Julie.

JULIE. Most of them. Sometimes one is weak—

JEAN. You hate me?

JULIE. Excessively. I could see you shot—

JEAN. Like a mad dog?

JULIE. Exactly!

JEAN. But there is nothing here to shoot with. What shall we do then?

JULIE [*Rousing herself*].We must get away from here—travel.

JEAN. And torture each other to death?

JULIE. No—to enjoy, a few days, a week—as long as we can. And then to die.

JEAN. Die! How silly. I think it's better to start the hotel.

JULIE [*Not heeding him*]. By the Lake of Como where the sun is always shining, where the laurel is green at Christmas and the oranges glow.

JEAN. The Lake of Como is it rain hole, I never saw any oranges there except on fruit stands. But it's a good resort, and there are many villas to rent to loving couples. That's a very paying industry. You know why? They take leases for half a year at least, but they usually leave in three weeks.

JULIE [*Naïvely*]. Why after three weeks?

JEAN. Why? They quarrel of course, but the rent must be paid all the same. Then you re-let, and so one after another they come and go, for there is plenty of love, although it doesn't last long.

JULIE. Then you don't want to die with me?

JEAN. I don't want to die at all, both because I enjoy living and because I regard suicide as a crime to Him who has given us life.

JULIE. Then you believe in God?

JEAN. Yes. Of course I do, and I go to church every other Sunday—But I'm tired of all this and I'm going to bed.

JULIE. Do you think I would allow myself to be satisfied with such an ending? Do you know what a man owes to a woman he hits— —

JEAN [*Takes out a silver coin and throws it on the table*]. Allow me, I don't want to owe anything to anyone.

JULIE [*Pretending not to notice the insult*]. Do you know what the law demands?

JEAN. I know that the law demands nothing of a woman who seduces a man.

JULIE [*Again not heeding him*]. Do you see any way out of it but to travel?—wed—and separate?

JEAN. And if I protest against this misalliance?

JULIE. Misalliance!

JEAN. Yes, for me. For you see I have a finer ancestry than you, for I have no fire-bug in my family.

JULIE. How do you know?

JEAN. You can't prove the contrary. We have no family record except that which the police keep. But your pedigree I have read in a book on the drawing room table. Do you know who the founder of your family was? It was a miller whose wife found favor with the king during the Danish War. Such ancestry I have not.

JULIE. This is my reward for opening my heart to anyone so unworthy, with whom I have talked about my family honor.

JEAN. Dishonor—yes, I said it. I told you not to drink because then one talks too freely and one should never talk.

JULIE. Oh, how I repent all this. If at least you loved me!

JEAN. For the last time—what do you mean? Shall I weep, shall I jump over your riding whip, shall I kiss you, lure you to Lake Como for three weeks, and then—what do you want anyway? This is getting tiresome. But that's the way it always is when you get mixed up in women's affairs. Miss Julie, I see that you are unhappy, I know that you suffer, but I can't understand you. Among my kind there is no nonsense of this sort; we love as we play when work gives us time. We haven't the whole day and night for it like you.

JULIE. You must be good to me and speak to me as though I were a human being.

JEAN. Be one yourself. You spit on me and expect me to stand it.

JULIE. Help me, help me. Only tell me what to do—show me a way out of this!

JEAN. In heaven's name, if I only knew myself.

JULIE. I have been raving, I have been mad, but is there no means of deliverance?

JEAN. Stay here at home and say nothing. No one knows.

JULIE. Impossible. These people know it, and Kristin.

JEAN. They don't know it and could never suspect such a thing.

JULIE [*Hesitating*]. But—it might happen again.

JEAN. That is true.

JULIE. And the consequences?

JEAN [*Frightened*]. Consequences—where were my wits not to have thought of that! There is only one thing to do. Get away from here immediately. I can't go with you or they will suspect. You must go alone—away from here—anywhere.

JULIE. Alone? Where? I cannot.

JEAN. You must—and before the Count returns. If you stay, we know how it will be. If one has taken a false step it's likely to happen again as the harm has already been done, and one grows more and more daring until at last all is discovered. Write the Count afterward and confess all—except that it was I. That he could never guess, and I don't think he'll be so anxious to know who it was, anyway.

JULIE. I will go if you'll go with me.

JEAN. Are you raving again? Miss Julie running away with her coachman? All the papers would be full of it and that the Count could never live through.

JULIE. I can't go—I can't stay. Help me, I'm so tired—so weary. Command me, set me in motion—I can't think any more,—can't act—

JEAN. See now, what creatures you aristocrats are! Why do you bristle up and stick up your noses as though you were lords of creation. Very well—I will command you! Go up and dress yourself and see to it that you have travelling money and then come down. [*She hesitates.*] Go immediately.

[*She still hesitates. He takes her hand and leads her to door.*]

JULIE. Speak gently to me, Jean.
JEAN. A command always sounds harsh. Feel it yourself now.

[*Exit Julie.*]
[*Jean draws a sigh of relief, seats himself by the table, takes out a notebook and pencil and counts aloud now and then until, Kristin comes in, dressed for church.*]

KRISTIN. My heavens, how it looks here. What's been going on?
JEAN. Oh, Miss Julie dragged in the people. Have you been sleeping so soundly that you didn't hear anything?
KRISTIN. I've slept like a log.
JEAN. And already dressed for church!
KRISTIN. Ye-es, [*Sleepily*] didn't you promise to go to early service with me?
JEAN. Yes, quite so, and there you have my stock and front. All right.

[*He seats himself. Kristin putting on his stock.*]

JEAN [*Sleepily*]. What is the text today?
KRISTIN. St. John's Day! It is of course about the beheading of John the Baptist.
JEAN. I'm afraid it will be terribly long drawn out—that. Hey, you're choking me. I'm so sleepy, so sleepy.
KRISTIN. What have you been doing up all night? You are actually green in the face.
JEAN. I have been sitting here talking to Miss Julie.
KRISTIN. Oh you don't know your place.

[*Pause.*]

JEAN. Listen, Kristin.
KRISTIN. Well?
JEAN. It's queer about her when you think it over.
KRISTIN. What is queer?
JEAN. The whole thing.

[*Pause. Kristin looks at half empty glasses on table.*]

KRISTIN. Have you been drinking together, too?
JEAN. Yes!
KRISTIN. For shame. Look me in the eye.
JEAN. Yes.
KRISTIN. Is it possible? Is it possible?
JEAN [*After reflecting*]. Yes, it is.
KRISTIN. Ugh! That I would never have believed. For shame, for shame!
JEAN. You are not jealous of her?
KRISTIN. No, not of her. But if it had been Clara or Sophie—then I would have

scratched your eyes out. So that is what has happened—how I can't understand! No, that wasn't very nice!

JEAN. Are you mad at her?

KRISTIN. No, but with you. That was bad of you, very bad. Poor girl. Do you know what—I don't want to be here in this house any longer where one cannot respect one's betters.

JEAN. Why should one respect them?

KRISTIN. Yes, you can say that, you are so smart. But I don't want to serve people who behave so. It reflects on oneself, I think.

JEAN. Yes, but it's a comfort that they're not a bit better than we.

KRISTIN. No, I don't, think so, for if they are not better there's no use in our trying to better ourselves in this world. And to think of the Count! Think of him who has had so much sorrow all his days? No, I don't want to stay in this house any longer! And to think of it being with such as you! If it had been the Lieutenant— if it had been a better man—

JEAN. What's that?

KRISTIN. Yes! He was good enough, to be sure, but there's a difference between people just the same. No, this I can never forget. Miss Julie who was always so proud and indifferent to men! One never would believe that she would give herself—and to one like you! She who was ready to have Diana shot because she would run after the gatekeeper's mongrels. Yes, I say it—and here I won't stay any longer and on the twenty-fourth of October I go my way.

JEAN. And then?

KRISTIN. Well, as we've come to talk about it, it's high time you looked around for something else, since we're going to get married.

JEAN. Well, what'll I look for? A married man couldn't get a place like this.

KRISTIN. No, of course not. But you could take a gatekeeper's job or look for it watchman's place in some factory. The government's plums are few, but they are sure. And then the wife and children get a pension—

JEAN [*With a grimace*]. That's all very fine—all that, but it's not exactly in my line to think about dying for my wife and children just now. I must confess that I have slightly different aspirations.

KRISTIN. Aspirations? Aspirations—anyway you have obligations. Think of those, you.

JEAN. Don't irritate me with talk about my obligations. I know my own business. [*He listens.*] We'll have plenty of time for all this some other day. Go and get ready and we'll be off to church.

KRISTIN [*Listening*]. Who's that walking upstairs?

JEAN. I don't know—unless it's Clara.

KRISTIN [*Starting to go*]. It could never be the Count who has come home without anyone hearing him?

JEAN [*Frightened*]. The Count! I can't believe that. He would have rung the bell.

KRISTIN. God help us! Never have I been mixed up in anything like this!

[*Exit Kristin. The sun has risen and lights up the scene. Presently the sunshine comes in through windows at an angle. Jean goes to door and motions. Enter Julie, dressed for travelling, carrying a small bird cage covered with a cloth, which she places on a chair.*]

JULIE. I am ready!
JEAN. Hush, Kristin is stirring!

[*Julie frightened and nervous throughout following scene.*]

JULIE. Does she suspect anything?
JEAN. She knows nothing. But, good heavens, how you look!
JULIE. Why?
JEAN. You are pale as a ghost.
JULIE [*Sighs*]. Am I? Oh, the sun is rising, the sun!
JEAN. And now the troll's spell is broken.
JULIE. The trolls have indeed been at work this night. But, Jean, listen—come with me, I have money enough.
JEAN. Plenty?
JULIE. Enough to start with. Go with me for I can't go alone—today, midsummer day. Think of the stuffy train, packed in with the crowds of people staring at one; the long stops at the stations when one would be speeding away. No, I cannot, I cannot! And then the memories, childhood's memories of midsummer day—the church decorated with birch branches and syringa blossoms; the festive dinner table with relations and friends, afternoon in the park, music, dancing, flowers and games—oh, one may fly, fly, but anguish and remorse follow in the pack wagon.
JEAN. I'll go with you—if we leave instantly—before it's too late.
JULIE. Go and dress then.

[*She takes up bird cage.*]

JEAN. But no baggage! That would betray us.
JULIE. Nothing but what we can take in the coupé.

[*Jean has picked up his hat.*]

JEAN. What have you there?
JULIE. It's only my canary. I cannot, will not, leave it behind.
JEAN. So we are to lug a bird cage with us. Are you crazy? Let go of it.
JULIE. It is all I take from home. The only living creature that cares for me. Don't be hard—let me take it with me.
JEAN. Let go the cage and don't talk so loud. Kristin will hear us.
JULIE. No, I will not leave it to strange hands. I would rather see it dead.
JEAN. Give me the creature. I'll fix it.
JULIE. Yes, but don't hurt it. Don't—no, I cannot.
JEAN. Let go. I can.
JULIE [*Takes the canary from cage*]. Oh, my little siren. Must your mistress part with you?
JEAN. Be so good as not to make a scene. Your welfare, your life, is at stake. So—quickly. [*Snatches bird from her and goes to chopping block and takes up meat chopper*]. You should have learned how to chop off a chicken's head instead of shooting with a revolver. [*He chops off the bird's head*]. Then you wouldn't swoon at a drop of blood.

JULIE [*Shrieks*]. Kill me, too. Kill me! You who can butcher an innocent bird without a tremble. Oh, how I shrink from you. I curse the moment I first saw you. I curse the moment I was conceived in my mother's womb.

JEAN. Come now! What good is your cursing, let's be off.

JULIE [*Looks toward chopping block as though obsessed by thought of the slain bird*]. No, I cannot. I must see— —hush, a carriage is passing. Don't you think I can stand the sight of blood? You think I am weak. Oh, I should like to see your blood flowing—to see your brain on the chopping block, all your sex swimming in a sea of blood. I believe I could drink out of your skull, bathe my feet in your breast and eat your heart cooked whole. You think I am weak; you believe that I love you because my life has mingled with yours; you think that I would carry your offspring under my heart, and nourish it with my blood—give birth to your child and take your name! Hear, you, what are you called, what is your family name? But I'm sure you have none. I should be "Mrs. Gate-Keeper," perhaps, or "Madame Dumpheap." You dog with my collar on, you lackey with my father's hallmark on your buttons. I play rival to my cook—oh—oh—oh! You believe that I am cowardly and want to run away. No, now I shall stay. The thunder may roll. My father will return—and find his desk broken into—his money gone! Then he will ring—that bell. A scuffle with his servant—then sends for the police—and then I tell all—everything! Oh, it will be beautiful to have it all over with—if only that were the end! And my father—he'll have a shock and die, and then that will be the end. Then they will place his swords across the coffin—and the Count's line is extinct. The serf's line will continue in an orphanage, win honors in the gutter and end in prison.

JEAN. Now it is the king's blood talking. Splendid, Miss Julie! Only keep the miller in his sack.

[*Enter Kristin with prayer-book in hand.*]

JULIE [*Hastening to Kristin and falls in her arms as though seeking protection*]. Help me, Kristin, help me against this man.

KRISTIN [*Cold and unmoved*]. What kind of performance is this for a holy day morning? What does this mean—this noise and fuss?

JULIE. Kristin, you are a woman,—and my friend. Beware of this wretch.

JEAN [*A little embarrassed and surprised*]. While the ladies are arguing I'll go and shave myself.

[*Jean goes,* R.]

JULIE. You must understand me—you must listen to me.

KRISTIN. No—I can't understand all this bosh. Where may you be going in your traveling dress?—and he had his hat on! Hey?

JULIE. Listen to me, Kristin, listen to me and I'll tell you everything.

KRISTIN. I don't want to know anything—

JULIE. You must listen to me—

KRISTIN. What about? Is it that foolishness with Jean? That doesn't concern me at all. That I won't be mixed up with, but if you're trying to lure him to run away with you then we must put a stop to it.

JULIE [*Nervously*]. Try to be calm now Kristin, and listen to me. I can't stay here and

Jean can't stay here. That being true, we must leave— —Kristin.

KRISTIN. Hm, hm!

JULIE [*Brightening up*]. But I have an idea—what if we three should go—away—to foreign parts. To Switzerland and set up a hotel together—I have money you see— and Jean and I would back the whole thing, you could run the kitchen. Won't that be fine? Say yes, now—and come with us—there everything would be arranged—say yes!

[*Throws her arms around Kristin and coaxes her*].

KRISTIN [*Cold and reflecting*]. Hm—hm!

JULIE [*Presto tempo*]. You leave never been out and traveled, Kristin. You shall look about you in the world. You can't believe how pleasant traveling on a train is—new faces continually, new countries—and we'll go to Hamburg—'and passing through we'll see the zoological gardens—that you will like—then we'll go to the theatre and hear the opera—and when we reach Munich there will be the museum—there are Rubens and Raphaels and all the big painters that you know—you have heard of Munich—where King Ludwig lived—the King, you know, who went mad. Then we'll see his palace—a palace like those in the Sagas—and from there it isn't far to Switzerland—and the Alps, the Alps mind you with snow in mid-summer. And there oranges grow and laurel—green all the year round if—

[*Jean is seen in the doorway R. stropping his razor on the strop which he holds between his teeth and left hand. He listens and nods his head favorably now and then. Julie continues, tempo prestissimo*]

And there we'll take a hotel and I'll sit taking the cash while Jean greets the guests— goes out and markets writes letters—that will be life, you may believe—then the train whistles—then the omnibus comes—then a bell rings upstairs, then in the restaurant—and then I make out the bills—and I can salt them—you can't think how people tremble when they receive their bill—and you—you can sit like a lady—of course you won't have to stand over the stove—you can dress finely and neatly when you show yourself to the people—and you with your appearance—Oh, I'm not flattering, you can catch a husband some fine day—a rich Englishman perhaps—they are so easy to—[Slowing up] to catch— —Then we'll be rich—and then we'll build a villa by Lake Como—to be sure it rains sometimes—but [becoming languid] the sun must shine too sometimes— — —although it seems dark— — —and if not—we can at least travel homeward—and come back—here—or some other place.

KRISTIN. Listen now. Does Miss Julie believe in all this?

[*Julie going to pieces.*]

JULIE. Do I believe in it?

KRISTIN. Yes.

JULIE [*Tired*]. I don't know. I don't believe in anything any more. [*Sinks down on bench, and takes head in her hand on table.*] In nothing—nothing!

KRISTIN [*Turns to R. and looks toward Jean*]. So—you intended to run away?

JEAN [*Rather shamefaced comes forward and puts razor on table*]. Run away? That's putting it rather strong. You heard Miss Julie's project, I think it might be carried out.

KRISTIN. Now listen to that! Was it meant that I should be her cook—

JEAN [*Sharply*]. Be so good as to use proper language when you speak of your mistress.

KRISTIN. Mistress?

JEAN. Yes.

KRISTIN. No—hear! Listen to him!

JEAN. Yes, you listen—you need to, and talk less. Miss Julie is your mistress and for the same reason that you do not respect her now you should not respect yourself.

KRISTIN. I have always had so much respect for myself—

JEAN. That you never had any left for others!

KRISTIN. I have never lowered my position. Let any one say, if they can, that the Count's cook has had anything to do with the riding master or the swineherd. Let them come and say it!

JEAN. Yes, you happened to get a fine fellow. That was your good luck.

KRISTIN. Yes, a fine fellow—who sells the Count's oats from his stable.

JEAN. Is it for you to say anything—you who get a commission on all the groceries and a bribe from the butcher?

KRISTIN. What's that?

JEAN. And you can't have respect for your master and mistress any longer—you, you!

KRISTIN [*Glad to change the subject*]. Are you coming to church with me? You need a good sermon for your actions.

JEAN. No, I'm not going to church today. You can go alone—and confess your doings.

KRISTIN. Yes, that I shall do, and I shall return with so much forgiveness that there will be enough for you too. The Savior suffered and died on the cross for all our sins, and when we go to Him in faith and a repentant spirit he takes our sins on Himself.

JULIE. Do you believe that, Kristin?

KRISTIN. That is my life's belief, as true as I stand here. And that was my childhood's belief that I have kept since my youth, Miss Julie. And where sin overflows, there mercy overflows also.

JULIE. Oh, if I only had your faith. Oh, if—

KRISTIN. Yes, but you see that is not given without God's particular grace, and that is not allotted to all, that!

JULIE. Who are the chosen?

KRISTIN. That is the great secret of the Kingdom of Grace, and the Lord has no respect for persons. But there the last shall be first.

JULIE. But then has he respect for the last—the lowliest person?

KRISTIN [*Continuing*]. It is easier for a camel to pass through the eye of a needle than for a rich man to enter the Kingdom of Heaven. That's the way it is, Miss Julie. However—now I am going—alone. And on any way I shall stop in and tell the stable boy not to let any horses go out in case any one wants to get away before the Count comes home. Good bye.

[*Exit Kristin.*]

JEAN. Such a devil. And all this on account of your confounded canary!

JULIE [*Tired*]. Oh, don't speak of the canary—do you see any way out—any end to this?

JEAN [*Thinking*]. No.

JULIE. What would you do in my place?

JEAN. In your place—wait. As a noble lady, as a woman—fallen—I don't know. Yes, now I know.

JULIE [*She takes up razor from table and makes gestures saying*] This?

JEAN. Yes. But *I* should not do it, mark you, for there is a difference between us.

JULIE. Because you are a man and I am a woman? What other difference is there?

JEAN. That very difference—of man and woman.

JULIE [*Razor in hand*]. I want to do it—but I can't. My father couldn't either that time when he should have done it.

JEAN. No, he was right, not to do it—he had to avenge himself first.

JULIE. And now my mother revenges herself again through me.

JEAN. Haven't you loved your father, Miss Julie?

JULIE. Yes, deeply. But I have probably hated him too, I must have—without being aware of it. And it is due to my father's training that I have learned to scorn my own sex. Between them both they have made me half man, half woman. Whose is the fault for what has happened—my father's? My mother's? My own? I haven't anything of my own. I haven't a thought which was not nay father's—not a passion that wasn't my mother's. And last of all from my betrothed the idea that all people are equal. For that I now call him a wretch. How can it be my own fault then? Throw the burden on Jesus as Kristin did? No, I am too proud, too intelligent, thanks to my father's teaching.— —And that a rich man cannot enter the Kingdom of Heaven—that is a lie, and Kristin, who has money in the savings bank—she surely cannot enter there. Whose is the fault? What does it concern us whose fault it is? It is I who must bear the burden and the consequences.

JEAN. Yes, but— —

[*Two sharp rings on bell are heard. Julie starts to her feet. Jean changes his coat.*]

JEAN. The Count—has returned. Think if Kristin has— [*Goes up to speaking tube and listens.*]

JULIE. Now he has seen the desk!

JEAN [*Speaking in the tube*]. It is Jean, Excellency. [*Listens*]. Yes, Excellency. [*Listens*].Yes, Excellency,—right away—immediately, Excellency. Yes—in half an hour.

JULIE [*In great agitation*]. What did he say? In Heaven's name, what did he say?

JEAN. He wants his boots and coffee in a half hour.

JULIE. In half an hour then. Oh, I'm so tired—I'm incapable of feeling, not able to be sorry, not able to go, not able to stay, not able to live—not able to die. Help me now. Command me—I will obey like a dog. Do me this last service save my honor. Save his name. You know what I have the will to do—but cannot do. You will it and command me to execute your will.

JEAN. I don't know why—but now I can't either.—I don't understand myself. It is absolutely as though this coat does it—but I can't command you now. And since the Count spoke to me— —I can't account for it—but oh, it is that damned servant in my back—I believe if the Count came in here now and told me to cut my throat I would do it on the spot.

JULIE. Make believe you are he—and I you. You could act so well a little while ago when you knelt at my feet. Then you were a nobleman—or haven't you ever been at the theatre and seen the hypnotist—[*Jean nods*] He says to his subject "Take the broom," and he takes it; he says, "Sweep," and he sweeps.

JEAN. Then the subject must be asleep!

JULIE [*Ecstatically*]. I sleep already. The whole room is like smoke before me—and you are like a tall black stove, like a man clad in black clothes with a high hat; and your eyes gleam like the hot coals when the fire is dying; and your face a white spot like fallen ashes. [*The sunshine is coming in through the windows and falls on Jean. Julie rubs her hands as though warming them before a fire*]. It is so warm and good—and so bright and quiet!

JEAN [*Takes razor and puts it in her hand*]. There is the broom, go now while it's bright—out to the hay loft—and—[*He whispers in her ear.*]

JULIE [*Rousing herself*]. Thanks. And now I go to rest. But tell me this—the foremost may receive the gift of Grace? Say it, even if you don't believe it.

JEAN. The foremost? No, I can't say that. But wait, Miss Julie—you are no longer among the foremost since you are of the lowliest.

JULIE. That's true, I am the lowliest—the lowliest of the lowly. Oh, now I can't go. Tell me once more that I must go.

JEAN. No, now I cannot either—I cannot.

JULIE. And the first shall be last— — —

JEAN. Don't think. You take my strength from me, too, so that I become cowardly.— What— —I thought I heard the bell!— — No! To be afraid of the sound of is bell! But it's not the bell—it's someone behind the bell, the hand that sets the lull in motion—and something else that sets the land in motion. But stop your cars, stop your ears. Then he will only ring louder and keep on ringing until it's answered—and then it is too late! Then come the police and then—[*Two loud rings on bell are heard, Jean falls in a heap for a moment, but straightens up immediately.*] It is horrible! But there is no other way. Go!

[*Countess Julie goes out resolutely.*]

CURTAIN.

THE DANCE OF DEATH

PART I

CHARACTERS

EDGAR, *Captain in the Coast Artillery*
ALICE, his *wife, a former actress*
CURT, *Master of Quarantine*
JENNY }
THE OLD WOMAN } *Subordinate characters*
THE SENTRY }

THE DANCE OF DEATH

PART I

The scene is laid inside of a round fort built of granite.
In the background, a gateway, closed by huge, swinging double doors; in these, small, square window panes, through which may be seen a sea shore with batteries and the sea beyond.
On either side of the gateway, a window with flower pots and bird cages.
To the right of the gateway, an upright piano; further down the stage, a sewing-table and two easy-chairs.
On the left, half-way down the stage, a writing-table with a telegraph instrument on it; further down, a what-not full of framed photographs. Beside it, a couch that can be used to sleep on. Against the wall, a buffet.
A lamp suspended from the ceiling. On the wall near the piano hang two large laurel wreaths with ribbons. Between them, the picture of a woman in stage dress.
Beside the door, a hat-stand on which hang accoutrements, sabers, and so forth. Near it, a chiffonier.
To the left of the gateway hangs a mercurial barometer.
It is a mild. Fall evening. The doors stand open, and a sentry is seen pacing back and forth on the shore battery. He wears a helmet with a forward pointed brush for a crest. Now and then his drawn saber catches the red glare of the setting sun. The sea lies dark and quiet.
The CAPTAIN *sits in the easy-chair to the left of the sewing-table, fumbling an extinguished cigar. He has on a much-worn undress uniform and riding-boots with spurs. Looks tired and bored.*
ALICE *sits in the easy-chair on the right, doing nothing at all. Looks tired and expectant.*

CAPTAIN. Won't you play something for me?
ALICE. [*Indifferently, but not snappishly*] What am I to play?
CAPTAIN. Whatever suits you.
ALICE. You don't like my repertory.
CAPTAIN. Nor you mine.

ALICE. [*Evasively*] Do you want the doors to stay open?

CAPTAIN. If you wish it.

ALICE. Let them be, then. [*Pause*] Why don't you smoke?

CAPTAIN. Strong tobacco is beginning not to agree with me.

ALICE. [*In an almost friendly tone*] Get weaker tobacco then. It is your only pleasure, as you call it.

CAPTAIN. Pleasure—what is that?

ALICE. Don't ask me. I know it as little as you—Don't you want your whiskey yet?

CAPTAIN. I'll wait a little. What have you for supper?

ALICE. How do I know? Ask Christine.

CAPTAIN. The mackerel ought to be in season soon—now the Fall is here.

ALICE. Yes, it is Fall!

CAPTAIN. Within and without. But leaving aside the cold that comes with the Fall, both within and without, a little broiled mackerel, with a slice of lemon and a glass of white Burgundy, wouldn't be so very bad.

ALICE. Now you grow eloquent.

CAPTAIN. Have we any Burgundy left in the wine-cellar?

ALICE. So far as I know, we have had no wine-cellar these last five years—

CAPTAIN. You never know anything. However, we *must* stock up for our silver wedding.

ALICE. Do you actually mean to celebrate it?

CAPTAIN. Of course!

ALICE. It would be more seemly to hide our misery—our twenty-five years of misery—

CAPTAIN. My dear Alice, it has been a misery, but we have also had some fun—now and then. One has to avail oneself of what little time there is, for afterward it is all over.

ALICE. Is it over? Would that it were!

CAPTAIN. It is over! Nothing left but what can be put on a wheel-barrow and spread on the garden beds.

ALICE. And so much trouble for the sake of the garden beds!

CAPTAIN. Well, that's the way of it. And it is not of my making.

ALICE. So much trouble! [*Pause*] Did the mail come?

CAPTAIN. Yes.

ALICE. Did the butcher send his bill?

CAPTAIN. Yes.

ALICE. How large is it?

CAPTAIN. [*Takes a paper from his pocket and puts on his spectacles, but takes them off again at once*] Look at it yourself. I cannot see any longer.

ALICE. What is wrong with your eyes?

CAPTAIN. Don't know.

ALICE. Growing old?

CAPTAIN. Nonsense! I?

ALICE. Well, not I!

CAPTAIN. Hm!

ALICE. [*Looking at the bill*] Can you pay it?

CAPTAIN. Yes, but not this moment.

ALICE. Some other time, of course! In a year, when you have been retired with a small pension, and it is too late! And then, when your trouble returns—

CAPTAIN. Trouble? I never had any trouble—only a slight indisposition once. And I can live another twenty years.

ALICE. The doctor thought otherwise.

CAPTAIN. The doctor!

ALICE. Yes, who else could express any valid opinion about sickness?

CAPTAIN. I have no sickness, and never had. I am not going to have it either, for I shall die all of a sudden—like an old soldier.

ALICE. Speaking of the doctor—you know they are having a party to-night?

CAPTAIN. [*Agitated*] Yes, what of it? We are not invited because we don't associate with those people, and we don't associate with them because we don't want to—because we despise both of them. Rabble—that's what they are!

ALICE. You say that of everybody.

CAPTAIN. Because everybody is rabble.

ALICE. Except yourself.

CAPTAIN. Yes, because I have behaved decently under all conditions of life. That's why I don't belong to the rabble.

[*Pause.*]

ALICE. Do you want to play cards?

CAPTAIN. All right

ALICE. [*Takes a pack of cards from the drawer in the sewing table and begins to shuffle them*] Just think, the doctor is permitted to use the band for a private entertainment!

CAPTAIN. [*Angrily*] That's because he goes to the city and truckles to the Colonel. Truckle, you know—if one could only do that!

ALICE. [*Deals*] I used to be friendly with Gerda, but she played me false—

CAPTAIN. They are all false! What did you turn up for trumps?

ALICE. Put on your spectacles.

CAPTAIN. They are no help—Well, well!

ALICE. Spades are trumps.

CAPTAIN. [*Disappointed*] Spades—?

ALICE. [*Leads*] Well, be that as it may, our case is settled in advance with the wives of the new officers.

CAPTAIN. [*Taking the trick*] What does it matter? We never give any parties anyhow, so nobody is the wiser. I can live by myself—as I have always done.

ALICE. I, too. But the children? The children have to grow up without any companionship.

CAPTAIN. Let them find it for themselves in the city—I take that! Got any trumps left?

ALICE. One—That's mine!

CAPTAIN. Six and eight make fifteen—

ALICE. Fourteen—fourteen!

CAPTAIN. Six and eight make fourteen. I think I am also forgetting how to count. And two makes sixteen—[*Yawns*] It is your deal.

ALICE. You are tired?

CAPTAIN. [*Dealing*] Not at all.

ALICE. [*Listening in direction of the open doors*] One can hear the music all this way. [*Pause*] Do you think Curt is invited also?

CAPTAIN. He arrived this morning, so I guess he has had time to get out his evening clothes, though he has not had time to call on us.

ALICE. Master of Quarantine—is there to be a quarantine station here?

CAPTAIN. Yes.

ALICE. He is my own cousin after all, and once I bore the same name as he—

CAPTAIN. In which there was no particular honor—

ALICE. See here! [*Sharply*] You leave my family alone, and I'll leave yours!

CAPTAIN. All right, all right—don't let us begin again!

ALICE. Must the Master of Quarantine be a physician?

CAPTAIN. Oh, no, he's merely a sort of superintendent or book-keeper—and Curt never became anything in particular.

ALICE. He was not much good—

CAPTAIN. And he has cost us a lot of money. And when he left wife and children, he became disgraced.

ALICE. Not quite so severe, Edgar!

CAPTAIN. That's what happened! What has he been doing in America since then? Well, I cannot say that I am longing for him—but he was a nice chap, and I liked to argue with him.

ALICE. Because he was so tractable—

CAPTAIN. [*Haughtily*] Tractable or not, he was at least a man one could talk to. Here, on this island here is not one person who understands what I say—it's a community of idiots!

ALICE. It is rather strange that Curt should arrive just in time for our silver wedding—whether we celebrate it or not—

CAPTAIN. Why is that strange? Oh, I see! It was he who brought us together, or got you married, as they put it.

ALICE. Well, didn't he?

CAPTAIN. Certainly! It was a kind of fixed idea with him—I leave it for you to say what kind.

ALICE. A wanton fancy—

CAPTAIN. For which we have had to pay, and not he!

ALICE. Yes, think only if I had remained on the stage! All my friends are stars now.

CAPTAIN. [*Rising*] Well, well, well! Now I am going to have a drink. [*Goes over to the buffet and mixes a drink, which he takes standing up*] There should be a rail here to put the foot on, so that one might dream of being at Copenhagen, in the American Bar.

ALICE. Let us put a rail there, if it will only remind us of Copenhagen. For there we spent our best moments.

CAPTAIN. [*Drinks quickly*] Yes, do you remember that "navarin aux pommes"?

ALICE. No, but I remember the concerts at the Tivoli.

CAPTAIN. Yes, your tastes are so—exalted!

ALICE. It ought to please you to have a wife whose taste is good.

CAPTAIN. So it does.

ALICE. Sometimes, when you need something to brag of—

CAPTAIN. [*Drinking*] I guess they must be dancing at the doctor's—I catch the three-four time of the tuba: boom—boom-boom!

ALICE. I can hear the entire melody of the Alcazar Waltz. Well, it was not yesterday I danced a waltz—

CAPTAIN. You think you could still manage?

ALICE. Still?

CAPTAIN. Ye-es. I guess you are done with dancing, you like me!

ALICE. I am ten years younger than you.

CAPTAIN. Then we are of the same age, as the lady should be ten years younger.

ALICE. Be ashamed of yourself! You are an old man—and I am still in my best years.

CAPTAIN. Oh, I know, you can be quite charming—to others, when you make up your mind to it.

ALICE. Can we light the lamp now?

CAPTAIN. Certainly.

ALICE. Will you ring, please.

[*The* CAPTAIN *goes languidly to the writing-table and rings a bell.*]
[JENNY *enters from the right.*]

CAPTAIN. Will you be kind enough to light the lamp, Jenny?

ALICE. [*Sharply*] I want you to light the hanging lamp.

JENNY. Yes, ma'am.

[*Lights the lamp while the* CAPTAIN *watches her.*]

ALICE. [*Stiffly*] Did you wipe the chimney?

JENNY. Sure.

ALICE. What kind of an answer is that?

CAPTAIN. Now—now—

ALICE. [*To* JENNY] Leave us. I will light the lamp myself. That will be better.

JENNY. I think so too. [*Starts for the door.*]

ALICE. [*Rising*] Go!

JENNY. [*Stops*] I wonder, ma'am, what you'd say if I did go?

[ALICE *remains silent.*]
[JENNY *goes out.*]
[*The* CAPTAIN *comes forward and lights the lamp.*]

ALICE. [*With concern*] Do you think she will go?

CAPTAIN. Shouldn't wonder. And then we are in for it—

ALICE. It's your fault! You spoil them.

CAPTAIN. Not at all. Can't you see that they are always polite to me?

ALICE. Because you cringe to them. And you always cringe to inferiors, for that matter, because, like all despots, you have the nature of a slave.

CAPTAIN. There—there!

ALICE. Yes, you cringe before your men, and before your sergeants, but you cannot get on with your equals or your superiors.

CAPTAIN. Ugh!

ALICE. That's the way of all tyrants—Do you think she will go?

CAPTAIN. Yes, if you don't go out and say something nice to her.

ALICE. I?

CAPTAIN. Yes, for if I should do it, you would say that I was flirting with the maids.

ALICE. Mercy, if she should leave! Then I shall have to do the work, as I did the last time, and my hands will be spoiled.

CAPTAIN. That is not the worst of it. But if Jenny leaves, Christine will also leave, and then we shall never get a servant to the island again. The mate on the steamer scares away every one that comes to look for a place—and if he should miss his chance, then my corporals attend to it.

ALICE. Yes, your corporals, whom I have to feed in my kitchen, and whom you dare not show the door—

CAPTAIN. No, for then they would also go when their terms were up—and we might have to close up the whole gun shop!

ALICE. It will be our ruin.

CAPTAIN. That's why the officers have proposed to petition His Royal Majesty for special expense money.

ALICE. For whom?

CAPTAIN. For the corporals.

ALICE. [*Laughing*] You are crazy!

CAPTAIN. Yes, laugh a little for me. I need it.

ALICE. I shall soon have forgotten how to laugh—

CAPTAIN. [*Lighting his cigar*] That is something one should never forget—it is tedious enough anyhow!

ALICE. Well, it is not very amusing—Do you want to play anymore?

CAPTAIN. No, it tires me. [*Pause.*]

ALICE. Do you know, it irritates me nevertheless that my cousin, the new Master of Quarantine, makes his first visit to our enemies.

CAPTAIN. Well, what's the use of talking about it?

ALICE. But did you see in the paper that he was put down as *rentier?* He must have come into some money then.

CAPTAIN. *Rentier!* Well, well—a rich relative. That's really the first one in this family.

ALICE. In your family, yes. But among my people many have been rich.

CAPTAIN. If he has money, he's conceited, I suppose, but I'll hold him in check—and he won't get a chance to look at my cards.

[*The telegraph receiver begins to click.*]

ALICE. Who is it?

CAPTAIN. [*Standing still*] Keep quiet, please.

ALICE. Well, are you not going to look—

CAPTAIN. I can hear—I can hear what they are saying—It's the children.

[*Goes over to the instrument and sends an answer; the receiver continues to click for awhile, and then the* CAPTAIN *answers again.*]

ALICE. Well?

CAPTAIN. Wait a little—[*Gives a final click*] The children are at the guard-house in the city. Judith is not well again and is staying away from school.

ALICE. Again! What more did they say?

CAPTAIN. Money, of course!

ALICE. Why is Judith in such a hurry? If she didn't pass her examinations until next year, it would be just as well.

CAPTAIN. Tell her, and see what it helps.

ALICE. You should tell her.

CAPTAIN. How many times have I not done so? But children have their own wills, you know.

ALICE. Yes, in this house at least. [*The* CAPTAIN *yawns*] So, you yawn in your wife's presence!

CAPTAIN. Well, what can I do? Don't you notice how day by day we are saying the same things to each other? When, just now, you sprang that good old phrase of yours, "in this house at least," I should have come back with my own stand-by, "it is not my house only." But as I have already made that reply some five hundred times, I yawned instead. And my yawn could be taken to mean either that I was too lazy to answer, or "right you are, my angel," or "supposing we quit."

ALICE. You are very amiable to-night.

CAPTAIN. Is it not time for supper soon?

ALICE. Do you know that the doctor ordered supper from the city—from the Grand Hotel?

CAPTAIN. No! Then they are having ptarmigans—tschk! Ptarmigan, you know, is the finest bird there is, but it's clear barbarism to fry it in bacon grease—

ALICE. Ugh! Don't talk of food.

CAPTAIN. Well, how about wines? I wonder what those barbarians are drinking with the ptarmigans?

ALICE. Do you want me to play for you?

CAPTAIN. [*Sits down at the writing-table*] The last resource! Well, if you could only leave your dirges and lamentations alone—it sounds too much like music with a moral. And I am always adding within myself: "Can't you hear how unhappy I am! Meow, meow! Can't you hear what a horrible husband I have! Brum, brum, brum! If he would only die soon! Beating of the joyful drum, flourishes, the finale of the Alcazar Waltz, Champagne Galop!" Speaking of champagne, I guess there are a couple of bottles left. What would you say about bringing them up and pretending to have company?

ALICE. No, we won't, for they are mine—they were given to me personally.

CAPTAIN. You are so economical.

ALICE. And you are always stingy—to your wife at least!

CAPTAIN. Then I don't know what to suggest. Perhaps I might dance for you?

ALICE. No, thank you—I guess you are done with dancing.

CAPTAIN. You should bring some friend to stay with you.

ALICE. Thanks! You might bring a friend to stay with you.

CAPTAIN. Thanks! It has been tried, and with mutual dissatisfaction. But it was interesting in the way of an experiment, for as soon as a stranger entered the house, we became quite happy—to begin with—

ALICE. And then!

CAPTAIN. Oh, don't talk of it!

[*There is a knock at the door on the left.*]

ALICE. Who can be coming so late as this?

CAPTAIN. Jenny does not knock.

ALICE. Go and open the door, and don't yell "come"—it has a sound of the workshop.

CAPTAIN. [*Goes toward the door on the left*] You don't like workshops.

ALICE. Please, open!

CAPTAIN. [*Opens the door and receives a visiting-card that is held out to him*] It is Christine—Has Jenny left? [*As the public cannot hear the answer, to* ALICE] Jenny has left.

ALICE. Then I become servant girl again!

CAPTAIN. And I man-of-all-work.

ALICE. Would it not be possible to get one of your gunners to help along in the kitchen?

CAPTAIN. Not these days.

ALICE. But it couldn't be Jenny who sent in her card?

CAPTAIN. [*Looks at the card through his spectacles and then turns it over to* ALICE] You see what it is—I cannot.

ALICE. [*Looks at the card*] Curt—it is Curt! Hurry up and bring him in.

CAPTAIN. [*Goes out to the left*] Curt! Well, that's a pleasure!

[ALICE *arranges her hair and seems to come to life.*]

CAPTAIN. [*Enters from the left with* CURT] Here he is, the, traitor! Welcome, old man! Let me hug you!

ALICE. [*Goes to* CURT] Welcome to my home, Curt!

CURT. Thank you—it is some time since we saw each other.

CAPTAIN. How long? Fifteen years! And we have grown old—

ALICE. Oh, Curt has not changed, it seems to me.

CAPTAIN. Sit down, sit down! And first of all—the programme. Have you any engagement for to-night?

CURT. I am invited to the doctor's, but I have not promised to go.

ALICE. Then you will stay with your relatives.

CURT. That would seem the natural thing, but the doctor is my superior, and I might have trouble afterward.

CAPTAIN. What kind of talk is that? I have never been afraid of my superiors—

CURT. Fear or no fear, the trouble cannot be escaped.

CAPTAIN. On this island I am master. Keep behind my back, and nobody will dare to touch you.

ALICE. Oh, be quiet, Edgar! [*Takes* CURT *by the hand*] Leaving both masters and superiors aside, you must stay with us. That will be found both natural and proper.

CURT. Well, then—especially as I feel welcome here.

CAPTAIN. Why should you not be welcome? There is nothing between us—[CURT *tries vainly to hide a sense of displeasure*] What could there be? You were a little careless as a young man, but I have forgotten all about it. I don't let things rankle.

[ALICE *looks annoyed. All three sit down at the sewing table.*]

ALICE. Well, you have strayed far and wide in the world?

CURT. Yea, and now I have found a harbour with you—

CAPTAIN. Whom you married off twenty-five years ago.

CURT. It was not quite that way, but it doesn't matter. It is pleasing to see that you have stuck together for twenty-five years.

CAPTAIN. Well, we have borne with it. Now and then it has been so-so, but, as you say, we have stuck together. And Alice has had nothing to complain of. There has been plenty of everything—heaps of money. Perhaps you don't know that I am a celebrated author—an author of text-books—

CURT. Yes, I recall that, when we parted, you had just published a volume on rifle practice that was selling well. Is it still used in the military schools?

CAPTAIN. It is still in evidence, and it holds its place as number one, though they have tried to substitute a worse one—which is being used now, but which is totally worthless.

[*Painful silence.*]

CURT. You have been travelling abroad, I have heard.

ALICE. We have been down to Copenhagen five times—think of it?'

CAPTAIN. Well, you see, when I took Alice away from the stage—

ALICE. Oh, you took me?

CAPTAIN. Yes, I took you as a wife should be taken—

ALICE. How brave you have grown!

CAPTAIN. But as it was held up against me afterward that I had spoiled her brilliant career—hm!—I had to make up for it by promising to take my wife to Copenhagen—and this I have kept—fully! Five times we have been there. Five [*holding up the five fingers of the left hand*] Have you been in Copenhagen?

CURT. [*Smiling*] No, I have mostly been in America.

CAPTAIN. America? Isn't that a rotten sort of a country?

CURT. [*Unpleasantly impressed*] It is not Copenhagen.

ALICE. Have you—heard anything—from your children?

CURT. No.

ALICE. I hope you pardon me—but was it not rather inconsiderate to leave them like that—

CURT. I didn't leave them, but the court gave them to the mother.

CAPTAIN. Don't let us talk of that now. I for my part think it was lucky for you to get out of that mess.

CURT. [*To* ALICE] How are your children?

ALICE. Well, thank you. They are at school in the city and will soon be grown up.

CAPTAIN. Yes, they're splendid kids, and the boy has a brilliant head—brilliant! He is going to join the General Staff—

ALICE. If they accept him!

CAPTAIN. Him? Who has the making of a War Minister in him!

CURT. From one thing to another. There is to be a quarantine station here—against plague, cholera, and that sort of thing. And the doctor will be my superior, as you know—what sort of man is he?

CAPTAIN. Man? He is no man! He's an ignorant rascal!

CURT. [*To* ALICE] That is very unpleasant for me.

ALICE. Oh, it is not quite as bad as Edgar makes it out, but I must admit that I have small sympathy for the man—

CAPTAIN. A rascal, that's what he is. And that's what the others are, too—the Collector of Customs, the Postmaster, the telephone girl, the druggist, the pilot—what is it they call him now?—the Pilot Master—rascals one and all—and that's why I don't associate with them.

CURT. Are you on bad terms with all of them?

CAPTAIN. Every one!

ALICE. Yes, it is true that intercourse with those people is out of the question.

CAPTAIN. It is as if all the tyrants of the country had been sent to this island for safe-keeping.

ALICE. [*Ironically*] Exactly!

CAPTAIN. [*Good-naturedly*] Hm! Is that meant for me? I am no tyrant—not in my own house at least.

ALICE. You know better!

CAPTAIN. [*To* CURT] Don't believe her! I am a very reasonable husband, and the old lady is the best wife in the world.

ALICE. Would you like something to drink, Curt?

CURT. No, thank you, not now.

CAPTAIN. Have you turned—

CURT. A little moderate only—

CAPTAIN. Is that American?

CURT. Yes.

CAPTAIN. No moderation for me, or I don't care at all. A man should stand his liquor.

CURT. Returning to our neighbours on the island—my position will put me in touch with all of them—and it is not easy to steer clear of everything, for no matter how little you care to get mixed up in other people's intrigues, you are drawn into them just the same.

ALICE. You had better take up with them—in the end you will return to us, for here you find your true friends.

CURT. Is it not dreadful to be alone among a lot of enemies as you are?

ALICE. It is not pleasant.

CAPTAIN. It isn't dreadful at all. I have never had anything but enemies all my life, and they have helped me on instead of doing me harm. And when my time to die comes, I may say that I owe nothing to anybody and that I have never got a thing for nothing. Every particle of what I own I have had to fight for.

ALICE. Yes, Edgar's path has not been strewn with roses—

CAPTAIN. No, with thorns and stones—pieces of flint—but a man's own strength: do you know what that means?

CURT. [*Simply*] Yes, I learned to recognize its insufficiency about ten years ago.

CAPTAIN. Then you are no good!

ALICE. [*To the* CAPTAIN] Edgar!

CAPTAIN. He is no good, I say, if he does not have the strength within himself. Of course it is true that when the mechanism goes to pieces there is nothing left but a barrowful to chuck out on the garden beds; but as long as the mechanism holds together the thing to do is to kick and fight, with hands and feet, until there is nothing left. That is my philosophy.

CURT. [*Smiling*] It is fun to listen to you.

CAPTAIN. But you don't think it's true?

CURT. No, I don't.

CAPTAIN. But true it is, for all that.

[*During the preceding scene the wind has begun to blow hard, and now one of the big doors is closed with a bang.*]

CAPTAIN. [*Rising*] It's blowing. I could just feel it coming.

[*Goes back and closes both doors. Knocks on the barometer.*]

ALICE. [*To* CURT] You will stay for supper?

CURT. Thank you.

ALICE. But it will be very simple, as our housemaid has just left us.

CURT. Oh, it will do for me, I am sure.

ALICE. You ask for so little, dear Curt.

CAPTAIN. [*At the barometer*] If you could only see how the mercury is dropping! Oh, I felt it coming!

ALICE. [*Secretly to* CURT] He is nervous.

CAPTAIN. We ought to have supper soon.

ALICE. [*Rising*] I am going to see about it now. You can sit here and philosophize— [*secretly to* CURT], but don't contradict him, for then he gets into bad humor. And don't ask him why he was not made a major.

[CURT *nods assent.*]
[ALICE *goes toward the right.*]

CAPTAIN. See that we get something nice now, old lady!

ALICE. You give me money, and you'll get what you want.

CAPTAIN. Always money!

[ALICE *goes out.*]

CAPTAIN. [*To* ALICE] Money, money, money! All day long I have to stand ready with the purse, until at last I have come to feel as if I myself were nothing but a purse. Are you familiar with that kind of thing?

CURT. Oh, yes—with the difference that I took myself for a pocket-book.

CAPTAIN. Ha-ha! So you know the flavor of the brand! Oh, the ladies! Ha-ha! And you had one of the proper kind!

CURT. [*Patiently*] Let that be buried now.

CAPTAIN. She was a jewel! Then I have after all—in spite of everything—one that's pretty decent. For she is straight, in spite of everything.

CURT. [*Smiling good-humoredly*] In spite of everything.

CAPTAIN. Don't you laugh!

CURT. [*As before*] In spite of everything!

CAPTAIN. Yes, she has been a faithful mate, a splendid mother—excellent—but [*with a glance at the door on the right*] she has a devilish temper. Do you know, there have been moments when I cursed you for saddling me with her.

CURT. [*Good-naturedly*] But I didn't. Listen, man—

CAPTAIN. Yah, yah, yah! You talk nonsense and forget things that are not pleasant to remember. Don't take it badly, please—I am accustomed to command and raise Cain, you see, but you know me, and don't get angry!

CURT. Not at all. But I have not provided you with a wife—on the contrary.

CAPTAIN. [*Without letting his flow of words be checked*] Don't you think life is queer anyhow?]

CURT. I suppose so.

CAPTAIN. And to grow old—it is no fun, but it is interesting. Well, my age is nothing to speak of, but it does begin to make itself felt. All your friends die off, and then you become so lonely.

CURT. Lucky the man who can grow old in company with a wife.

CAPTAIN. Lucky? Well, it is luck, for the children go their way, too. You ought not to have left yours.

CURT. Well, I didn't. They were taken away from me—

CAPTAIN. Don't get mad now, because I tell you—

CURT. But it was not so.

CAPTAIN. Well, whichever way it was, it has now become forgotten—but you are alone!

CURT. You get accustomed to everything.

CAPTAIN. Do you—is it possible to get accustomed—to being quite alone also?

CURT. Here am I!

CAPTAIN. What have you been doing these fifteen years?

CURT. What a question! These fifteen years!

CAPTAIN. They say you have got hold of money and grown rich.

CURT. I can hardly be called rich—

CAPTAIN. I am not going to ask for a loan.

CURT. If you were, you would find me ready.

CAPTAIN. Many thanks, but I have my bank account. You see [*with a glance toward the door on the right*], nothing must be lacking in this house; and the day I had no more money— she would leave me!

CURT. Oh, no!

CAPTAIN. No? Well, I know better. Think of it, she makes a point of asking me when I happen to be short, just for the pleasure of showing me that I am not supporting my family.

CURT. But I heard you say that you have a large income.

CAPTAIN. Of course, I have a large income—but it is not enough.

CURT. Then it is not large, as such things are reckoned

CAPTAIN. Life is queer, and we as well!

[*The telegraph receiver begins to click.*]

CURT. What is that?

CAPTAIN. Nothing but a time correction.

CURT. Have you no telephone?

CAPTAIN. Yes, in the kitchen. But we use the telegraph because the girls at the central report everything we say.

CURT. Social conditions out here by the sea must be frightful!

CAPTAIN. They are simply horrible! But all life is horrible. And you, who believe in a sequel, do you think there will be any peace further on?

CURT. I presume there will be storms and battles there also.

CAPTAIN. There also—if there be any "there"! I prefer annihilation!

CURT. Are you sure that annihilation will come without pain?

CAPTAIN. I am going to die all of a sudden, without pain.

CURT. So you know that?

CAPTAIN. Yes, I know it.

CURT. You don't appear satisfied with your life?

CAPTAIN. [*Sighing*] Satisfied? The day I could die, I should be satisfied.

CURT. [*Rising*] That you don't know! But tell me: what is going on in this house? What is happening here? There is a smell as of poisonous wall-paper, and one feels sick the moment one enters. I should prefer to get away from here, had I not promised Alice to stay. There are dead bodies beneath the flooring, and the place is so filled with hatred that one can hardly breathe. [*The* CAPTAIN *sinks together and sits staring into vacancy*] What is the matter with you? Edgar! [*The* CAPTAIN *does not move. Slaps the* CAPTAIN *on the shoulder*] Edgar!

CAPTAIN. [*Recovering consciousness*] Did you say anything? [*Looks around*] I thought it was—Alice!—Oh, is that you?— Say— [*Relapses into apathy.*]

CURT. This is horrible! [*Goes over to the door on the right and opens it*] Alice!

ALICE. [*Enters, wearing a kitchen apron*] What is it?

CURT. I don't know. Look at him.

ALICE. [*Calmly*] He goes off like that at times—I'll play and then he will wake up.

CURT. No, don't! Not that way! Leave it to me—Does he hear? Or see?

ALICE. Just now he neither hears nor sees.

CURT. And you can speak of that with such calm? Alice, what is going on in this house?

ALICE. Ask him there.

CURT. Him there? But he is your husband!

ALICE. A stranger to me—as strange as he was twenty-five years ago. I know nothing at all about that man—nothing but—

CURT. Stop! He may overhear you.

ALICE. Now he cannot hear anything.

[*A trumpet signal is sounded outside.*]

CAPTAIN. [*Leaps to his feet and grabs saber and cap*] Pardon me. I have to inspect the sentries.

[*Goes out through the door in the background.*]

CURT. Is he ill?

ALICE. I don't know.

CURT. Has he lost his reason?

ALICE. I don't know.

CURT. Does he drink?

ALICE. He boasts more of it than he really drinks.

CURT. Sit down and talk—but calmly and truthfully.

ALICE. [*Sitting down*] What am I to talk about? That I have spent a lifetime in this tower, locked up, guarded by a man whom I have always hated, and whom I now hate so beyond all bounds that the day he died I should be laughing until the air shook.

CURT. Why have you not parted?

ALICE. You may well ask! While still engaged we parted twice; since then we have been trying to part every single day—but we are chained together and cannot break away. Once we were separated—within the same house—for five whole years. Now nothing but death can part us. This we know, and for that reason we are waiting for him as for a liberator.

CURT. Why are you so lonely?

ALICE. Because he isolates me. First he "exterminated" all my brothers and sisters from our home—he speaks of it himself as "extermination"—and then my girl friends and everybody else.

CURT. But *his* relatives? He has not "exterminated" them?

ALICE. Yes, for they came near taking my life, after having taken my honor and good name. Finally I became forced to keep up my connection with the world and with other human beings by means of that telegraph—for the telephone was watched by the operators. I have taught myself telegraphy, and he doesn't know it. You must not tell him, for then he would kill me.

CURT. Frightful! Frightful!— But why does he hold me responsible for your marriage? Let me tell you now how it was. Edgar was my childhood friend. When he saw you he fell in love at once. He came to me and asked me to plead his cause. I said no at once—and, my dear Alice, I knew your tyrannical and cruel temperament. For that reason I warned him—and when he persisted, I sent him to get your brother for his spokesman.

ALICE. I believe what you say. But he has been deceiving himself all these years, so that now you can never get him to believe anything else.

CURT. Well, let him put the blame on me if that can relieve his sufferings.

ALICE. But that is too much—

CURT. I am used to it. But what does hurt me is his unjust charge that I have deserted my children—

ALICE. That's the manner of man he is. He says what suits him, and then he believes it. But he seems to be fond of you, principally because you don't contradict him. Try not to grow tired of us now. I believe you have come in what was to us a fortunate moment; I think it was even providential—Curt, you must not grow tired of us, for we are undoubtedly the most unhappy creatures in the whole world!

[*She weeps.*]

CURT. I have seen one marriage at close quarters, and it was dreadful—but this is almost worse!

ALICE. Do you think so?

CURT. Yes.

ALICE. Whose fault is it?

CURT. The moment you quit asking whose fault it is, Alice, you will feel a relief. Try to regard it as a fact, a trial that has to be borne—

ALICE. I cannot do it! It is too much! [*Rising*] It is beyond help!

CURT. I pity both of you!—Do you know why you are hating each other?

ALICE. No, it is the most unreasoning hatred, without cause, without purpose, but also without end. And can you imagine why he is principally afraid of death? He fears that I may marry again.

CURT. Then he loves you.

ALICE. Probably. But that does not prevent him from hating me.

CURT. [*As if to himself*] It is called love-hatred, and it hails from the pit!—Does he like you to play for him?

ALICE. Yes, but only horrid melodies—for instance, that awful "The Entry of the Boyars." When he hears it he loses his head and wants to dance.

CURT. Does he dance?

ALICE. Oh, he is very funny at times.

CURT. One thing—pardon me for asking. Where are the children?

ALICE. Perhaps you don't know that two of them are dead?

CURT. So you have had that to face also?

ALICE. What is there I have not faced?

CURT. But the other two?

ALICE. In the city. They couldn't stay at home. For he set them against me.

CURT. And you set them against him?

ALICE. Of course. And then parties were formed, votes bought, bribes given—and in order not to spoil the children completely we had to part from them. What should have been the uniting link became the seed of dissension: what is held the blessing of the home turned into a curse—well, I believe sometimes that we belong to a cursed race!

CURT. Yes, is it not so—ever since the Fall?

ALICE. [*With a venomous glance and sharp voice*] What fall?

CURT. That of our first parents.

ALICE. Oh, I thought you meant something else!

[*Embarrassed silence.*]

ALICE. [*With folded hands*] Curt, my kinsman, my childhood friend—I have not always acted toward you as I should. But now I am being punished, and you are having your revenge.

CURT. No revenge! Nothing of that kind here! Hush!

ALICE. Do you recall one Sunday while you were engaged—and I had invited you for dinner—

CURT. Never mind!

ALICE. I must speak! Have pity on me! When you came to dinner, we had gone away, and you had to leave again.

CURT. You had received an invitation yourselves—what is that to speak of!

ALICE. Curt, when to-day, a little while ago, I asked you to stay for supper, I thought we had something left in the pantry. [*Hiding her face in her hands*] And there is not a thing, not even a piece of bread—

CURT. [*Weeping*] Alice—poor Alice!

ALICE. But when he comes home and wants something to eat, and there is nothing—then he gets angry. You have never seen him angry! O, God, what humiliation!

CURT. Will you not let me go out and arrange for something?

ALICE. There is nothing to be had on this island.

CURT. Not for my sake, but for his and yours—let me think up something—something. We must make the whole thing seem laughable when he comes. I'll propose that we have a drink, and in the meantime I'll think of something. Put him in good humor; play for him, any old nonsense. Sit down at the piano and make yourself ready—

ALICE. Look at my hands—are they fit to play with? I have to wipe glasses and polish brass, sweep floors, and make fires—

CURT. But you have two servants?

ALICE. So we have to pretend because he is an officer—but the servants are leaving us all the time, so that often we have none at all—most of the time, in fact. How am I to get out of this—this about supper? Oh, if only fire would break out in this house!

CURT. Don't, Alice, don't!

ALICE. If the sea would rise and take us away!

CURT. No, no, no, I cannot listen to you!

ALICE. What will he say, what will he say—Don't go, Curt, don't go away from me!

CURT. No, dear Alice—I shall not go.

ALICE. Yes, but when you are gone—

CURT. Has he ever laid hands on you?

ALICE. On me? Oh, no, for he knew that then I should have left him. One has to preserve some pride.

[*From without is heard: "Who goes there?—Friend."*]

CURT. [*Rising*] Is he coming?

ALICE. [*Frightened*] Yes, that's he. [*Pause.*]

CURT. What in the world are we to do?

ALICE. I don't know, I don't know!

CAPTAIN. [*Enters from the background, cheerful*] There! Leisure now! Well, has she had time to make her complaints? Is she not unhappy—hey?

CURT. How's the weather outside?

CAPTAIN. Half storm—[*Facetiously; opening one of the doors ajar*] Sir Bluebeard with the maiden in the tower; and outside stands the sentry with drawn saber to guard the pretty maiden—and then come the brothers, but the sentry is there. Look at him. Hip—hip! That's a fine sentry. Look at him. *Malbrough s'en va-t-en guerre!* Let us dance the sword dance! Curt ought to see it!

CURT. No, let us have "The Entry of the Boyars" instead!

CAPTAIN. Oh, you know that one, do you?—Alice in the kitchen apron, come and play. Come, I tell you!

[ALICE *goes reluctantly to the piano.*]

CAPTAIN. [*Pinching her arm*] Now you have been blackguarding me!

ALICE. I?

[CURT *turns away from them.*]

[ALICE *plays "The Entry of the Boyars."*]

[*The* CAPTAIN *performs some kind of Hungarian dance step behind the writing-table so that his spurs are set jingling. Then he sinks down on the floor without being noticed by* CURT *and* ALICE, *and the latter goes on playing the piece to the end.*]

ALICE. [*Without turning around*] Shall we have it again? [*Silence. Turns around and becomes aware of the* CAPTAIN, *who is lying unconscious on the floor in such a way that he is hidden from the public by the writing-table*] Lord Jesus!

[*She stands still, with arms crossed over her breast, and gives vent to a sigh of gratitude and relief.*]

CURT. [*Turns around; hurries over to the* CAPTAIN] What is it? What is it?

ALICE. [*In a high state of tension*] Is he dead?
CURT. I don't know. Come and help me.
ALICE. [*Remains still*] I cannot touch him—is he dead?
CURT. No—he lives.

[ALICE *sighs.*]
[CURT *helps the* CAPTAIN *to his feet and places him in a chair.*]

CAPTAIN. What was it? [*Silence*] What was it?
CURT. You fell down.
CAPTAIN. Did anything happen?
CURT. You fell on the floor. What is the matter with you?
CAPTAIN. With me? Nothing at all. I don't know of anything. What are you staring at me for?
CURT. You are ill.
CAPTAIN. What nonsense is that? You go on playing, Alice—Oh, now it's back again!

[*Puts both hands up to his head.*]

ALICE. Can't you see that you are ill?
CAPTAIN. Don't shriek! It is only a fainting spell.
CURT. We must call a doctor—I'll use your telephone—
CAPTAIN. I don't want any doctor.
CURT. You must! We have to call him for our own sake—otherwise we shall be held responsible—
CAPTAIN. I'll show him the door if he comes here. I'll shoot him. Oh, now it's there again!

[*Takes hold of his head.*]

CURT. [*Goes toward the door on the right*] Now I am going to telephone! [*Goes out.*]

[Alice *takes off her apron.*]

CAPTAIN. Will you give me a glass of water?
ALICE. I suppose I have to! [*Gives him a glass of water.*]
CAPTAIN. How amiable!
ALICE. Are you ill?
CAPTAIN. Please pardon me for not being well.
ALICE. Will you take care of yourself then?
CAPTAIN. *You* won't do it, I suppose?
ALICE. No, of that you may be sure!
CAPTAIN. The hour is come for which you have been waiting so long.
ALICE. The hour you believed would never come.
CAPTAIN. Don't be angry with me!
CURT. [*Enters from the right*] Oh, it's too bad—
ALICE. What did he say?
CURT. He rang off without a word.
ALICE. [*To the* CAPTAIN] There is the result of your limitless arrogance!

CAPTAIN. I think I am growing worse—Try to get a doctor from the city.

ALICE. [*Goes to the telegraph instrument*] We shall have to use the telegraph then.

CAPTAIN. [*Rising half-way from the chair; startled*] Do you—know—how to use it?

ALICE. [*Working the key*] Yes, I do.

CAPTAIN. So-o! Well, go on then—But isn't she treacherous! [*To* CURT] Come over here and sit by me. [CURT *sits down beside the* CAPTAIN] Take my hand. I sit here and fall—can you make it out? Down something—such a queer feeling.

CURT. Have you had any attack like this before?

CAPTAIN. Never—

CURT. While you are waiting for an answer from the city, I'll go over to the doctor and have a talk with him. Has he attended you before?

CAPTAIN. He has.

CURT. Then he knows your case. [*Goes toward the left.*]

ALICE. There will be an answer shortly. It is very kind of you, Curt. But come back soon.

CURT. As soon as I can. [*Goes out.*]

CAPTAIN. Curt *is* kind! And how he has changed.

ALICE. Yes, and for the better. It is too bad, however, that he must be dragged into our misery just now.

CAPTAIN. But good for us—I wonder just how he stands. Did you notice that he wouldn't speak of his own affairs?

ALICE. I did notice it, but then I don't think anybody asked him.

CAPTAIN. Think, what a life! And ours! I wonder if it is the same for all people?

ALICE. Perhaps, although they don't speak of it as we do.

CAPTAIN. At times I have thought that misery draws misery, and that those who are happy shun the unhappy. That is the reason why we see nothing but misery.

ALICE. Have you known anybody who was happy?

CAPTAIN. Let me see! No—Yes—the Ekmarks.

ALICE. You don't mean it! She had to have an operation last year—

CAPTAIN. That's right. Well, then I don't know—yes, the Von Kraffts.

ALICE. Yes, the whole family lived an idyllic life, well off, respected by everybody, nice children, good marriages—right along until they were fifty. Then that cousin of theirs committed a crime that led to a prison term and all sorts of after-effects. And that was the end of their peace. The family name was dragged in the mud by all the newspapers. The Krafft murder case made it impossible for the family to appear anywhere, after having been so much thought of. The children had to be taken out of school. Oh, heavens!

CAPTAIN. I wonder what my trouble is?

ALICE. What do you think?

CAPTAIN. Heart or head. It is as if the soul wanted to fly off and turn into smoke.

ALICE. Have you any appetite?

CAPTAIN. Yes, how about the supper?

ALICE. [*Crosses the stage, disturbed*] I'll ask Jenny.

CAPTAIN. Why, she's gone!

ALICE. Yes, yes, yes!

CAPTAIN. Ring for Christine so that I can get some fresh water.

ALICE. [*Rings*] I wonder—[*Rings again*] She doesn't hear.

CAPTAIN. Go and look—just think, if she should have left also!

ALICE. [*Goes over to the door on the left, and opens it*] What is this? Her trunk is in the hallway—packed.

CAPTAIN. Then she has gone.

ALICE. This is hell!

[*Begins to cry, falls on her knees, and puts her head on a chair, sobbing.*]

CAPTAIN. And everything at once! And then Curt had to turn up just in time to get a look into this mess of ours! If there be any further humiliation in store, let it come this moment!

ALICE. Do you know what I suspect? Curt went away and will not come back.

CAPTAIN. I believe it of him.

ALICE. Yes, we are cursed—

CAPTAIN. What are you talking of?

ALICE. Don't you see how everybody shuns us?

CAPTAIN. I don't mind! [*The telegraph receiver clicks*] There is the answer. Hush, I can hear it—Nobody can spare the time. Evasions! The rabble!

ALICE. That's what you get because you have despised your physicians—and failed to pay them.

CAPTAIN. That is not so!

ALICE. Even when you could, you didn't care to pay their bills because you looked down upon their work, just as you have looked down upon mine and everybody else's. They don't want to come. And the telephone is cut off because you didn't think that good for anything either. Nothing is good for anything but your rifles and guns!

CAPTAIN. Don't stand there and talk nonsense—

ALICE. Everything comes back.

CAPTAIN. What sort of superstition is that? Talk for old women!

ALICE. You will see! Do you know that we owe Christine six months' wages?

CAPTAIN. Well, she has stolen that much.

ALICE. But I have also had to borrow money from her.

CAPTAIN. I think you capable of it.

ALICE. What an ingrate you are! You know I borrowed that money for the children to get into the city.

CAPTAIN. Curt had a fine way of coming back! A rascal, that one, too! And a coward! He didn't dare to say he had had enough, and that he found the doctor's party more pleasant—He's the same rapscallion as ever!

CURT. [*Enters quickly from the left*] Well, my dear Edgar, this is how the matter stands— the doctor knows everything about your heart—

CAPTAIN. My heart?

CURT. You have long been suffering from calcification of the heart—

CAPTAIN. Stone heart?

CURT. And—

CAPTAIN. Is it serious?

CURT. Well, that is to say—

CAPTAIN. It is serious.

CURT. Yes.

CAPTAIN. Fatal?

CURT. You must be very careful. First of all: the cigar must go. [*The* CAPTAIN *throws away his cigar*] And next: no more whiskey! Then, to bed!

CAPTAIN. [*Scared*] No, I don't want *that*! Not to bed! That's the end! Then you never get up again. I shall sleep on the couch to-night. What more did he say?

CURT. He was very nice about it and will come at once if you call him.

CAPTAIN. Was he nice, the hypocrite? I don't want to see him! I can at least eat?

CURT. Not to-night. And during the next few days nothing but milk.

CAPTAIN. Milk! I cannot take that stuff into my mouth.

CURT. Better learn how!

CAPTAIN. I am too old to learn. [*Puts his hand up to his head*] Oh, there it is again now!

[*He sits perfectly still, staring straight ahead.*]

ALICE. [*To* CURT] What did the doctor tell you?

CURT. That he *may* die.

ALICE. Thank God!

CURT. Take care, Alice, take care! And now, go and get a pillow and a blanket and I'll put him here on the couch. Then I'll sit on the chair here all night.

ALICE. And I?

CURT. You go to bed. Your presence seems only to make him worse.

ALICE. Command! I shall obey, for you seem to mean well toward both of us. [*Goes out to the left.*]

CURT. Mark you—toward both of you! And I shall not mix in any partisan squabbles.

[CURT *takes the water bottle and goes out to the right. The noise of the wind outside is clearly heard. Then one of the doors is blown open and an old woman of shabby, unprepossessing appearance peeps into the room.*]

CAPTAIN. [*Wakes up, rises, and looks around*] So, they have left me, the rascals! [*Catches sight of the old woman and is frightened by her*] Who is it? What do you want?

Old Woman. I just wanted to close the door, sir.

CAPTAIN. Why should you? Why should you?

OLD WOMAN. Because it blew open just as I passed by.

CAPTAIN. Wanted to steal, did you?

OLD WOMAN. Not much here to take away, Christine said.

CAPTAIN. Christine?

OLD WOMAN. Good night, sir, and sleep well!

[*Closes the door and disappears.*]
[ALICE *comes in from the left with pillows and a blanket.*]

CAPTAIN. Who was that at the door? Anybody?

ALICE. Why, it was old Mary from the poorhouse who just went by.

CAPTAIN. Are you sure?

ALICE. Are you afraid?

CAPTAIN. I, afraid? Oh, no!

ALICE. As you don't want to go to bed, you can lie here.

CAPTAIN. [*Goes over to the couch and lies down*] I'll lie here. [*Tries to take Alice's hand, but she pulls it away.*]

[CURT *comes in with the water bottle.*]

CAPTAIN. Curt, don't go away from me!
CURT. I am going to stay up with you all night. Alice is going to bed.
CAPTAIN. Good night then, Alice.
ALICE. [*To* CURT] Good night, Curt.
CURT. Good night.

[ALICE *goes out.*]

CURT. [*Takes a chair and sits down beside the couch*] Don't you want to take off your boots?
CAPTAIN. No, a warrior should always be armed.
CURT. Are you expecting a battle then?
CAPTAIN. Perhaps! [*Rising up in bed*] Curt, you are the only human being to whom I ever disclosed anything of myself. Listen to me!—If I die to-night—look after my children!
CURT. I will do so.
CAPTAIN. Thank you—I trust in you!
CURT. Can you explain why you trust me?
CAPTAIN. We have not been friends, for friendship is something I don't believe in, and our families were born enemies and have always been at war—
CURT. And yet you trust me?
CAPTAIN. Yes, and I don't know why. [*Silence*] Do you think I am going to die?
CURT. You as well as everybody. There will be no exception made in your case.
CAPTAIN. Are you bitter?
CURT. Yes—are you afraid of death? Of the wheelbarrow and the garden bed?
CAPTAIN. Think, if it were not the end!
CURT. That's what a great many think!
CAPTAIN. And then?
CURT. Nothing but surprises, I suppose.
CAPTAIN. But nothing at all is known with certainty?
CURT. No, that's just it! That is why you must be prepared for everything.
CAPTAIN. You are not childish enough to believe in a hell?
CURT. Do you not believe in it—you, who are right in it?
CAPTAIN. That is metaphorical only.
CURT. The realism with which you have described yours seems to preclude all thought of metaphors, poetical or otherwise. [*Silence.*]
CAPTAIN. If you only knew what pangs I suffer!
CURT. Of the body?
CAPTAIN. No, not of the body.
CURT. Then it must be of the spirit, for no other alternative exists. [*Pause.*]
CAPTAIN. [*Rising up in bed*] I don't want to die!
CURT. Not long ago you wished for annihilation.
CAPTAIN. Yes, if it be painless.
CURT. Apparently it is not!
CAPTAIN. Is this annihilation then?

CURT. The beginning of it.
CAPTAIN. Good night.
CURT. Good night.

Curtain.

The same setting, but now the lamp is at the point of going out. Through the windows and the glass panes of the doors a gray morning is visible. The sea is stirring. The sentry is on the battery as before.

> *The* CAPTAIN *is lying on the couch, asleep.* CURT *sits on a chair beside him, looking pale and wearied from his watch.*

ALICE. [*In from the left*] Is he asleep?
CURT. Yes, since the time when the sun should have risen.
ALICE. What kind of night did he have?
CURT. He slept now and then, but he talked a good deal.
ALICE. Of what?
CURT. He argued about religion like a schoolboy, but with a pretension of having solved all the world riddles. Finally, toward morning, he invented the immortality of the soul.
ALICE. For his own glory.
CURT. Exactly! He is actually the most conceited person I have ever met. "I am; consequently God must be."
ALICE. You have become aware of it? Look at those boots. With those he would have trampled the earth flat, had he been allowed to do so. With those he has trampled down other people's fields and gardens. With those he has trampled on some people's toes and other people's heads—Man-eater, you have got your bullet at last!
CURT. He would be comical were he not so tragical; and there are traces of greatness in all his narrow-mindedness—Have you not a single good word to say about him?
ALICE. [*Sitting down*] Yes, if he only does not hear it; for if he hears a single word of praise he develops megalomania on the spot.
CURT. He can hear nothing now, for he has had a dose of morphine.
ALICE. Born in a poor home, with many brothers and sisters, Edgar very early had to support the family by giving lessons, as the father was a ne'er-do-well if nothing worse. It must be hard for a young man to give up all the pleasures of youth in order to slave for a bunch of thankless children whom he has not brought into the world. I was a little girl when I saw him, as a young man, going without an overcoat in the winter while the mercury stood at fifteen below zero—his little sisters wore kersey coats—it was fine, and I admired him, but his ugliness repelled me. Is he not unusually ugly?
CURT. Yes, and his ugliness has a touch of the monstrous at times. Whenever we fell out, I noticed it particularly. And when, at such times, he went away, his image assumed enormous forms and proportions, and he literally haunted me.
ALICE. Think of me then! However, his earlier years as an officer were undoubtedly a martyrdom. But now and then he was helped by rich people. This he will never admit, and whatever has come to him in that way he has accepted as a due tribute, without giving thanks for it.
CURT. We were to speak well of him.

ALICE. Yes—after he is dead. But then I recall nothing more.

CURT. Have you found him cruel?

ALICE. Yes—and yet he can show himself both kind and susceptible to sentiment. As an enemy he is simply horrible.

Curt. Why did he not get the rank of major?

ALICE. Oh, you ought to understand that! They didn't want to raise a man above themselves who had already proved himself a tyrant as an inferior. But you must never let on that you know this. He says himself that he did not want promotion— Did he speak of the children?

CURT. Yes, he was longing for Judith.

ALICE. I thought so—Oh! Do you know what Judith is? His own image, whom he has trained for use against me. Think only, that my own daughter—has raised her hand against me!

CURT. That is too much!

ALICE. Hush! He is moving—Think if he overheard us! He is full of trickery also.

CURT. He is actually waking up.

ALICE. Does he not look like an ogre? I am afraid of him!

[*Silence.*]

CAPTAIN. [*Stirs, wakes up, rises in bed, and looks around*] It is morning—at last!

CURT. How are you feeling?

CAPTAIN. Not so very bad.

CURT. Do you want a doctor?

CAPTAIN. No—I want to see Judith—my child!

CURT. Would it not be wise to set your house in order before—or if something should happen?

CAPTAIN. What do you mean? What could happen?

CURT. What may happen to all of us.

CAPTAIN. Oh, nonsense! Don't you believe that I die so easily! And don't rejoice prematurely, Alice!

CURT. Think of your children. Make your will so that your wife at least may keep the household goods.

CAPTAIN. Is she going to inherit from me while I am still alive?

CURT. No, but if something happens she ought not to be turned into the street. One who has dusted and polished and looked after these things for twenty-five years should have some right to remain in possession of them. May I send word to the regimental lawyer?

CAPTAIN. No!

CURT. You are a cruel man—more cruel than I thought you!

CAPTAIN. Now it is back again!

[*Falls back on the bed unconscious.*]

ALICE. [*Goes toward the right*] There are some people in the kitchen—I have to go down there.

CURT. Yes, go. Here is not much to be done.

[ALICE *goes out.*]

CAPTAIN. [*Recovers*] Well, Curt, what are you going to do about your quarantine?

CURT. Oh, that will be all right.

CAPTAIN. No; I am in command on this island, so you will have to deal with me—don't forget that!

CURT. Have you ever seen a quarantine station?

CAPTAIN. Have I? Before you were born. And I'll give you a piece of advice: don't place your disinfection plant too close to the shore.

CURT. I was thinking that the nearer I could get to the water the better—

CAPTAIN. That shows how much you know of your business. Water, don't you see, is the element of the bacilli, their life element?

CURT. But the salt water of the sea is needed to wash away all the impurity.

CAPTAIN. Idiot! Well, now, when you get a house for yourself I suppose you'll bring home your children?

CURT. Do you think they will let themselves be brought?

CAPTAIN. Of course, if you have got any backbone! It would make a good impression on the people if you fulfilled your duties in that respect also—

CURT. I have always fulfilled my duties in that respect.

CAPTAIN. [*Raising his voice*]—in the one respect where you have proved yourself most remiss—

CURT. Have I not told you—

CAPTAIN. [*Paying no attention*]—for one does not desert one's children like that—

CURT. Go right on!

CAPTAIN. As your relative—a relative older than yourself—I feel entitled to tell you the truth, even if it should prove bitter—and you should not take it badly—

CURT. Are you hungry?

CAPTAIN. Yes, I am.

CURT. Do you want something light?

CAPTAIN. No, something solid.

CURT. Then you would be done for.

CAPTAIN. Is it not enough to be sick, but one must starve also?

CURT. That's how the land lies.

CAPTAIN. And neither drink nor smoke? Then life is not worth much!

CURT. Death demands sacrifices, or it comes at once.

ALICE. [*Enters with several bunches of flowers and some telegrams and letters*] These are for you.

[*Throws the flowers on the writing-table.*]

CAPTAIN. [*Flattered*] For me! Will you please let me look?

ALICE. Oh, they are only from the non-commissioned officers, the bandmen, and the gunners.

CAPTAIN. You are jealous.

ALICE. Oh, no. If it were laurel wreaths, that would be another matter—but those you can never get.

CAPTAIN. Hm!—Here's a telegram from the Colonel— read it, Curt. The Colonel is a gentleman after all—though he is something of an idiot. And this is from—what does it say? It is from Judith! Please telegraph her to come with the next boat. And here—yes, one is not quite without friends after all, and it is fine to see them take thought of a sick man, who is also a man of deserts above his rank, and a man free of fear or blemish.

ALICE. I don't quite understand—are they congratulating you because you are sick?

CAPTAIN. Hyena!

ALICE. Yes, we had a doctor here on the island who was so hated that when he left they gave a banquet—after him, and not for him!

CAPTAIN. Put the flowers in water—I am not easily caught, and all people are a lot of rabble, but, by heavens, these simple tributes are genuine—they cannot be anything but genuine!

ALICE. Fool!

CURT. [*Reading the telegram*] Judith says she cannot come because the steamer is held back by the storm.

CAPTAIN. Is that all?

CURT. No-o—there is a postscript.

CAPTAIN. Out with it!

CURT. Well, she asks her father not to drink so much.

CAPTAIN. Impudence! That's like children! That's my only beloved daughter—my Judith—my idol!

ALICE. And your image!

CAPTAIN. Such is life. Such are its best joys—Hell!

ALICE. Now you get the harvest of your sowing. You have set her against her own mother and now she turns against the father. Tell me, then, that there is no God!

CAPTAIN. [*To* CURT] What does the Colonel say?

CURT. He grants leave of absence without any comment.

CAPTAIN. Leave of absence? I have not asked for it.

ALICE. No, but I have asked for it.

CAPTAIN. I don't accept it.

ALICE. Order has already been issued.

CAPTAIN. That's none of my concern!

ALICE. Do you see, Curt, that for this man exist no laws, no constitutions, no prescribed human order? He stands above everything and everybody. The universe is created for his private use. The sun and the moon pursue their courses in order to spread his glory among the stars. Such is this man: this insignificant captain, who could not even reach the rank of major, and at whose strutting everybody laughs, while he thinks himself feared; this poor wretch who is afraid in the dark and believes in barometers: and all this in conjunction with and having for its climax—a barrowful of manure that is not even prime quality!

CAPTAIN. [*Fanning himself with a bunch of flowers, conceitedly, without listening to* ALICE] Have you asked Curt to breakfast?

ALICE. No.

CAPTAIN. Get us, then, at once two nice tenderloin steaks.

ALICE. Two?

CAPTAIN. I am going to have one myself.

ALICE. But we are three here.

CAPTAIN. Oh, you want one also? Well, make it three then.

ALICE. Where am I to get them? Last night you asked Curt to supper, and there was not a crust of bread in the house. Curt has been awake all night without anything to eat, and he has had no coffee because there is none in the house and the credit is gone.

CAPTAIN. She is angry at me for not dying yesterday.

ALICE. No, for not dying twenty-five years ago—for not dying before you were born!

CAPTAIN. [*To* CURT] Listen to her! That's what happens when you institute a marriage, my dear Curt. And it is perfectly clear that it was not instituted in heaven.

[ALICE *and* CURT *look at each other meaningly.*]

CAPTAIN. [*Rises and goes toward the door*] However, say what you will, now I am going on duty. [*Puts on an old-fashioned helmet with a brush crest, girds on the saber, and shoulders his cloak*] If anybody calls for me, I am at the battery. [ALICE *and* CURT *try vainly to hold him back*] Stand aside!

[*Goes out.*]

ALICE. Yes, go! You always go, always show your back, whenever the fight becomes too much for you. And then you let your wife cover the retreat—you hero of the bottle, you arch-braggart, you arch-liar! Fie on you!

CURT. This is bottomless!

ALICE. And you don't know everything yet.

CURT. Is there anything more—

ALICE. But I am ashamed—

CURT. Where is he going now? And where does he get the strength?

ALICE. Yes, you may well ask! Now he goes down to the non-commissioned officers and thanks them for the flowers—and then he eats and drinks with them. And then he speaks ill of all the other officers—If you only knew how many times he has been threatened with discharge! Nothing but sympathy for his family has saved him. And this he takes for fear of his superiority. And he hates and maligns the very women— wives of other officers—who have been pleading our cause.

CURT. I have to confess that I applied for this position in order to find peace by the sea— and of your circumstances I knew nothing at all.

ALICE. Poor Curt! And how will you get something to eat?

CURT. Oh, I can go over to the doctor's—but you? Will you not permit me to arrange this for you?

ALICE. If only he does not learn of it, for then he would kill me.

CURT. [*Looking out through the window*] Look, he stands right in the wind out there on the rampart.

ALICE. He is to pitied—for being what he is!

CURT. Both of you are to be pitied! But what can be done?

ALICE. I don't know—The mail brought a batch of unpaid bills also, and those he did not see.

CURT. It may be fortunate to escape seeing things at times.

ALICE. [*At the window*] He has unbuttoned his cloak and lets the wind strike his chest. Now he wants to die!

CURT. That is not what he wants, I think, for a while ago, when he felt his life slipping away, he grabbed hold of mine and began to stir in my affairs as if he wanted to crawl into me and live my life.

ALICE. That is just his vampire nature—to interfere with other people's destinies, to suck interest out of other existences, to regulate and arrange the doings of others, since he can find no interest whatever in his own life. And remember, Curt, don't ever admit him into your family life, don't ever make him acquainted with your friends, for he will take them away from you and make them his own. He is a perfect magician in this respect. Were he to meet your children, you would soon find them intimate with *him*, and he would be advising them and educating them to suit himself—but principally in opposition to *your* wishes.

CURT. Alice, was it not he who took my children away from me at the time of the divorce?

ALICE. Since it is all over now—yes, it was he.

CURT. I have suspected it, but never had any certainty. It was he!

ALICE. When you placed your full trust in my husband and sent him to make peace between yourself and your wife, he made love to her instead, and taught her the trick that gave her the children.

CURT. Oh, God! God in heaven!

ALICE. There you have another side of him. [*Silence.*]

CURT. Do you know, last night—when he thought himself dying—then—he made me promise that I should look after his children!

ALICE. But you don't want to revenge yourself on my children?

CURT. Yes—by keeping my promise. I shall look after your children.

ALICE. You could take no worse revenge, for there is nothing he hates so much as generosity.

CURT. Then I may consider myself revenged—without any revenge.

ALICE. I love revenge as a form of justice, and I am yearning to see evil get its punishment!

CURT. You still remain at that point?

Alice. There I shall always remain, and the day I forgave or loved an enemy I should be a hypocrite.

Curt. It may be a duty not to say everything, Alice, not to see everything. It is called forbearance, and all of us need it.

ALICE. Not I! My life lies clear and open, and I have always played my cards straight.

CURT. That is saying a good deal.

ALICE. No, it is not saying enough. Because what I have suffered innocently for the sake of this man, whom I never loved—

CURT. Why did you marry?

ALICE. Who can tell? Because he took me, seduced me! I don't know. And then I was longing to get up on the heights—

CURT. And deserted your art?

ALICE. Which was despised! But you know, he cheated me! He held out hopes of a pleasant life, a handsome home—and there was nothing but debts; no gold except on the uniform—and even that was not real gold. He cheated me!

CURT. Wait a moment! When a young man falls in love, he sees the future in a hopeful light: that his hopes are not always realized, one must pardon. I have the same kind of deceit on my own conscience without thinking myself dishonest—What is it you see on the rampart?

ALICE. I want to see if he has fallen down.

CURT. Has he?

ALICE. No—worse luck! He is cheating me all the time.

CURT. Then I shall call on the doctor and the lawyer.

ALICE. [*Sitting down at the window*] Yes, dear Curt, go. I shall sit here and wait. And I have learned how to wait!

Curtain.

Same setting in full daylight. The sentry is pacing back and forth on the battery as before. ALICE *sits in the right-hand easy-chair. Her hair is now gray.*

CURT. [*Enters from the left after having knocked*] Good day, Alice.

ALICE. Good day, Curt. Sit down.

CURT. [*Sits down in the left-hand easy-chair*] The steamer is just coming in.

ALICE. Then I know what's in store, for he is on board.

CURT. Yes, he is, for I caught the glitter of his helmet—What has he been doing in the city?

ALICE. Oh, I can figure it out. He dressed for parade, which means that he saw the Colonel, and he put on white gloves, which means that he made some calls.

CURT. Did you notice his quiet manner yesterday? Since he has quit drinking and become temperate, he is another man: calm, reserved, considerate—

ALICE. I know it, and if that man had always kept sober he would have been a menace to humanity. It is perhaps fortunate for the rest of mankind that he made himself ridiculous and harmless through his whiskey.

CURT. The spirit in the bottle has chastised him—But have you noticed since death put its mark on him that he has developed a dignity which elevates? And is it not possible that with this new idea of immortality may have come a new outlook upon life?

ALICE. You are deceiving yourself. He is conjuring up something evil. And don't you believe what he says, for he lies with premeditation, and he knows the art of intriguing as no one else—

CURT. [*Watching* ALICE] Why, Alice, what does this mean? Your hair has turned gray in these two nights!

ALICE. No, my friend, it has long been gray, and I have simply neglected to darken it since my husband is as good as dead. Twenty-five years in prison—do you know that this place served as a prison in the old days?

CURT. Prison—well, the walls show it.

ALICE. And my complexion! Even the children took on prison color in here.

CURT. I find it hard to imagine children prattling within these walls.

ALICE. There was not much prattling done either. And those two that died perished merely from lack of light.

CURT. What do you think is coming next?

ALICE. The decisive blow at us two. I caught a familiar glimmer in his eye when you read out that telegram from Judith. It ought, of course, to have been directed against her, but she, you know, is inviolate, and so his hatred sought you.

CURT. What are his intentions in regard to me, do you think?

ALICE. Hard to tell, but he possesses a marvellous skill in nosing out other people's secrets—and did you notice how, all day yesterday, he seemed to be living in your quarantine; how he drank a life-interest out of your existence; how he ate your children alive? A cannibal, I tell you—for I know him. His own life is going, or has gone—

CURT. I also have that impression of his being already on the other side. His face seems to phosphoresce, as if he were in a state of decay—and his eyes flash like will-o'-the-wisps over graves or morasses—Here he comes! Tell him you thought it possible he might be jealous.

ALICE. No, he is too self-conceited. "Show me the man of whom I need to be jealous!" Those are his own words.

CURT. So much the better, for even his faults carry with them a certain merit—Shall I get up and meet him anyhow?

ALICE. No, be impolite, or he will think you false. And if he begins to lie, pretend to believe him. I know perfectly how to translate his lies, and get always at the truth with the help of my dictionary. I foresee something dreadful—but, Curt, don't lose your self-control! My own advantage in our long struggle has been that I was always sober, and for that reason in full control of myself. He was always tripped by his whiskey—Now we shall see!

CAPTAIN. [*In from the left in full uniform, with helmet, cloak, and white gloves. Calm, dignified, but pale and hollow-eyed. Moves forward with a tottering step and sinks down, his helmet and cloak still on, in a chair at the right of the stage, far from* CURT *and* ALICE] Good day. Pardon me for sitting down like this, but I feel a little tired.

ALICE *and* Curt. Good day. Welcome home.

ALICE. How are you feeling?

CAPTAIN. Splendid! Only a little tired—

ALICE. What news from the city?

CAPTAIN. Oh, a little of everything. I saw the doctor, among other things, and he said it was nothing at all—that I might live twenty years, if I took care of myself.

ALICE. [*To* CURT] Now he is lying. [*To the* CAPTAIN] Why, that's fine, my dear.

CAPTAIN. So much for that.

[*Silence, during which the* CAPTAIN *is looking at* ALICE *and* CURT *as if expecting them to speak.*]

ALICE. [*To* CURT] Don't say a word, but let him begin—then he will show his cards.

CAPTAIN. [*To* Alice] Did you say anything?

ALICE. No, not a word.

CAPTAIN. [*Dragging on the words*] Well, Curt!

ALICE. [*To* CURT] There—now he is coming out.

CAPTAIN. Well, I went to the city, as you know. [CURT *nods assent*] Mm-mm, I picked up acquaintances—and among others—a young cadet [*dragging*] in the artillery. [*Pause, during which* CURT *shows some agitation*] As—we are in need of cadets right here, I arranged with the Colonel to let him come here. This ought to please you, especially when I inform you that—he is—your own son!

ALICE. [*To* CURT] The vampire—don't you see?

CURT. Under ordinary circumstances that ought to please a father, but in my case it will merely be painful.

CAPTAIN. I don't see why it should!

CURT. You don't need to—it is enough that I don't want it.

CAPTAIN. Oh, you think so? Well, then, you ought to know that the young man has been ordered to report here, and that from now on he has to obey me.

CURT. Then I shall force him to seek transfer to another regiment.

CAPTAIN. You cannot do it, as you have no rights over your son.

CURT. No?

CAPTAIN. No, for the court gave those rights to the mother.

CURT. Then I shall communicate with the mother.

CAPTAIN. You don't need to.

CURT. Don't need to?

CAPTAIN. No, for I have already done so. Yah!

[CURT *rises but sinks back again.*]

ALICE. [To CURT] Now he must die!

CURT. Why, he *is* a cannibal!

CAPTAIN. So much for that! [*Straight to* ALICE *and* CURT] Did you say anything?

ALICE. No—have you grown hard of hearing?

CAPTAIN. Yes, a little—but if you come nearer to me I can tell you something between ourselves.

ALICE. That is not necessary—and a witness is sometimes good to have for both parties.

CAPTAIN. You are right; witnesses are sometimes good to have! But, first of all, did you get that will?

ALICE. [*Hands him a document*] The regimental lawyer drew it up himself.

CAPTAIN. In your favor—good! [*Reads the document and then tears it carefully into strips which he throws on the floor*] So much for that! Yah!

ALICE. [To CURT] Did you ever see such a man?

CURT. That is no man!

CAPTAIN. Well, Alice, this was what I wanted to say—

ALICE. [*Alarmed*] Go on, please.

CAPTAIN. [*Calmly as before*] On account of your long cherished desire to quit this miserable existence in an unhappy marriage; on account of the lack of feeling with which you have treated your husband and children, and on account of the carelessness you have shown in the handling of our domestic economy, I have, during this trip to the city, filed an application for divorce in the City Court.

ALICE. Oh—and your grounds?

CAPTAIN. [*Calmly as before*] Besides the grounds already mentioned, I have others of a purely personal nature. As it has been found that I may live another twenty years, I am contemplating a change from this unhappy marital union to one that suits me better, and I mean to join my fate to that of some woman capable of devotion to her husband, and who also may bring into the home not only youth, but—let us say—a little beauty!

ALICE. [*Takes the wedding-ring from her finger and throws it at the* CAPTAIN] You are welcome!

CAPTAIN. [*Picks up the ring and puts it in his vest pocket*] She throws away the ring. The witness will please take notice.

ALICE. [*Rises in great agitation*] And you intend to turn me out in order to put another woman into my home?

CAPTAIN. Yah!

ALICE. Well, then, we'll speak plain language! Cousin Curt, that man is guilty of an attempt to murder his wife.

CURT. An attempt to murder?

ALICE. Yes, he pushed me into the water.

CAPTAIN. Without witnesses!

ALICE. He lies again—Judith saw it!

CAPTAIN. Well, what of it?

ALICE. She can testify to it.

CAPTAIN. No, she cannot, for she says that she didn't see anything.

ALICE. You have taught the child to lie!

CAPTAIN. I didn't need to, for you had taught her already.

ALICE. You have met Judith?

CAPTAIN. Yah!

ALICE. Oh, God! Oh, God!

CAPTAIN. The fortress has surrendered. The enemy will be permitted to depart in safety on ten minutes' notice. [*Places his watch on the table*] Ten minutes—watch on the table! [*Stops and puts one hand up to his heart.*]

ALICE. [*Goes over to the Captain and takes his arm*] What is it?

CAPTAIN. I don't know.

ALICE. Do you want anything—a drink?

CAPTAIN. Whiskey? No, I don't want to die—You! [*Straightening himself up*] Don't touch me! Ten minutes, or the garrison will be massacred. [*Pulls the saber partly from the scabbard*] Ten minutes!

[*Goes out through the background.*]

CURT. What kind of man is this?

ALICE. He is a demon, and no man!

CURT. What does he want with my son?

ALICE. He wants him as hostage in order to be your master—he wants to isolate you from the authorities of the island—Do you know that the people around here have named this island "Little Hell"?

CURT. I didn't know that—Alice, you are the first woman who ever inspired me with compassion—all others have seemed to me to deserve their fate.

ALICE. Don't desert me now! Don't leave me, for he will beat me—he has been doing so all these twenty-five years—in the presence of the children—and he has pushed me into the water—

CURT. Having heard this, I place myself absolutely against him. I came here without an angry thought, without memory of his former slanders and attempts to humiliate me. I forgave him even when you told me that he was the man who had parted me from my children—for he was ill and dying—but now, when he wants to steal my son, he must die—he or I!

ALICE. Good! No surrender of the fortress! But blow it up instead, with him in it, even if we have to keep him company! I am in charge of the powder!

CURT. There was no malice in me when I came here, and I wanted to run away when I felt myself infected with your hatred, but now I am moved by an irresistible impulse to hate this man, as I hate everything that is evil. What can be done?

ALICE. I have learned the tactics from him. Drum up his enemies and seek allies.

CURT. Just think—that he should get hold of my wife! Why didn't those two meet a lifetime ago? Then there would have been a battle-royal that had set the earth quaking.

ALICE. But now these souls have spied each other—and yet they must part. I guess what is his most vulnerable spot—I have long suspected it—

CURT. Who is his most faithful enemy on the island?

ALICE. The Quartermaster.

CURT. Is he an honest man?

ALICE. He is. And he knows what I—I know too—he knows what the Sergeant-Major and the Captain have been up to.

CURT. What they have been up to? You don't mean—

ALICE. Defalcations!

CURT. This is terrible! No, I don't want to have any finger in that mess!

ALICE. Ha-ha! You cannot hit an enemy.

CURT. Formerly I could, but I can do so no longer.

ALICE. Why?

CURT. Because I have discovered—that justice is done anyhow.

ALICE. And you could wait for that? Then your son would already have been taken away from you. Look at my gray hairs—just feel how thick it still is, for that matter—He intends to marry again, and then I shall be free—to do the same—I am free! And in ten minutes he will be under arrest down below, right under us—[*stamps her foot on the floor*] right under us—and I shall dance above his head—I shall dance "The Entry of the Boyars"—[*makes a few steps with her arms akimbo*] ha-ha-ha-ha! And I shall play on the piano so that he can hear it. [*Hammering on the piano*] Oh, the tower is opening its gates, and the sentry with the drawn saber will no longer be guarding me, but him—*Malrough s'en va-t-en guerre!* Him, him, him, the sentry is going to guard!

CURT. [*Has been watching her with an intoxicated look in his eyes*] Alice, are you, too, a devil?

ALICE. [*Jumps up on a chair and pulls down the wreaths*] These we will take along when we depart—the laurels of triumph! And fluttering ribbons! A little dusty, but eternally green—like my youth—I am not old, Curt?

CURT. [*With shining eyes*] You are a devil!

ALICE. In "Little Hell"— Listen! Now I shall fix my hair—[*loosens her hair*], dress in two minutes—go to the Quartermaster in two minutes—and then, up in the air with the fortress!

CURT. [*As before*] You are a devil!

ALICE. That's what you always used to say when we were children. Do you remember when we were small and became engaged to each other? Ha-ha! You were bashful, of course—

CURT. [*Seriously*] Alice!

ALICE. Yes, you were! And it was becoming to you. Do you know there are gross women who like modest men? And there are said to be modest men who like gross women— You liked me a little bit, didn't you?

CURT. I don't know where I am!

ALICE. With an actress whose manners are free, but who is an excellent lady otherwise. Yes! But now I am free, free, free! Turn away and I'll change my waist!

[*She opens her waist. Curt rushes up to her, grabs her in his arms, lifts her high up, and bites her throat so that she cries out. Then he drops her on the couch and runs out to the left.*]

Curtain and intermission.

Same stage setting in early evening light. The sentry on the battery is still visible through the windows in the background. The laurel wreaths are hung over the arms of an easy chair. The hanging lamp is lit. Faint music.

The CAPTAIN, *pale and hollow-eyed, his hair showing touches of gray, dressed in a worn undress uniform, with riding-boots, sits at the writing-table and plays solitaire. He wears his spectacles. The entr'acte music continues after the curtain has been raised and until another person enters.*

The CAPTAIN *plays away at his solitaire, but with a sudden start now and then, when he looks up and listens with evident alarm.*

He does not seem able to make the solitaire come out, so he becomes impatient and gathers up the cards. Then he goes to the left-hand window, opens it, and throws out the cards. The window (of the French type) remains open, rattling on its hinges.

He goes over to the buffet, but is frightened by the noise made by the window, so that he turns around to see what it is. Takes out three dark-coloured square whiskey bottles, examines them carefully—and throws them out of the window. Takes out some boxes of cigars, smells at one, and throws them out of the window.

Next he takes off his spectacles, cleans them carefully, and tries how far he can see with them. Then he throws them out of the window, stumbles against the furniture as if he could not see, and lights six candles in a candelabrum on the chiffonier. Catches sight of the laurel wreaths, picks them up, and goes toward the window, but turns back. Folds the wreaths carefully in the piano cover, fastens the corners together with pins taken from the writing-table, and puts the bundle on a chair. Goes to the piano, strikes the keyboard with his fists, locks the piano, and throws the key out through the window. Then he lights the candles on the piano. Goes to the what-not, takes his wife's picture from it, looks at this and tears it to pieces, dropping the pieces on the floor. The window rattles on its hinges, and again he becomes frightened.

Then, after having calmed himself, he takes the pictures of his son and daughter, kisses them in an off-hand way, and puts them, into his pocket. All the rest of the pictures he sweeps down with his elbow and pokes together into a heap with his foot.

Then he sits down at the writing-table, tired out, and puts a hand up to his heart. Lights the candle on the table and sighs; stares in front of himself as if confronted with unpleasant visions. Rises and goes over to the chiffonier, opens the lid, takes out a bundle of letters tied together with a blue silk ribbon, and throws the bundle into the fireplace of the glazed brick oven. Closes the chiffonier. The telegraph receiver sounds a single click. The CAPTAIN *shrinks together in deadly fear and stands fixed to the spot, listening. But hearing nothing more from the instrument, he turns to listen in the direction of the door on the left. Goes over and opens it, takes a step inside the doorway, and returns, carrying on his arm a cat whose back he strokes. Then he goes old to the right. Now the music ceases.*

ALICE *enters from the background, dressed in a walking suit, with gloves and hat on; her hair is black; she looks around with surprise at the many lighted candles.*

CURT *enters from the left, nervous.*

ALICE. It looks like Christmas Eve here.

CURT. Well?

ALICE. [*Holds out her hand for him to kiss*] Thank me! [CURT *kisses her hand unwillingly*] Six witnesses, and four of them solid as rock. The report has been made, and the answer will come here by telegraph—right here, into the heart of the fortress.

CURT. So!

ALICE. You should say "thanks" instead of "so."

CURT. Why has he lit so many candles?

ALICE. Because he is afraid of the dark, of course. Look at the telegraph key—does it not look like the handle of a coffee mill? I grind, I grind, and the beans crack as when you pull teeth—

CURT. What has he been doing in the room here?

ALICE. It looks as if he intended to move. Down below, that's where you are going to move!

CURT. Don't. Alice—I think it's distressing! He was the friend of my youth, and he showed me kindness many times when I was in difficulty—He should be pitied!

ALICE. And how about me, who have done nothing wrong, and who have had to sacrifice my career to that monster?

CURT. How about that career? Was it so very brilliant?

ALICE. [*Enraged*] What are you saying? Do you know who I am, what I have been?

CURT. Now, now!

ALICE. Are you beginning already?

CURT. Already?

[ALICE *throws her arms around* CURT'S *neck and kisses him.*]
[CURT *takes her by the arms and bites her neck so that she screams.*]

ALICE. You bite me!

CURT. [*Beyond himself*] Yes, I want to bite your throat and. suck your blood like a lynx. You have aroused the wild beast in me—that beast which I have tried for years to kill by privations and self-inflicted tortures. I came here believing myself a little better than you two, and now I am the vilest of all. Since I first saw you—in all your odious nakedness—and since my vision became warped by passion, I have known the full strength of evil. What is ugly becomes beautiful; what is good becomes ugly and mean—Come here and I'll choke you—with a kiss! [*He locks her in his arms.*]

ALICE. [*Holds up her left hand*] Behold the mark of the shackles that you have broken. I was a slave, and you set me free.

CURT. But I am going to bind you—

ALICE. You?

CURT. I!

ALICE. For a moment I thought you were—

CURT. Pious?

ALICE. Yes, you prated about the fall of man—

CURT. Did I?

ALICE. And I thought you had come here to preach—

CURT. You thought so? In an hour we shall be in the city, and then you shall see what I am—

ALICE. Then we will go to the theatre to-night, just to show ourselves. The shame will be his if I run away, don't you see!

CURT. I begin to understand that prison is not enough—

ALICE. No, it is not—there must be shame also.

CURT. A strange world! You commit a shameful act, and the shame falls on him.

ALICE. Well, if the world be so stupid—

CURT. It is as if these prison walls had absorbed all the corruption of the criminals, and it gets into you if you merely breathe this air. You were thinking of the theatre and the supper, I suppose. I was thinking of my son.

ALICE. [*Strikes him on the month with her glove*] Fogey!

[CURT *lifts his hand as if to strike her.*]

ALICE. [*Drawing back*] Tout beau!

CURT. Forgive me!

ALICE. Yes—on your knees! [CURT *kneels down*] Down on your face! [CURT *touches the ground with his forehead*] Kiss my foot! [CURT *kisses her foot*] And don't you ever do it again! Get up!

CURT. [*Rising*] Where have I landed? Where am I?

ALICE. Oh, you know!

CURT. [*Looking around with horror*] I believe almost—

CAPTAIN. [*Enters from the right, looking wretched, leaning on a cane*] Curt, may I have a talk with you—alone?

ALICE. Is it about that departure in safety?

CAPTAIN. [*Sits down at the sewing-table*] Curt, will you kindly sit down here by me a little while? And, Alice, will you please grant me a moment—of peace!

ALICE. What is up now? New signals! [*To* CURT] Please be seated. [CURT *sits down reluctantly*] And listen to the words of age and wisdom—And if a telegram should come—tip me off! [*Goes out to the left.*]

CAPTAIN. [*With dignity, after a pause*] Can you explain a fate like mine, like ours?

CURT. No more than I can explain my own!

CAPTAIN. What can be the meaning of this jumble?

CURT. In my better moments I have believed that just this was the meaning—that we should not be able to catch a meaning, and yet submit—

CAPTAIN. Submit? Without a fixed point outside myself I cannot submit.

CURT. Quite right, but as a mathematician you should be able to seek that unknown point when several known ones are given—

CAPTAIN. I have sought it, and—I have not found it!

CURT. Then you have made some mistake in your calculations—do it all over again!

CAPTAIN. I should do it over again? Tell me, where did you get your resignation?

CURT. I have none left. Don't overestimate me.

CAPTAIN. As you may have noticed, my understanding of the art of living has been— elimination! That means: wipe out and pass on! Very early in life I made myself a bag into which I chucked my humiliations, and when it was full I dropped it into the sea. I don't think any man ever suffered so many humiliations as I have. But when I wiped them out and passed on they ceased to exist.

CURT. I have noticed that you have wrought both your life, and your environment out of your poetical imagination.

CAPTAIN. How could I have lived otherwise? How could I have endured? [*Puts his hand over his heart.*]

CURT. How are you doing?

CAPTAIN. Poorly. [*Pause*] Then comes a moment when the faculty for what you call poetical imagination gives out. And then reality leaps forth in all its nakedness—It is frightful! [*He is now speaking in a voice of lachrymose senility, and with his lower jaw drooping*] Look here, my dear friend—[*controls himself and speaks in his usual voice*] forgive me!—When I was in the city and consulted the doctor [*now the tearful voice returns*] he said that I was played out—[*in his usual voice*] and that I couldn't live much longer.

CURT. Was *that* what he said?

CAPTAIN. [*With tearful voice*] That's what he said!

CURT. So it was not true?

CAPTAIN. What? Oh—no, that was not true. [*Pause.*]

CURT. Was the rest of it not true either?

CAPTAIN. What do you mean?

CURT. That my son was ordered to report here as cadet?

CAPTAIN. I never heard of it.

CURT. Do you know—your ability to wipe out your own misdeeds is miraculous!

CAPTAIN. I don't understand what you are talking of.

CURT. Then you have come to the end!

CAPTAIN. Well, there is not much left!

CURT. Tell me, perhaps you never applied for that divorce which would bring your wife into disgrace?

CAPTAIN. Divorce? No, I have not heard of it.

CURT. [*Rising*] Will you admit, then, that you have been lying?

CAPTAIN. You employ such strong words, my friend. All of us need forbearance.

CURT. Oh, you have come to see that?

CAPTAIN. [*Firmly, with clear voice*] Yes, I have come to see that—And for this reason, Curt, please forgive me! Forgive everything!

CURT. That was a manly word! But I have nothing to forgive you. And I am not the man you believe me to be. No longer now! Least of all one worthy of receiving your confessions!

CAPTAIN. [*With clear voice*] Life seemed so peculiar—so contrary, so malignant—ever since my childhood—and people seemed so bad that I grew bad also—

CURT. [*On his feet, perturbed, and glancing at the telegraph instrument*] Is it possible to close off an instrument like that?

CAPTAIN. Hardly.

CURT. [*With increasing alarm*] Who is Sergeant-Major Östberg?

CAPTAIN. An honest fellow, but something of a busybody, I should say.

CURT. And who is the Quartermaster?

CAPTAIN. He is my enemy, of course, but I have nothing bad to say of him.

CURT. [*Looking out through the window, where a lantern is seen moving to and fro*] What are they doing with the lantern out on the battery?

CAPTAIN. Do you see a lantern?

CURT. Yes, and people moving about.

CAPTAIN. I suppose it is what we call a service squad.

CURT. What is that?

CAPTAIN. A few men and a corporal. Probably some poor wretch that has to be locked up.

CURT. Oh! [*Pause.*]

CAPTAIN. Now, when you know Alice, how do you like her?

CURT. I cannot tell—I have no understanding of people at all. She is as inexplicable to me as you are, or as I am myself. For I am reaching the age when wisdom makes this acknowledgment: I know nothing, I understand nothing! But when I observe an action, I like to get at the motive behind it. Why did you push her into the water?—

CAPTAIN. I don't know. It merely seemed quite natural to me, as she was standing on the pier, that she ought to be in the water.

CURT. Have you ever regretted it?

CAPTAIN. Never!

CURT. That's strange!

CAPTAIN. Of course, it is! So strange that I cannot realize that I am the man who has been guilty of such a mean act.

CURT. Have you not expected her to take some revenge?

CAPTAIN. Well, she seems to have taken it in full measure; and that, too, seems no less natural to me.

CURT. What has so suddenly brought you to this cynical resignation?

CAPTAIN. Since I looked death in the face, life has presented itself from a different viewpoint. Tell me, if you were to judge between Alice and myself, whom would you place in the right?

CURT. Neither of you. But to both of you I should give endless compassion—perhaps a little more of it to you!

CAPTAIN. Give me your hand, Curt!

CURT. [*Gives him one hand and puts the other one on the* CAPTAIN'S *shoulder*] Old boy!

ALICE. [*In from the left, carrying a sunshade*] Well, how harmonious! Oh, friendship! Has there been no telegram yet?

CURT. [*Coldly*] No.

ALICE. This delay makes me impatient, and when I grow impatient I push matters along—Look, Curt, how I give him the final bullet. And now he'll bite the grass! First, I load—I know all about rifle practice, the famous rifle practice of which less than 5,000 copies were sold—and then I aim—fire! [*She takes aim with her sunshade*] How is your new wife? The young, beautiful, unknown one? You don't know! But I know how my lover is doing. [*Puts her arms around the neck of* CURT *and kisses him; he thrusts her away from himself*] He is well, although still a little bashful! You wretch, whom I have never loved—you, who were too conceited to be jealous—you never saw how I was leading you by the nose!

[*The* CAPTAIN *draws the saber and makes a leap at her, aiming at her several futile blows that only hit the furniture.*]

ALICE. Help! Help!

[CURT *does not move.*]

CAPTAIN. [*Falls with the saber in his hand*] Judith, avenge me!

ALICE. Hooray! He's dead!

[CURT *withdraws toward the door in the background.*]

CAPTAIN. [*Gets on his feet*] Not yet! [*Sheathes the saber and sits down in the easy-chair by the sewing-table*] Judith! Judith!

ALICE. [*Drawing nearer to* CURT] Now I go—with you!

CURT. [*Pushes her back with such force that she sinks to her knees*] Go back to the hell whence you came! Good-bye forever! [*Goes to the door.*]

CAPTAIN. Don't leave me Curt; she will kill me!

ALICE. Don't desert me, Curt—don't desert us!

CURT. Good-bye! [*Goes out.*]

ALICE. [*With a sudden change of attitude*] The wretch! That's a friend for you!

CAPTAIN. [*Softly*] Forgive me Alice, and come here—come quick!

ALICE. [*Over to the* CAPTAIN] That's the worst rascal and hypocrite I have met in my life! Do you know, you are a man after all!

CAPTAIN. Listen, Alice! I cannot live much longer.

ALICE. Is that so?

CAPTAIN. The doctor has said so.

ALICE. Then there was no truth in the rest either?

CAPTAIN. No.

ALICE. [*In despair*] Oh, what have I done!

CAPTAIN. There is help for everything.

ALICE. No, this is beyond helping!

CAPTAIN. Nothing is beyond helping, if you only wipe it out and pass on.

ALICE. But the telegram—the telegram!

CAPTAIN. Which telegram?

ALICE. [*On her knees beside the* CAPTAIN] Are we then cast out? Must this happen? I have sprung a mine under myself, under us. Why did you have to tell untruths? And why should that man come here to tempt me? We are lost! Your magnanimity might have helped everything, forgiven everything!

CAPTAIN. What is it that cannot be forgiven? What is it that I have not already forgiven you?

ALICE. You are right—but there is no help for this.

CAPTAIN. I cannot guess it, although I know your ingenuity when it comes to villanies—

ALICE. Oh, if I could only get out of this, I should care for you—I should love you, Edgar!

CAPTAIN. Listen to me! Where do I stand?

ALICE. Don't you think anybody can help us—well, no man can!

CAPTAIN. Who could then help?

ALICE. [*Looking the* CAPTAIN *straight in the eye*] I don't know—Think of it, what is to become of the children with their name dishonored—?

CAPTAIN. Have you dishonored that name?

ALICE. Not I! Not I! And then they must leave school! And as they go out into the world, they will be lonely as we, and cruel as we—Then you didn't meet Judith either, I understand now?

CAPTAIN. No, but wipe it out!

[*The telegraph receiver clicks.* ALICE *flies up.*]

ALICE. [*Screams*] Now ruin is overtaking us! [*To the* CAPTAIN] Don't listen!

CAPTAIN. [*Quietly*] I am not going to listen, dear child—just calm yourself!

ALICE. [*Standing by the instrument, raises herself on tip-toe in order to look out through the window*] Don't listen! Don't listen!

CAPTAIN. [*Holding his hands over his ears*] Lisa, child, I am stopping up my ears.

ALICE. [*On her knees, with lifted hands*] God, help us! The squad is coming—[*Weeping and sobbing*] God in heaven!

[*She appears to be moving her lips as if in silent prayer.*]

[*The telegraph receiver continues to click for a while and a long white strip of paper seems to crawl out of the instrument. Then complete silence prevails once more.*]

ALICE. [*Rises, tears off the paper strip, and reads it in silence. Then she turns her eyes upward for a moment. Goes over to the Captain and kisses him on the forehead*] That is over now! It was nothing!

[*Sits down in the other chair, puts her handkerchief to her face, and breaks into a violent spell of weeping.*]

CAPTAIN. What kind of secrets are these?

ALICE. Don't ask! It is over now!

CAPTAIN. As you please, child.

ALICE. You would not have spoken like that three days ago—what has done it?

CAPTAIN. Well, dear, when I fell down that first time, I went a little way on the other side of the grave. What I saw has been forgotten, but the impression of it still remains.

ALICE. And it was?

CAPTAIN. A hope—for something better!

ALICE. Something better?

CAPTAIN. Yes. That this could be the real life, I have, in fact, never believed: it is death— or something still worse!

ALICE. And we—

CAPTAIN. Have probably been set to torment each other—so it seems at least!

ALICE. Have we tormented each other enough?

CAPTAIN. Yes, I think so! And upset things! [*Looks around*] Suppose we put things to rights? And clean house?

ALICE. Yes, if it can be done.

CAPTAIN. [*Gets up to survey the room*] It can't be done in one day—no, it can't!

ALICE. In two, then! Many days!

CAPTAIN. Let us hope so! [*Pause. Sits down again*] So you didn't get free this time after all! But then, you didn't get me locked up either! [ALICE *looks staggered*] Yes, I know you wanted to put me in prison, but I wipe it out. I suppose you have done worse than that—[ALICE *is speechless*] And I was innocent of those defalcations.

ALICE. And now you intend me to become your nurse?

CAPTAIN. If you are willing!

ALICE. What else could I do?

CAPTAIN. I don't know!

ALICE. [*Sits down, numbed and crushed*] These are the eternal torments! Is there, then, no end to them?

CAPTAIN. Yes, if we are patient. Perhaps life begins when death comes.

ALICE. If it were so! [*Pause.*]

CAPTAIN. You think Curt a hypocrite?

ALICE. Of course I do!

CAPTAIN. And I don't! But all who come near us turn evil and go their way. Curt was weak, and the evil is strong [*Pause*] How commonplace life has become! Formerly blows were struck; now you shake your fist at the most! I am fairly certain that, three months from now, we shall celebrate our silver wedding—with Curt as best man—and with the Doctor and Gerda among the guests. The Quartermaster will make the speech and the Sergeant-Major will lead the cheering. And if I know the Colonel right, he will come on his own invitation—Yes, you may laugh! But do you recall the silver wedding of Adolph—in the Fusiliers? The bride had to carry her wedding ring on the right hand, because the groom in a tender moment had chopped off her left ring finger with his dirk. [ALICE *puts her handkerchief to her mouth in order to repress her laughter*] Are you crying? No, I believe J you are laughing! Yes, child, partly we weep and partly we laugh. Which is the right thing to do?—Don't ask me! The other day I read in a newspaper that a man had been divorced seven times—which means that he had been married seven times—and finally, at the age of ninety-eight, he ran away with his first wife and married her again. Such is love! If life be serious, or merely a joke, is more than I can decide. Often it is most painful when a joke, and its seriousness is after all more agreeable and peaceful. But when at last you try to be serious, somebody comes and plays a joke on you—as Curt, for instance! Do you want a silver wedding? [ALICE *remains silent*] Oh, say yes! They will laugh at us, but what does it matter? We may laugh also, or keep serious, as the occasion may require.

ALICE. Well, all right!

CAPTAIN. Silver wedding, then! [*Rising*] Wipe out and pass on! Therefore, let us pass on!

Curtain.

THE DANCE OF DEATH

PART II

CHARACTERS

EDGAR
ALICE
CURT
ALLAN, *the son of* CURT
JUDITH, *the daughter of* EDGAR
THE LIEUTENANT

THE DANCE OF DEATH

PART II

A rectangular drawing-room in white and gold. The rear wall is broken by several French windows reaching down to the floor. These stand open, revealing a garden terrace outside. Along this terrace, serving as a public promenade, runs a stone balustrade, on which are ranged pots of blue and white faïence, with petunias and scarlet geraniums in them. Beyond, in the background, can be seen the shore battery with a sentry pacing back and forth. In the far distance, the open sea.

At the left of the drawing-room stands a sofa with gilded woodwork. In front of it are a table and chairs. At the right is a grand piano, a writing-table, and an open fireplace.

In the foreground, an American easy-chair.

By the writing-table is a standing lamp of copper with a table attached to it.

On the walls are several old-fashioned oil paintings.

ALLAN is sitting at the writing-table, engrossed in some mathematical problem. JUDITH enters from the background, in summer dress, short skirt, hair in a braid down her back, hat in one hand and tennis racket in the other. She stops in the doorway. ALLAN rises, serious and respectful.

JUDITH. [*In serious but friendly tone*] Why don't you come and play tennis?

ALLAN. [*Bashful, struggling with his emotion*] I am very busy—

JUDITH. Didn't you see that I had made my bicycle point toward the oak, and not away from it?

ALLAN. Yes, I saw it.

JUDITH. Well, what does it mean?

ALLAN. It means—that you want me to come and play tennis—but my duty—I have some problems to work out—and your father is a rather exacting teacher—

JUDITH. Do you like him?

ALLAN. Yes, I do. He takes such interest in all his pupils—

JUDITH. He takes an interest in everything and everybody. Won't you come?

ALLAN. You know I should like to—but I must not!

JUDITH. I'll ask papa to give you leave.

ALLAN. Don't do that. It will only cause talk.

JUDITH. Don't you think I can manage him? He wants what I want.

ALLAN. I suppose that is because you are so hard.

JUDITH. You should be hard also.

ALLAN. I don't belong to the wolf family.

JUDITH. Then you are a sheep.

ALLAN. Rather that.

JUDITH. Tell me why you don't want to come and play tennis?

ALLAN. You know it.

JUDITH. Tell me anyhow. The Lieutenant—

ALLAN. Yes, you don't care for me at all, but you cannot enjoy yourself with the Lieutenant unless I am present, so you can see me suffer.

JUDITH. Am I as cruel as that? I didn't know it.

ALLAN. Well, now you know it.

JUDITH. Then I shall do better hereafter, for I don't want to be cruel, I don't want to be bad—in your eyes.

ALLAN. You say this only to fasten your hold on me. I am already your slave, but it does not satisfy you. The slave must be tortured and thrown to the wild beasts. You have already that other fellow in your clutches—what do you want with me then? Let me go my own way, and you can go yours.

JUDITH. Do you send me away? [ALLAN *does not answer*] Then I go! As second cousins, we shall have to meet now and then, but I am not going to bother you any longer.

[ALLAN *sits down at the table and returns to his problem.*]

JUDITH. [*Instead of going away, comes down the stage and approaches gradually the table where* ALLAN *is sitting*] Don't be afraid, I am going at once—I wanted only to see how the Master of Quarantine lives—[*Looks around*] White and gold—a Bechstein grand—well, well! We are still in the fort since-papa was pensioned—in the tower where mamma has been kept twenty-five years—and we are there on sufferance at that. You—you are rich—

ALLAN. [*Calmly*] We are not rich.

JUDITH. So you say, but you are always wearing fine clothes—but whatever you wear, for that matter, is becoming to you. Do you hear what I say? [*Drawing nearer.*]

ALLAN. [*Submissively*] I do.

JUDITH. How can you hear when you keep on figuring, or whatever you are doing?

ALLAN. I don't use my eyes to listen with.

JUDITH. Your eyes—have you ever looked at them in the mirror?

ALLAN. Go away!

JUDITH. You despise me, do you?

ALLAN. Why, girl, I am not thinking of you at all.

JUDITH. [*Still nearer*] Archimedes is deep in his figures when the soldier comes and cuts him down.

[*Stirs his papers about with the racket.*]

ALLAN. Don't touch my papers!

JUDITH. That's what Archimedes said also. Now you are thinking something foolish—you are thinking that I cannot live without you—

ALLAN. Why can't you leave me alone?

JUDITH. Be courteous, and I'll help you with your examinations—

ALLAN. You?

JUDITH. Yes, I know the examiners—

ALLAN. [*Sternly*] And what of it?

JUDITH. Don't you know that one should stand well with the teachers?

ALLAN. Do you mean your father and the Lieutenant?

JUDITH. And the Colonel!

ALLAN. And then you mean that your protection would enable me to shirk my work?

JUDITH. You are a bad translator—

ALLAN. Of a bad original—

JUDITH. Be ashamed!

ALLAN. So I am—both on your behalf and my own! I am ashamed of having listened to you—Why don't you go?

JUDITH. Because I know you appreciate my company—Yes, you manage always to pass by my window. You have always some errand that brings you into the city with the same boat that I take. You cannot go for a sail without having me to look after the jib.

ALLAN. But a young girl shouldn't say that kind of things!

JUDITH. Do you mean to say that I am a child?

ALLAN. Sometimes you are a good child, and sometimes a bad woman. Me you seem to have picked to be your sheep.

JUDITH. You are a sheep, and that's why I am going to protect you.

ALLAN. [*Rising*] The wolf makes a poor shepherd! You want to eat me—that is the secret of it, I suppose. You want to put your beautiful eyes in pawn to get possession of my head.

JUDITH. Oh, you have been looking at my eyes? I didn't expect that much courage of you.

[ALLAN *collects his papers and starts to go out toward the right.*]
[JUDITH *places herself in front of the door.*]

ALLAN. Get out of my way, or—

JUDITH. Or?

ALLAN. If you were a boy—bah! But you are a girl.

JUDITH. And then?

ALLAN. If you had any pride at all, you would be gone, as you may regard yourself as shown the door.

JUDITH. I'll get back at you for that!

ALLAN. I don't doubt it!

JUDITH. [*Goes enraged toward the background*] I—shall—get—back—at you for that! [*Goes out.*]

CURT. [*Enters from the left*] Where are you going, Allan?

ALLAN. Oh, is that you?

CURT. Who was it that left in such hurry—so that the bushes shook?

ALLAN. It was Judith.

CURT. She is a little impetuous, but a fine girl.

ALLAN. When a girl is cruel and rude, she is always said to be a fine girl.

CURT. Don't be so severe, Allan! Are you not satisfied with your new relatives?

ALLAN. I like Uncle Edgar—

CURT. Yes, he has many good sides. How about your other teachers—the Lieutenant, for instance?

ALLAN. He's so uncertain. Sometimes he seems to have a grudge against me.

CURT. Oh, no! You just go here and make people "seem" this or that. Don't brood, but look after your own affairs, do what is proper, and leave others to their own concerns.

ALLAN. So I do, but—they won't leave me alone. They pull you in—as the cuttlefish down at the landing—they don't bite, but they stir up vortices that suck—

CURT. You have some tendency to melancholia, I think. Don't you feel at home here with me? Is there anything you miss?

ALLAN. I have never been better off, but—there is something here that smothers me.

CURT. Here by the sea? Are you not fond of the sea?

ALLAN. Yes, the open sea. But along the shores you find eelgrass, cuttlefish, jellyfish, sea-nettles, or whatever they are called.

CURT. You shouldn't stay indoors so much. Go out and play tennis.

ALLAN. Oh, that's no fun!

CURT. You are angry with Judith, I guess?

ALLAN. Judith?

CURT. You are so exacting toward people—it is not wise, for then you become isolated.

ALLAN. I am not exacting, but—It feels as if I were lying at the bottom of a pile of wood and had to wait my turn to get into the fire—and it weighs on me—all that is above weighs me down.

CURT. Bide your turn. The pile grows smaller—

ALLAN. Yes, but so slowly, so slowly. And in the meantime I lie here and grow mouldy.

CURT. It is not pleasant to be young. And yet you young ones are envied.

ALLAN. Are we? Would you change?

CURT. No, thanks!

ALLAN. Do you know what is worse than anything else? It is to sit still and keep silent while the old ones talk nonsense—I know that I am better informed than they on some matters—and yet I must keep silent. Well, pardon me, I am not counting you among the old.

CURT. Why not?

ALLAN. Perhaps because we have only just now become acquainted—

CURT. And because—your ideas of me have undergone a change?

ALLAN. Yes.

CURT. During the years we were separated, I suppose you didn't always think of me in a friendly way?

ALLAN. No.

CURT. Did you ever see a picture of me?

ALLAN. One, and it was very unfavorable.

CURT. And old-looking?

ALLAN. Yes.

CURT. Ten years ago my hair turned gray in a single night—it has since then resumed its natural color without my doing anything for it—Let us talk of something else! There comes your aunt—my cousin. How do you like her?

ALLAN. I don't want to tell!

CURT. Then I shall not ask you.

ALICE. [*Enters dressed in a very light-colored walking-suit and carrying a sunshade*] Good morning, Curt.

[*Gives him a glance signifying that* ALLAN *should leave.*]

CURT. [*To* ALLAN] Leave us, please.

[ALLAN *goes out to the right.*]
[ALICE *takes a seat on the sofa to the left.*]
[CURT *sits down on a chair near her.*]

ALICE. [*In some confusion*] He will be here in a moment, so you need not feel embarrassed.

CURT. And why should I?

ALICE. You, with your strictness—

CURT. Toward myself, yes—

ALICE. Of course—Once I forgot myself, when in you I saw the liberator, but you kept your self-control—and for that reason we have a right to forget—what has never been.

CURT. Forget it then!

ALICE. However—I don't think *he* has forgotten—

CURT. You are thinking of that night when his heart gave out and he fell on the floor—and when you rejoiced too quickly, thinking him already dead?

ALICE. Yes. Since then he has recovered; but when he gave up drinking, he learned to keep silent, and now he is terrible. He is up to something that I cannot make out—

CURT. Your husband, Alice, is a harmless fool who has shown me all sorts of kindnesses—

ALICE. Beware of his kindnesses. I know them.

CURT. Well, well—

ALICE. He has then blinded you also? Can you not see the danger? Don't you notice the snares?

CURT. No.

ALICE. Then your ruin is certain.

CURT. Oh, mercy!

ALICE. Think only, I have to sit here and see disaster stalking you like a cat—I point at it, but you cannot see it.

CURT. Allan, with his unspoiled vision, cannot see it either. He sees nothing but Judith, for that matter, and this seems to me a safeguard of our good relationship.

ALICE. Do you know Judith?

CURT. A flirtatious little thing, with a braid down her back and rather too short skirts—

ALICE. Exactly! But the other day I saw her dressed up in long skirts—and then she was a young lady—and not so very young either, when her hair was put up.

CURT. She is somewhat precocious, I admit.

ALICE. And she is playing with Allan.

CURT. That's all right, so long as it remains play.

ALICE. So *that* is all right?—Now Edgar will be here soon, and he will take the easy-chair—he loves it with such passion that he could steal it.

CURT. Why, he can have it!

ALICE. Let him sit over there, and we'll stay here. And when he talks—he is always talkative in the morning—when he talks of insignificant things, I'll translate them for you—

CURT. Oh, my dear Alice, you are too deep, far too deep. What could I have to fear as long as I look after my quarantine properly and otherwise behave decently?

ALICE. You believe in justice and honor and all that sort of thing.

CURT. Yes, and it is what experience has taught me. Once I believed the very opposite—and paid dearly for it!

ALICE. Now he's coming!

CURT. I have never seen you so frightened before.

ALICE. My bravery was nothing but ignorance of the danger.

CURT. Danger? Soon you'll have me frightened too!

ALICE. Oh, if I only could—There!

> [*The* CAPTAIN *enters from the background, in civilian dress, black Prince Albert buttoned all the way, military cap, and a cane with silver handle. He greets them with a nod and goes straight to the easy-chair, where he sits down.*]

ALICE. [*To* CURT] Let him speak first.

CAPTAIN. This is a splendid chair you have here, dear Curt; perfectly splendid.

CURT. I'll give it to you, if you will accept it.

CAPTAIN. That was not what I meant—

CURT. But I mean it seriously. How much have I not received from you?

CAPTAIN. [*Garrulously*] Oh, nonsense! And when I sit here, I can overlook the whole island, all the walks; I can see all the people on their verandahs, all the ships on the sea, that are coming in and going out. You have really happened on the best piece of this island, which is certainly not an island of the blessed. Or what do you say, Alice? Yes, they call it "Little Hell," and here Curt has built himself a paradise, but without an Eve, of course, for when she appeared, then the paradise came to an end. I say—do you know that this was a royal hunting lodge?

CURT. So I have heard.

CAPTAIN. You live royally, you, but, if I may say so myself, you have me to thank for it.

ALICE. [*To* CURT] There—now he wants to steal you.

CURT. I have to thank you for a good deal.

CAPTAIN. Fudge! Tell me, did you get the wine cases?

CURT. Yes.

CAPTAIN. And you are satisfied?

CURT. Quite satisfied, and you may tell your dealer so.

CAPTAIN. His goods are always prime quality—

ALICE. [*To* CURT] At second-rate prices, and you have to pay the difference.

CAPTAIN. What did you say, Alice?

ALICE. I? Nothing!

CAPTAIN. Well, when this quarantine station was about to be established, I had in mind applying for the position—and so I made a study of quarantine methods.

ALICE. [*To* CURT] Now he's lying!

CAPTAIN. [*Boastfully*] And I did not share the antiquated ideas concerning disinfection which were then accepted by the government. For I placed myself on the side of the Neptunists—so called because they emphasize the use of water—

CURT. Beg your pardon, but I remember distinctly that it was I who preached water, and you fire, at that time.

CAPTAIN. I? Nonsense!

ALICE. [*Aloud*] Yes, I remember that, too.

CAPTAIN. You?

CURT. I remember it so much the better because—

CAPTAIN. [*Cutting him short*] Well, it's possible, but it does not matter. [*Raising his voice*] However—we have now reached a point where a new state of affairs—[*To* CURT, *who wants to interrupt*] just a moment!—has begun to prevail—and when the methods of quarantining are about to become revolutionized.

CURT. By the by, do you know who is writing those stupid articles in that periodical?

CAPTAIN. [*Flushing*] No, I don't know, but why do you call them stupid?

ALICE. [*To* CURT] Look out! It is he who writes them.

CURT. He?—[*To the* Captain] Not very well advised, at least.

CAPTAIN. Well, are you the man to judge of that?

ALICE. Are we going to have a quarrel?

CURT. Not at all.

CAPTAIN. It is hard to keep peace on this island, but we ought to set a good example—

CURT. Yes, can you explain this to me? When I came here I made friends with all the officials and became especially intimate with the regimental auditor—as intimate as men are likely to become at our age. And then, in a little while—it was shortly after your recovery—one after another began to grow cold toward me—and yesterday the auditor avoided me on the promenade. I cannot tell you how it hurt me! [*The* CAPTAIN *remains silent*] Have you noticed any ill-feeling toward yourself?

CAPTAIN. No, on the contrary.

ALICE. [*To* CURT] Don't you understand that he has been stealing your friends?

CURT. [*To the* CAPTAIN] I wondered whether it might have anything to do with this new stock issue to which I refused to subscribe.

CAPTAIN. No, no—But can you tell me why you didn't subscribe?

CURT. Because I have already put my small savings into your soda factory. And also because a new issue means that the old stock is shaky.

CAPTAIN. [*Preoccupied*] That's a splendid lamp you have. Where did you get it?

CURT. In the city, of course.

ALICE. [*To* CURT] Look out for your lamp!

CURT. [*To the* CAPTAIN] You must not think that I am ungrateful or distrustful, Edgar.

CAPTAIN. No, but it shows small confidence to withdraw from an undertaking which you have helped to start.

CURT. Why, ordinary prudence bids everybody save himself and what is his.

CAPTAIN. Save? Is there any danger then? Do you think anybody wants to rob you?

CURT. Why such sharp words?

CAPTAIN. Were you not satisfied when I helped you to place your money at six per cent?

CURT. Yes, and even grateful.

CAPTAIN. You are not grateful—it is not in your nature, but this you cannot help.

ALICE. [To CURT] Listen to him!

CURT. My nature has shortcomings enough, and my struggle against them has not been very successful, but I do recognize obligations—

CAPTAIN. Show it then! [*Reaches out his hand to pick up a newspaper*] Why, what is this? A death notice? [*Reads*] The Health Commissioner is dead.

ALICE. [*To* CURT] Now he is speculating in the corpse—

CAPTAIN. [*As if to himself*] This is going to bring about certain—changes—

CURT. In what respect?

CAPTAIN. [*Rising*] That remains to be seen.

ALICE. [*To the* CAPTAIN] Where are you going?

CAPTAIN. I think I'll have to go to the city—[*Catches sight of a letter on the writing-table, picks it up as if unconsciously, reads the address, and puts it back*] Oh, I hope you will pardon my absent-mindedness.

CURT. No harm done.

CAPTAIN. Why, that's Allan's drawing case. Where is the boy?

CURT. He is out playing with the girls.

CAPTAIN. That big boy? I don't like it. And Judith must not be running about like that. You had better keep an eye on your young gentleman, and I'll look after my young lady. [*Goes over to the piano and strikes a few notes*] Splendid tone in this instrument. A Steinbech, isn't it?

CURT. A Bechstein.

CAPTAIN. Yes, you are well fixed. Thank me for bringing you here.

ALICE. [*To* CURT] He lies, for he tried to keep you away.

CAPTAIN. Well, good-bye for a while. I am going to take the next boat.

[*Scrutinizes the paintings on the walls as he goes out.*]

ALICE. Well?

CURT. Well?

ALICE. I can't see through his plans yet. But—tell me one thing. This envelope he looked at—from whom is the letter?

CURT. I am sorry to admit—it was my one secret.

ALICE. And he ferreted it out. Can you see that he knows witchery, as I have told you before? Is there anything printed on the envelope?

CURT. Yes—"The Citizens' Union."

ALICE. Then he has guessed your secret. You want to get into the Riksdag, I suppose. And now you'll see that he goes there instead of you.

CURT. Has he ever thought of it?

ALICE. No, but he is thinking of it now. I read it on his face while he was looking at the envelope.

CURT. That's why he has to go to the city?

ALICE. No, he made up his mind to go when he read the death notice.

CURT. What has he to gain by the death of the Health Commissioner?

ALICE. Hard to tell! Perhaps the man was an enemy who had stood in the way of his plans.

CURT. If he be as terrible as you say, then there is reason to fear him.

ALICE. Didn't you hear how he wanted to steal you, to tie your hands by means of pretended obligations that do not exist? For instance, he has done nothing to get you this position, but has, on the contrary, tried to keep you out of it. He is a man-thief, an insect, one of those wood-borers that eat up your insides so that one day you find yourself as hollow as a dying pine tree. He hates you, although he is bound to you by the memory of your youthful friendship—

CURT. How keen-witted we are made by our hatreds!

ALICE. And stupid by our loves—blind and stupid!

CURT. Oh, no, don't say that!

ALICE. Do you know what is meant by a vampire? They say it is the soul of a dead person seeking a body in which it may live as a parasite. Edgar is dead—ever since he fell down on the floor that time. You see, he has no interests of his own, no personality, no initiative. But if he can only get hold of some other person he hangs on to him, sends down roots into him, and begins to flourish and blossom. Now he has fastened himself on you.

CURT. If he comes too close I'll shake him off.

ALICE. Try to shake off a burr! Listen: do you know why he does not want Judith and Allan to play?

CURT. I suppose he is concerned about their feelings.

ALICE. Not at all. He wants to marry Judith to—the Colonel!

CURT. [Shocked] That old widower!

ALICE. Yes.

CURT. Horrible! And Judith?

ALICE. If she could get the General, who is eighty, she would take him in order to bully the Colonel, who is sixty. To bully, you know, that's the aim of her life. To trample down and bully—there you have the motto of *that* family.

CURT. Can this be Judith? That maiden fair and proud and splendid?

ALICE. Oh, I know all about that! May I sit here and write a letter?

CURT. [Puts the writing-table in order] With pleasure.

ALICE. [Takes off her gloves and sits down at the writing-table] Now we'll try our hand at the art of war. I failed once when I tried to slay my dragon. But now I have mastered the trade.

CURT. Do you know that it is necessary to load before you fire?

ALICE. Yes, and with ball cartridges at that!

> [CURT withdraws to the right.]
> [ALICE ponders and writes.]
> [ALLAN comes rushing in without noticing ALICE and throws himself face downward on the sofa. He is weeping convulsively into a lace handkerchief.]

ALICE. [Watches him for a while. Then she rises and goes over to the sofa. Speaks in a tender voice] Allan!

> [ALLAN sits up disconcertedly and hides the handkerchief behind his back.]

ALICE. [Tenderly, womanly, and with true emotion] You should not be afraid of me, Allan—I am not dangerous to you—What is wrong? Are you sick?

ALLAN. Yes.

ALICE. In what way?

ALLAN. I don't know.

ALICE. Have you a headache?

ALLAN. No.

ALICE. And your chest? Pain?

ALLAN. Yes.

ALICE. Pain—pain—as if your heart wanted to melt away. And it pulls, pulls—

ALLAN. How do you know?

ALICE. And then you wish to die—that you were already dead—and everything seems so hard. And you can only think of one thing—always the same—but if two are thinking of the same thing, then sorrow falls heavily on one of them. [ALLAN *forgets himself and begins to pick at the handkerchief*] That's the sickness which no one can cure. You cannot eat and you cannot drink; you want only to weep, and you weep so bitterly—especially out in the woods where nobody can see you, for at that kind of sorrow all men laugh—men who are so cruel! Dear me! What do you want of her? Nothing! You don't want to kiss her mouth, for you feel that you would die if you did. When your thoughts run to her, you feel as if death were approaching. And it is death, child—that sort of death—which brings life, But you don't understand it yet! I smell violets—it is herself. [*Steps closer to* ALLAN *and takes the handkerchief gently away from him*] It is she, it is she everywhere, none but she! Oh, oh, oh! [ALLAN *cannot help burying his face in* ALICE'S *bosom*] Poor boy! Poor boy! Oh, how it hurts, how it hurts! [*Wipes off his tears with the handkerchief*] There, there! Cry—cry to your heart's content. There now! Then the heart grows lighter—But now. Allan, rise up and be a man, or she will not look at you—she, the cruel one, who is not cruel. Has she tormented you? With the Lieutenant? You must make friends with the Lieutenant, so that you two can talk of her. That gives a little ease also.

ALLAN. I don't want to see the Lieutenant!

ALICE. Now look here, little boy, it won't be long before the Lieutenant seeks you out in order to get a chance to talk of her. For—[ALLAN *looks up with a ray of hope on his face*] Well, shall I be nice and tell you? [ALLAN *droops his head*] He is just as unhappy as you are.

ALLAN. [*Happy*] No?

ALICE. Yes, indeed, and he needs somebody to whom he may unburden his heart when Judith has wounded him. You seem to rejoice in advance?

ALLAN. Does she not want the Lieutenant?

ALICE. She does not want you either, dear boy, for she wants the Colonel. [ALLAN *is saddened again*] Is it raining again? Well, the handkerchief you cannot have, for Judith is careful about her belongings and wants her dozen complete. [ALLAN *looks dashed*] Yes, my boy, such is Judith. Sit over there now, while I write another letter, and then you may do an errand for me.

[*Sits down at the writing-table and begins to write again.*]

LIEUTENANT. [*Enters from the background, with a melancholy face, but without being ridiculous. Without noticing* ALICE *he makes straight for* ALLAN] I say, Cadet—[ALLAN *rises and stands at attention*] Please be seated.

[ALICE *watches them.*]
[*The* LIEUTENANT *goes up to Allan and sits down beside him. Sighs, takes out a lace handkerchief just like the other one, and wipes his forehead with it.*]
[ALLAN *stares greedily at the handkerchief.*]
[*The* LIEUTENANT *looks sadly at Allan.*]
[ALICE *coughs.*]
[*The* LIEUTENANT *jumps up and stands at attention.*]

ALICE. Please be seated.

LIEUTENANT. I beg your pardon, madam—

ALICE. Never mind! Please sit down and keep the Cadet company—he is feeling a little lonely here on the island.

[*Writes.*]

LIEUTENANT. [*Conversing with* ALLAN *in low tone and uneasily*] It is awfully hot.

ALLAN. Rather.

LIEUTENANT. Have you finished the sixth book yet?

ALLAN. I have just got to the last proposition.

LIEUTENANT. That's a tough one. [*Silence*] Have you—[*seeking for words*] played tennis to-day?

Allan. No-o—the sun was too hot.

LIEUTENANT. [*In despair, but without any comical effect*] Yes, it's awfully hot to-day!

ALLAN. [*In a whisper*] Yes, it is very hot. [*Silence.*]

LIEUTENANT. Have you—been out sailing to-day?

ALLAN. No-o, I couldn't get anybody to tend the jib.

LIEUTENANT. Could you—trust me sufficiently to let me tend the jib?

ALLAN. [*Respectfully as before*] That would be too great an honor for me, Lieutenant.

LIEUTENANT. Not at all, not at all! Do you think—the wind might be good enough to-day—about dinner-time, say, for that's the only time I am free?

ALLAN. [*Slyly*] It always calms down about dinner-time, and—that's the time Miss Judith has her lesson.

LIEUTENANT. [*Sadly*] Oh, yes, yes! Hm! Do you think—

ALICE. Would one of you young gentlemen care to deliver a letter for me? [ALLAN *and the* LIEUTENANT *exchange glances of mutual distrust*]—to Miss Judith? [ALLAN *and the* LIEUTENANT *jump up and hasten over to* ALICE, *but not without a certain dignity meant to disguise their emotion*] Both of you? Well, the more safely my errand will be attended to. [*Hands the letter to the* LIEUTENANT] If you please, Lieutenant, I should like to have that handkerchief. My daughter is very careful about her things—there is a touch of pettiness in her nature—Give me that handkerchief! I don't wish to laugh at you, but you must not make yourself ridiculous—needlessly. And the Colonel does not like to play the part of an Othello. [*Takes the handkerchief*] Away with you now, young men, and try to hide your feelings as much as you can.

[*The* LIEUTENANT *bows and goes out, followed closely by* ALLAN.]

ALICE. [*Calls out*] Allan!

ALLAN. [*Stops unwillingly in the doorway*] Yes, Aunt.

ALICE. Stay here, unless you want to inflict more suffering on yourself than you can bear.

ALLAN. But he is going!

ALICE. Let him burn himself. But take care of yourself.

ALLAN. I don't want to take care of myself.

ALICE. And then you cry afterward. And so I get the trouble of consoling you.

ALLAN. I want to go!

ALICE. Go then! But come back here, young madcap, and I'll have the right to laugh at you.

    [ALLAN *runs after the* LIEUTENANT.]
    [ALICE *writes again.*]

CURT. [*Enters*] Alice, I have received an anonymous letter that is bothering me.

ALICE. Have you noticed that Edgar has become another person since he put off the uniform? I could never have believed that a coat might make such a difference.

CURT. You didn't answer my question.

ALICE. It was no question. It was a piece of information. What do you fear?

CURT. Everything!

ALICE. He went to the city. And his trips to the city are always followed by something dreadful.

CURT. But I can do nothing because I don't know from which quarter the attack will begin.

ALICE. [*Folding the letter*] We'll see whether I have guessed it.

CURT. Will you help me then?

ALICE. Yes—but no further than my own interests permit. My own—that is my children's.

CURT. I understand that! Do you hear how silent everything is—here on land, out on the sea, everywhere?

ALICE. But behind the silence I hear voices—mutterings, cries!

CURT. Hush! I hear something, too—no, it was only the gulls.

ALICE. But I hear something else! And now I am going to the post-office—with this letter!

Curtain.

Same stage setting. ALLAN *is sitting at the writing-table studying.* JUDITH *is standing in the doorway. She wears a tennis hat and carries the handle-bars of a bicycle in one hand.*

JUDITH. Can I borrow your wrench?

ALLAN. [*Without looking up*] No, you cannot.

JUDITH. You are discourteous now, because you think I am running after you.

ALLAN. [*Without crossness*] I am nothing at all, but I ask merely to be left alone.

JUDITH. [*Comes nearer*] Allan!

ALLAN. Yes, what is it?

JUDITH. You mustn't be angry with me!

ALLAN. I am not.

JUDITH. Will you give me your hand on that?

ALLAN. [*Kindly*] I don't want to shake hands with you, but I am not angry—What do you want with me anyhow?

JUDITH. Oh. but you're stupid!

ALLAN. Well, let it go at that.

JUDITH. You think me cruel, and nothing else.

ALLAN. No, for I know that you are kind too—you *can* be kind!

JUDITH. Well—how can I help—that you and the Lieutenant run around and weep in the woods? Tell me, why do you weep? [ALLAN *is embarrassed*] Tell me now—I never weep. And why have you become such good friends? Of what do you talk while you are walking about arm in arm? [ALLAN *cannot answer*] Allan, you'll soon see what kind I am and whether I can strike a blow for one I like. And I want to give you a piece of advice—although I have no use for tale-bearing. Be prepared!

ALLAN. For what?

JUDITH. Trouble.

ALLAN. From what quarter?

JUDITH. From the quarter where you least expect it.

ALLAN. Well, I am rather used to disappointment, and life has not brought me much that was pleasant What's in store now?

JUDITH. [*Pensively*] You poor boy—give me your hand! [ALLAN *gives her his hand*] Look at me! Don't you dare to look at me?

[ALLAN *rushes out to the left in order to hide his emotion.*]

LIEUTENANT. [*In from the background*] I beg your pardon! I thought that—

JUDITH. Tell me, Lieutenant, will you be my friend and ally?

LIEUTENANT. If you'll do me the honor—

JUDITH. Yes—a word only—don't desert Allan when disaster overtakes him.

LIEUTENANT. What disaster?

JUDITH. You'll soon see—this very day perhaps. Do you like Allan?

LIEUTENANT. The young man is my best pupil, and I value him personally also on account of his strength of character—Yes, life has moments when strength is required [*with emphasis*] to bear up, to endure, to suffer, in a word!

JUDITH. That was more than one word, I should say. However, you like Allan?

LIEUTENANT. Yes.

JUDITH. Look him up then, and keep him company.

LIEUTENANT. It was for that purpose I came here—for that and no other. I had no other object in my visit.

JUDITH. I had not supposed anything of that kind—of the kind you mean! Allan went that way.

[*Pointing to the left.*]

LIEUTENANT. [*Goes reluctantly to the left*] Yes—I'll do what you ask.

JUDITH. Do, please.

ALICE. [*In from the background*] What are you doing here?

JUDITH. I wanted to borrow a wrench.

ALICE. Will you listen to me a moment?

JUDITH. Of course, I will.

[ALICE *sits down on the sofa.*]

JUDITH. [*Remains standing*] But tell me quickly what you want to say. I don't like long lectures.

ALICE. Lectures? Well, then—put up your hair and put on a long dress.

JUDITH. Why?

ALICE. Because you are no longer a child. And you are young enough to need no coquetry about your age.

JUDITH. What does that mean?

ALICE. That you have reached marriageable age. And your way of dressing is causing scandal.

JUDITH. Then I shall do what you say.

ALICE. You have understood then?

JUDITH. Oh, yes.

ALICE. And we are agreed?

JUDITH. Perfectly.

ALICE. On all points?

JUDITH. Even the tenderest!

ALICE. Will you at the same time cease playing—with Allan?

JUDITH. It is going to be serious then?

ALICE. Yes.

JUDITH. Then we may just as well begin at once.

[*She has already laid aside the handle-bars. Now she lets down the bicycle skirt and twists her braid into a knot which she fastens on top of her head with a hairpin taken out of her mother's hair.*]

ALICE. It is not proper to make your toilet in a strange place.

JUDITH. Am I all right this way? Then I am ready. Come now who dares!

ALICE. Now at last you look decent. And leave Allan in peace after this.

JUDITH. I don't understand what you mean?

ALICE. Can't you see that he is suffering?

JUDITH. .Yes, I think I have noticed it, but I don't know why. I don't suffer!

ALICE. That is *your* strength. But the day will come—oh, yes, you shall know what it means. Go home now, and don't forget—that you are wearing a long skirt.

JUDITH. Must you walk differently then?

ALICE. Just try.

JUDITH. [*Tries to walk like a lady*] Oh, my feet are tied; I am caught, I cannot run any longer!

ALICE. Yes, child, now the walking begins, along the slow road toward the unknown, which you know already, but must pretend to ignore. Shorter steps, and much slower—much slower! The low shoes of childhood must go, Judith, and you have to wear boots. You don't remember when you laid aside baby socks and put on shoes, but I do!

JUDITH. I can never stand this!

ALICE. And yet you must—must!

JUDITH. [*Goes over to her mother and kisses her lightly on the cheek; then walks out with the dignified bearing of a lady, but forgetting the handle-bars*] Good-bye then!

CURT. [*Enters from the right*] So you're already here?

ALICE. Yes.

CURT. Has *he* come back?

ALICE. Yes.

CURT. How did he appear?

ALICE. In full dress—so he has called on the Colonel. And he wore two orders.

CURT. Two? I knew he was to receive the Order of the Sword on his retirement. But what can the other one be?

ALICE. I am not very familiar with those things, but there was a white cross within a red one.

CURT. It is a Portuguese order then. Let me see—tell me, didn't his articles in that periodical deal with quarantine stations in Portuguese harbours?

ALICE. Yes, as far as I can recall.

CURT. And he has never been in Portugal?

ALICE. Never.

CURT. But I have been there.

ALICE. You shouldn't be so communicative. His ears and his memory are so good.

CURT. Don't you think Judith may have helped him to this honor?

ALICE. Well, I declare! There are limits—[*rising*] and you have passed them.

CURT, Are we to quarrel now?

ALICE. That depends on you. Don't meddle with my interests.

CURT. If they cross my own, I have to meddle with them, although with a careful hand. Here he comes!

ALICE. And now it is going to happen.

CURT. What is—going to happen?

ALICE. We shall see!

CURT. Let it come to open attack then, for this state of siege is getting on my nerves. I have not a friend left on the island.

ALICE. Wait a minute! You sit on this side—he must have the easy-chair, of course—and then I can prompt you.

CAPTAIN. [*Enters from the background, in full dress uniform, wearing the Order of the Sword and the Portuguese Order of Christ*] Good day! Here's the meeting place.

ALICE. You are tired—sit down. [The CAPTAIN, *contrary to expectation, takes a seat on the sofa to the left*] Make yourself comfortable.

CAPTAIN. This is all right. You're too kind.

ALICE. [*To* CURT] Be careful—he's suspicious of us.

CAPTAIN. [*Crossly*] What was that you said?

ALICE. [*To* CURT] He must have been drinking.

CAPTAIN. [*Rudely*] No-o, he has not. [*Silence*] Well—how have you been amusing yourselves?

ALICE. And you?

CAPTAIN. Are you looking at my orders?

ALICE. No-o!

CAPTAIN. I guess not, because you are jealous—Otherwise it is customary to offer congratulations to the recipient of honors.

ALICE. We congratulate you.

CAPTAIN. We get things like these instead of laurel wreaths, such as they give to actresses.

ALICE. That's for the wreaths at home on the walls of the tower—

CAPTAIN. Which your brother gave you—

ALICE. Oh, how you talk!

CAPTAIN. Before which I have had to bow down these twenty-five years—and which it has taken me twenty-five years to expose.

ALICE. You have seen my brother?

CAPTAIN. Rather! [ALICE *is crushed. Silence*] And you, Curt—you don't say anything, do you?

CURT. I am waiting.

CAPTAIN. Well, I suppose you know the big news?

CURT. No.

CAPTAIN. It is not exactly agreeable for me to be the one who—

CURT. Oh, speak up!

CAPTAIN. The soda factory has gone to the wall—

CURT. That's decidedly unpleasant! Where does that leave you?

CAPTAIN. I am all right, as I sold out in time.

CURT. That was sensible.

CAPTAIN. But how about you?

CURT. Done for!

CAPTAIN. It's your own fault. You should have sold out in time, or taken new stock.

CURT. So that I could lose that too.

CAPTAIN. No, for then the company would have been all right.

CURT. Not the company, but the directors, for in my mind that new subscription was simply a collection for the benefit of the board.

CAPTAIN. And now I ask whether such a view of the matter will save your money?

CURT. No, I shall have to give up everything.

CAPTAIN. Everything?

CURT. Even my home, the furniture—

CAPTAIN. But that's dreadful!

CURT. I have experienced worse things. [*Silence.*]

CAPTAIN. That's what happens when amateurs want to speculate.

CURT. You surprise me, for you know very well that if I had not subscribed, I should have been boycotted. The supplementary livelihood of the coast population, toilers of the sea, inexhaustible capital, inexhaustible as the sea itself—philanthropy and national prosperity—Thus you wrote and printed—And now you speak of it as speculation!

CAPTAIN. [*Unmoved*] What are you going to do now?

CURT. Have an auction, I suppose.

CAPTAIN. You had better.

CURT. What do you mean?

CAPTAIN. What I said! For there [*slowly*] are going to be some changes—

CURT. On the island?

CAPTAIN. Yes—as, for instance,—your quarters are going to be exchanged for somewhat simpler ones.

CURT. Well, well.

CAPTAIN. Yes, the plan is to place the quarantine station on the outside shore, near the water.

CURT. My original idea!

CAPTAIN. [*Dryly*] I don't know about that—for I am not familiar with your ideas on the subject. However—it seems then quite natural that you dispose of the furniture, and it will attract much less notice—the scandal!

CURT. What?

CAPTAIN. The scandal! [*Egging himself on*] For it is a scandal to come to a new place and immediately get into financial troubles which must result in a lot of annoyance to the relatives—particularly to the relatives.

CURT. Oh, I guess I'll have to bear the worst of it.

CAPTAIN. I'll tell you one thing, my dear Curt: if I had not stood by you in this matter, you would have lost your position.

CURT. That too?

CAPTAIN. It comes rather hard for you to keep things in order—complaints have been made against your work.

CURT. Warranted complaints?

CAPTAIN. Yah! For you are—in spite of your other respectable qualities—a careless fellow—Don't interrupt me!—You are a very careless fellow!

CURT. How strange!

CAPTAIN. However—the suggested change is going to take place very soon. And I should advise you to hold the auction at once or sell privately.

CURT. Privately? And where could I find a buyer in this place?

CAPTAIN. Well, I hope you don't expect me to settle down in the midst of your things? That would make a fine story—[*staccato*] hm!—especially when I—think of what happened—once upon a time—

CURT. What was that? Are you referring to what did *not* happen?

CAPTAIN. [*Turning about*] You are so silent, Alice? What is the matter, old girl? Not blue, I hope?

ALICE. I sit here and think—

CAPTAIN. Goodness! Are you thinking? But you have to think quickly, keenly, and correctly, if it is to be of any help! So do your thinking now—one, two, three! Ha-ha! You can't! Well, then, I must try—Where is Judith?

ALICE. Somewhere.

CAPTAIN. Where is Allan? [ALICE *remains silent*] Where is the Lieutenant? [ALICE *as before*] I say, Curt—what are you going to do with Allan now?

CURT. Do with him?

CAPTAIN. Yes, you cannot afford to keep him in the artillery now.

CURT. Perhaps not.

CAPTAIN. You had better get him into some cheap infantry regiment—up in Norrland, or somewhere.

CURT. In Norrland?

CAPTAIN. Yes, or suppose you turned him into something practical at once? If I were in your place, I should get him into some business office—why not? [CURT *is silent*] In these enlightened times—yah! Alice is so *uncommonly* silent! Yes, children, this is the seesawing seesaw board of life—one moment high up, looking boldly around, and the next way down, and then upward again, and so on—So much for that—[*To* ALICE] Did you say anything? [ALICE *shakes her head*] We may expect company here in a few days.

ALICE. Were you speaking to me?

CAPTAIN. We may expect company in a few days—notable company!

ALICE. Who?

CAPTAIN. Behold—you're interested! Now you can sit there and guess who is coming, and between guesses you may read this letter over again. [*Hands her an opened letter.*]

ALICE. My letter? Opened? Back from the mail?

CAPTAIN. [*Rising*] Yes, as the head of the family and your guardian, I look after the sacred interests of the family, and with iron hand I shall cut short every effort to break the family ties by means of criminal correspondence. Yah! [ALICE *is crushed*] I am not dead, you know, but don't take offence now because I am going to raise us all out of undeserved humility—undeserved on my own part, at least!

ALICE. Judith! Judith!

CAPTAIN. And Holofernes? I, perhaps? Pooh!

[*Goes out through the background.*]

CURT. Who is that man?

ALICE. How can I tell?

CURT. We are beaten.

ALICE. Yes—beyond a doubt.

CURT. He has stripped me of everything, but so cleverly that I can accuse him of nothing.

ALICE. Why, no—you owe him a debt of gratitude instead!

CURT. Does he know what he is doing?

ALICE. No, I don't think so. He follows his nature and his instincts, and just now he seems to be in favor where fortune and misfortune are being meted out.

CURT. I suppose it's the Colonel who is to come here.

ALICE. Probably. And that is why Allan must go.

CURT. And you find that right?

ALICE. Yes.

CURT. Then our ways part.

ALICE. [*Ready to go*] A little—but we shall come together again.

CURT. Probably.

ALICE. And do you know where?

CURT. Here.

ALICE. You guess it?

CURT. That's easy! He takes the house and buys the furniture.

ALICE. I think so, too. But don't desert me!

CURT. Not for a little thing like that.

ALICE. Good-bye. [*Goes.*]

CURT. Good-bye.

Curtain.

Same stage setting, but the day is cloudy and it is raining outside. ALICE *and* CURT *enter from the background, wearing rain coats and carrying umbrellas.*

ALICE. At last I have got you to come here! But, I cannot be so cruel as to wish you welcome to your own home—

CURT. Oh, why not? I have passed through three forced sales—and worse than that—It doesn't matter to me.

ALICE. Did he call you?

CURT. It was a formal command, but on what basis I don't understand.

ALICE. Why, he is not your superior!

CURT. No, but he has made himself king of the island. And if there be any resistance, he has only to mention the Colonel's name, and everybody submits. Tell me, is it today the Colonel is coming?

ALICE. He is expected—but I know nothing with certainty—Sit down, please.

CURT. [*Sitting down*] Nothing has been changed here.

ALICE. Don't think of it! Don't renew the pain!

CURT. The pain? I find it merely a little strange. Strange as the man himself. Do you know, when I made his acquaintance as a boy, I fled him. But he was after me. Flattered, offered services, and surrounded me with ties—I repeated my attempt at escape, but in vain—And now I am his slave!

ALICE. And why? He owes you a debt, but you appear as the debtor.

CURT. Since I lost all I had, he has offered me help in getting Allan through his examinations—

ALICE. For which you will have to pay dearly! You are still a candidate for the Riksdag?

CURT. Yes, and, so far as I can see, there is nothing in my way. [*Silence.*]

ALICE. Is Allan really going to leave to-day?

CURT. Yes, if I cannot prevent it.

ALICE. That was a short-lived happiness.

CURT. Short-lived as everything but life itself, which lasts all too long.

ALICE. Too long, indeed!—Won't you come in and wait in the sitting-room? Even if it does not trouble you, it troubles me—these surroundings!

CURT. If you wish it—

ALICE. I feel ashamed, so ashamed that I could wish to die—but I can alter nothing!

CURT. Let us go then—as you wish it.

ALICE. And somebody is coming too.

[*They go out to the left.*]
[*The* CAPTAIN *and* ALLAN *enter from the background, both in uniform and wearing cloaks.*]

CAPTAIN. Sit down, my boy, and let me have a talk with you. [*Sits down in the easy-chair.*]

[ALLAN *sits down on the chair to the left.*]

CAPTAIN. It's raining to-day—otherwise I could sit here comfortably and look at the sea. [*Silence*] Well?—You don't like to go, do you?

ALLAN. I don't like to leave my father.

CAPTAIN. Yes, your father—he is rather an unfortunate man. [*Silence*] And parents rarely understand the true welfare of their children. That is to say—there are exceptions, of course. Hm! Tell me, Allan, have you any communication with your mother?

ALLAN. Yes, she writes now and then.

CAPTAIN. Do you know that she is your guardian?

ALLAN. Yes.

CAPTAIN. Now, Allan, do you know that your mother has authorized me to act in her place?

ALLAN. I didn't know that!

CAPTAIN. Well, you know it now. And, therefore, all discussions concerning your career are done with—And you are going to Norrland.

ALLAN. But I have no money.

CAPTAIN. I have arranged for what you need.

ALLAN. All I can do then is to thank you, Uncle.

CAPTAIN. Yes, *you* are grateful—which everybody is not. Hm!—[*Raising his voice*] The Colonel—do you know the Colonel?

ALLAN. [*Embarrassed*] No, I don't.

CAPTAIN. [*With emphasis*] The Colonel—is my special friend—[*a little more hurriedly*] as you know, perhaps. Hm! The Colonel has wished to show his interest in my family, including my wife's relatives. Through his intercession, the Colonel has been able to provide the means needed for the completion of your course. Now you understand the obligation under which you and your father are placed toward the Colonel. Have I spoken with sufficient plainness? [ALLAN *bows*] Go and pack your things now. The money will be handed to you at the landing. And now good-bye, my boy. [*Holds out a finger to* ALLAN] Good-bye then.

> [*Rises and goes out to the right.*]
> [ALLAN, *alone, stands still, looking sadly around the room.*]

JUDITH. [*Enters from the background, wearing a hooded rain coat and carrying an umbrella; otherwise exquisitely dressed, in long skirt and with her hair put up*] Is that you, Allan!

ALLAN. [*Turning around, surveys* JUDITH *carefully*] Is that you, Judith?

JUDITH. You don't know me any longer? Where have you been all this time? What are you looking at? My long dress—and my hair—You have not seen me like this before?

ALLAN. No-o—

JUDITH. Do I look like a married woman?

> [ALLAN *turns away from her.*]

JUDITH. [*Earnestly*] What are you doing here?

ALLAN. I am saying good-bye.

JUDITH. What? You are going—away?

ALLAN. I am transferred to Norrland.

JUDITH. [*Dumfounded*] To Norrland? When are you going?

ALLAN. To-day.

JUDITH. Whose doing is this?

ALLAN. Your father's.

JUDITH. That's what I thought! [*Walks up and down the floor, stamping her feet*] I wish you had stayed over to-day.

ALLAN. In order to meet the Colonel?

JUDITH. What do you know about the Colonel?—Is it certain that you are going?

ALLAN. There is no other choice. And now I want it myself. [*Silence.*]

JUDITH. Why do you want it now?

ALLAN. I want to get away from here—out into the world!

JUDITH. It's too close here? Yes, Allan, I understand you—it's unbearable here—here, where they speculate—in soda and human beings! [*Silence.*]

JUDITH. [*With genuine emotion*] As you know, Allan, I possess that fortunate nature which cannot suffer—but—now I am learning!

ALLAN. You?

JUDITH. Yes—now it's beginning! [She *presses both hands to her breast*] Oh, how it hurts—oh!

ALLAN. What is it?

JUDITH. I don't know—I choke—I think I'm going to die!

ALLAN. Judith?

JUDITH. [*Crying out*] Oh! Is this the way it feels? Is this the way—poor boys!

ALLAN. I should smile, if I were as cruel as you are.

JUDITH. I am not cruel, but I didn't know better—You must not go!

ALLAN. I have to!

JUDITH. Go then—but give me a keepsake!

ALLAN. What have I to give you?

JUDITH. [*With all the seriousness of deepest suffering*] You!—No, I can never live through this! [*Cries out, pressing her breast with both hands*] I suffer, I suffer— What have you done to me? I don't want to live any longer! Allan, don't go—not alone! Let us go together—we'll take the small boat, the little white one—and we'll sail far out, with the main sheet made fast—the wind is high—and we sail till we founder—out there, way out, where there is no eelgrass and no jellyfish—What do you say?—But we should have washed the sails yesterday—they should be white as snow—for I want to see white in that moment—and you swim with your arm about me until you grow tired—and then we sink—[*Turning around*] There would be style in that, a good deal more style than in going about here lamenting and smuggling letters that will be opened and jeered at by father—Allan! [*She takes hold of both his arms and shakes him*] Do you hear?

ALLAN. [*Who has been watching her with shining eyes*] Judith! Judith! Why were you not like this before?

JUDITH. I didn't know—how could I tell what I didn't know?

ALLAN. And now I must go away from you! But I suppose it is the better, the only thing! I cannot compete with a man—like—

JUDITH. Don't speak of the Colonel!

ALLAN. Is it not true?

JUDITH. It is true—and it is not true.

ALLAN. Can it become wholly untrue?

JUDITH. Yes, so it shall—within an hour!

ALLAN. And you keep your word? I can wait, I can suffer, I can work—Judith!

JUDITH. Don't go yet! How long must I wait?

ALLAN. A year.

JUDITH. [*Exultantly*] One? I shall wait a thousand years, and if you do not come then, I shall turn the dome of heaven upside down and make the sun rise in the west—Hush, somebody is coming! Allan, we must part—take me into your arms! [*They embrace each other*] But you must not kiss me. [*Turns her head away*] There, go now! Go now!

> [ALLAN *goes toward the background and puts on his cloak. Then they rush into each other's arms so that* JUDITH *disappears beneath the cloak, and for a moment they exchange kisses.* ALLAN *rushes out.* JUDITH *throws herself face downward on the sofa and sobs.*]

ALLAN. [*Comes back and kneels beside the sofa*] No, I cannot go! I cannot go away from you—not now!

JUDITH. [*Rising*] If you could only see how beautiful you are now! If you could only see yourself!

ALLAN. Oh, no, a man cannot be beautiful. But you, Judith! You—that you—oh, I saw that, when you were kind, another Judith appeared—and she's mine!—But if you don't keep faith with me now, then I shall die!

JUDITH. I think I am dying even now—Oh, that I might die now, just now, when I am so happy—

ALLAN. Somebody is coming!

JUDITH. Let them come! I fear nothing in the world hereafter. But I wish you could take me along under your cloak. [*She hides herself in play under his cloak*] And then I should fly with you to Norrland. What are we to do in Norrland? Become a Fusilier—one of those that wear plumes on their hats? There's style in that, and it will be becoming to you.

> [*Plays with his hair.*]
> [ALLAN *kisses the tips of her fingers, one by one—and then he kisses her shoe.*]

JUDITH. What are you doing, Mr. Madcap? Your lips will get black. [*Rising impetuously*] And then I cannot kiss you when you go! Come, and I'll go with you!

ALLAN. No, then I should be placed under arrest.

JUDITH. I'll go with you to the guard-room.

ALLAN. They wouldn't let you! We must part now!

JUDITH. I am going to swim after the steamer—and then you jump in and save me—and it gets into the newspapers, and we become engaged. Shall we do that?

ALLAN. You can still jest?

JUDITH. There will always be time for tears—Say goodbye now!—

> [*They rush into each other's arms; then* ALLAN *withdraws slowly through the door in the background,* JUDITH *following him; the door remains open after them; they embrace again outside, in the rain.*]

ALLAN. You'll get wet, Judith.

JUDITH. What do I care!

> [*They tear themselves away from each other.* ALLAN *leaves.* JUDITH *remains behind, exposing herself to the rain and to the wind, which strains at her hair and her clothes while she is waving her handkerchief. Then* JUDITH *runs back into the room and throws herself on the sofa, with her face buried in her hands.*]

ALICE. [*Enters and goes over to* JUDITH] What is this?—Get up and let me look at you.

> [JUDITH *sits up.*]

ALICE. [*Scrutinizing her*] You are not sick—And I am not going to console you. [*Goes out to the right.*]

[*The* LIEUTENANT *enters from the background.*]

JUDITH. [*Gets up and puts on the hooded coat*] Come along to the telegraph office, Lieutenant.
LIEUTENANT. If I can be of any service—but I don't think it's quite proper—
JUDITH. So much the better! I want you to compromise me—but without any illusions on your part—Go ahead, please! [*They go out through the background.*]

[*The* CAPTAIN *and* ALICE *enter from the right; he is in undress uniform.*]

CAPTAIN. [*Sits down in the easy-chair*] Let him come in.

[ALICE *goes over to the door on the left and opens it, whereupon she sits down on the sofa.*]

CURT. [*Enters from the left*] You want to speak to me?
CAPTAIN. [*Pleasantly, but somewhat condescendingly*] Yes, I have quite a number of important things to tell you. Sit down.
CURT. [*Sits down on the chair to the left*] I am all ears.
CAPTAIN. Well, then!—[*Bumptiously*] You know that our quarantine system has been neglected during nearly a century—hm!
ALICE. [*To* CURT] That's the candidate for the Riksdag who speaks now.
CAPTAIN. But with the tremendous development witnessed by our own day in—
ALICE. [*To* CURT] The communications, of course!
CAPTAIN. —all kinds of ways the government has begun to consider improvements. And for this purpose the Board of Health has appointed inspectors—hm!
ALICE. [*To* CURT] He's giving dictation.
CAPTAIN. You may as well learn it now as later—I have been appointed an inspector of quarantines. [*Silence.*]
CURT. I congratulate—and pay my respects to my superior at the same time.
CAPTAIN. On account of ties of kinship our personal relations will remain unchanged. However—to speak of other things—At my request your son Allan has been transferred to an infantry regiment in Norrland.
CURT. But I don't want it.
CAPTAIN. Your will in this case is subordinate to the mother's wishes—and as the mother has authorized me to decide, I have formed this decision.
CURT. I admire you!
CAPTAIN. Is that the only feeling you experience at this moment when you are to part from your son? Have you no other purely human feelings?
CURT. You mean that I ought to be suffering?
CAPTAIN. Yes.
CURT. It would please you if I suffered. You wish me to suffer.
CAPTAIN. *You* suffer?—Once I was taken sick—you were present and I can still remember that your face expressed nothing but undisguised pleasure.
ALICE. That is not true! Curt sat beside your bed all night and calmed you down when your qualms of conscience became too violent—but when you recovered you ceased to be thankful for it—

CAPTAIN. [*Pretending not to hear* ALICE] Consequently Allan will have to leave us.

CURT. And who is going to pay for it?

CAPTAIN. I have done so already—that is to say, we—a syndicate of people interested in the young man's future.

CURT. A syndicate?

CAPTAIN. Yes—and to make sure that everything is all right you can look over these subscription lists.

[*Hands him some papers.*]

CURT. Lists? [*Reading the papers*] These are begging letters?

CAPTAIN. Call them what you please.

CURT. Have you gone begging on behalf of my son?

CAPTAIN. Are you ungrateful again? An ungrateful man is the heaviest burden borne by the earth.

CURT. Then I am dead socially! And my candidacy is done for!

CAPTAIN. What candidacy?

CURT. For the Riksdag, of course.

CAPTAIN. I hope you never had any such notions—particularly as you might have guessed that I, as an older resident, intended to offer my own services, which you seem to underestimate.

CURT. Oh, well, then that's gone, too!

CAPTAIN. It doesn't seem to trouble you very much.

CURT. Now you have taken everything—do you want more?

CAPTAIN. Have you anything more? And have you anything to reproach me with? Consider carefully if you have anything to reproach me with.

CURT. Strictly speaking, no! Everything has been correct and legal as it should be between honest citizens in the course of daily life—

CAPTAIN. You say this with a resignation which I would call cynical. But your entire nature has a cynical bent, my dear Curt, and there are moments when I feel tempted to share Alice's opinion of you—that you are a hypocrite, a hypocrite of the first water.

CURT. [*Calmly*] So that's Alice's opinion?

ALICE. [*To* CURT] It was—once. But not now, for it takes true heroism to bear what you have borne—or it takes something else!

CAPTAIN. Now I think the discussion may be regarded as closed. You, Curt, had better go and say good-bye to Allan, who is leaving with the next boat.

CURT. [*Rising*] So soon? Well, I have gone through worse things than that.

CAPTAIN. You say that so often that I am beginning to wonder what you went through in America?

CURT. What I went through? I went through misfortunes. And it is the unmistakable right of every human being to suffer misfortune.

CAPTAIN. [*Sharply*] There are self-inflicted misfortunes—were yours of that kind?

CURT. Is not this a question of conscience?

CAPTAIN. [*Brusquely*] Do you mean to say you have a conscience?

CURT. There are wolves and there are sheep, and no human being is honored by being a sheep. But I'd rather be that than a wolf!

CAPTAIN. You don't recognize the old truth, that everybody is the maker of his own fortune?

CURT. Is *that* a truth?

CAPTAIN. And you don't know that a man's own strength—

CURT. Yes, I know that from the night when your own strength failed you, and you lay flat on the floor.

CAPTAIN. [*Raising his voice*] A deserving man like myself—yes, look at me—For fifty years I have fought—against a world—but at last I have won the game, by perseverance, loyalty, energy, and—integrity!

ALICE. You should leave that to be said by others!

CAPTAIN. The others won't say it because they are jealous. However—we are expecting company—my daughter Judith will to-day meet her intended—Where is Judith?

ALICE. She is out

CAPTAIN. In the rain? Send for her.

CURT. Perhaps I may go now?

CAPTAIN. No, you had better stay. Is Judith dressed—Properly?

ALICE. Oh, so-so—Have you definite word from the Colonel that he is coming?

CAPTAIN. [*Rising*] Yes—that is to say, he will take us by surprise, as it is termed. And I am expecting a telegram from him—any moment. [*Goes to the right*] I'll be back at once.

ALICE. There you see him as he is! Can he be called human?

CURT. When you asked that question once before, I answered no. Now I believe him to be the commonest kind of human being of the sort that possess the earth. Perhaps we, too, are of the same kind—making use of other people and of favorable opportunities?

ALICE. He has eaten you and yours alive—and you defend him?

CURT. I have suffered worse things. And this man-eater has left my soul unharmed—*that* he couldn't swallow!

ALICE. What "worse" have you suffered?

CURT. And *you* ask that?

ALICE. Do you wish to be rude?

CURT. No, I don't wish to—and therefore—don't ask again!

CAPTAIN. [*Enters from the right*] The telegram was already there, however—Please read it, Alice, for I cannot see—[*Seats himself pompously in the easy-chair*] Read it! You need not go, Curt.

[ALICE *glances through the telegram quickly and looks perplexed.*]

CAPTAIN. Well? Don't you find it pleasing?

[ALICE *stares in silence at the Captain.*]

CAPTAIN. [*Ironically*] Who is it from?

ALICE. From the Colonel.

CAPTAIN. [*With self-satisfaction*] So I thought—and what does the Colonel say?

ALICE. This is what he says: "On account of Miss Judith's impertinent communication over the telephone, I consider the relationship ended—forever!"

[*Looks intently at the* CAPTAIN.]

CAPTAIN. Once more, if you please.

ALICE. [*Reads rapidly*] "On account of Miss Judith's impertinent communication over the telephone, I consider the relationship ended—forever!"

CAPTAIN. [*Turns pale*] It is Judith!

ALICE. And there is Holofernes!

CAPTAIN. And what are you?

ALICE. Soon you will see!

CAPTAIN. This is your doing!

ALICE. No!

CAPTAIN. [*In a rage*] This is your doing!

ALICE. No! [*The* CAPTAIN *tries to rise and draw his saber, but falls back, touched by an apoplectic stroke*] There you got what was coming to you!

CAPTAIN. [*With senile tears in his voice*] Don't be angry at me—I am very sick—

ALICE. Are you? I am glad to hear it.

CURT. Let us put him to bed.

ALICE. No, I don't want to touch him. [*Rings.*]

CAPTAIN. [*As before*] You must not be angry at me! [*To* CURT] Look after my children!

CURT. This is sublime! I am to look after his children, and he has stolen mine!

ALICE. Always the same self-deception!

CAPTAIN. Look after my children! [*Continues to mumble unintelligibly*] Blub-blub-blub-blub.

ALICE. At last that tongue is checked! Can brag no more, lie no more, wound no more! You, Curt, who believe in God, give Him thanks on my behalf. Thank Him for my liberation from the tower, from the wolf, from the vampire!

CURT. Not that way, Alice!

ALICE. [*With her face close to the* CAPTAIN'S] Where is your own strength now? Tell me? Where is your energy? [*The* CAPTAIN, *speechless, spits in her face*] Oh, you can still squirt venom, you viper—then I'll tear the tongue out of your throat! [*Cuffs him on the ear*] The head is off, but still it blushes!—O, Judith, glorious girl, whom I have carried like vengeance under my heart—you, you have set us free, all of us!—If you have more heads than one, Hydra, we'll take them! [*Pulls his beard*] Think only that justice exists on the earth! Sometimes I dreamed it, but I could never believe it. Curt, ask God to pardon me for misjudging Him. Oh, there is justice! So I will become a sheep, too! Tell Him that, Curt! A little success makes us better, but adversity alone turns us into wolves.

[*The* LIEUTENANT *enters from the background.*]

ALICE. The Captain has had a stroke—will you please help us to roll out the chair?

LIEUTENANT. Madam—

ALICE. What is it?

LIEUTENANT. Well, Miss Judith—

ALICE. Help us with this first—then you can speak of Miss Judith afterward.

[*The* LIEUTENANT *rolls out the chair to the right.*]

ALICE. Away with the carcass! Out with it, and let's open the doors! The place must be aired! [*Opens the doors in the background; the sky has cleared*] Ugh!

CURT. Are you going to desert him?

ALICE. A wrecked ship is deserted, and the crew save their lives—I'll not act as undertaker to a rotting beast! Drainmen and dissectors may dispose of him! A garden bed would be too good for that barrowful of filth! Now I am going to wash and bathe myself in order to get rid of all this impurity—if I can ever cleanse myself completely!

[JUDITH *is seen outside, by the balustrade, waving her handkerchief toward the sea.*]

CURT. [*Toward the background*] Who is there? Judith! [*Calls out*] Judith!

JUDITH. [*Cries out as she enters*] He is gone!

CURT. Who?

JUDITH. Allan is gone!

CURT. Without saying good-bye?

JUDITH. He did to me, and he sent his love to you, Uncle.

ALICE. Oh, that was it!

JUDITH. [*Throwing herself into* CURT'S *arms*] He is gone!

CURT. He will come back, little girl.

ALICE. Or we will go after him!

CURT. [*With a gesture indicating the door on the right*] And leave him? What would the world—

ALICE. The world—bah! Judith, come into my arms! [JUDITH *goes up to* ALICE, *who kisses her on the forehead*] Do you want to go after him?

JUDITH. How can you ask?

ALICE. But your father is sick.

JUDITH. What do I care!

ALICE. This is Judith! Oh. I love you. Judith!

JUDITH. And besides, papa is never mean—and he doesn't like cuddling. There's style to papa, after all.

ALICE. Yes, in a way!

JUDITH. And I don't think he is longing for me after that telephone message—Well, why should he pester me with an old fellow? No, Allan, Allan! [*Throws herself into* CURT'S *arms*] I want to go to Allan!

[*Tears herself loose again and runs out to wave her handkerchief.*]
[CURT *follows her and waves his handkerchief also.*]

ALICE. Think of it, that flowers can grow out of dirt!

[*The* LIEUTENANT *in from the right.*]

ALICE. Well?

LIEUTENANT. Yes, Miss Judith—

ALICE. Is the feeling of those letters that form her name so sweet on your lips that it makes you forget him who is dying?

LIEUTENANT. Yes, but she said—

ALICE. She? Say rather Judith then! But first of all—how goes it in there?

LIEUTENANT. Oh, in there—it's all over!

ALICE. All over? O, God, on my own behalf and that of all mankind, I thank Thee for having freed us from this evil! Your arm, if you please—I want to go outside and get a breath—breathe!

[*The* LIEUTENANT *offers his arm.*]

ALICE. [*Checks herself*] Did he say anything before the end came?

LIEUTENANT. Miss Judith's father spoke a few words only.

ALICE. What did he say?

LIEUTENANT. He said: "Forgive them, for they know not what they do!"

ALICE. Inconceivable!

LIEUTENANT. Yes, Miss Judith's father was a good and noble man.

ALICE. Curt!

[CURT *Enters.*]

ALICE. It is over!

CURT. Oh!

ALICE. Do you know what his last words were? No, you can never guess it. "Forgive them, for they know not what they do!"

CURT. Can you translate it?

ALICE. I suppose he meant that he had always done right and died as one that had been wronged by life.

CURT. I am sure his funeral sermon will be fine.

ALICE. And plenty of flowers—from the non-commissioned officers.

CURT. Yes.

ALICE. About a year ago he said something like this: "It looks to me as if life were a tremendous hoax played on all of us!"

CURT. Do you mean to imply that he was playing a hoax on us up to the very moment of death?

ALICE. No—but now, when he is dead, I feel a strange inclination to speak well of him.

CURT. Well, let us do so!

LIEUTENANT. Miss Judith's father was a good and noble man.

ALICE. [*To* CURT] Listen to that!

CURT. "They know not what they do." How many times did I not ask you whether he knew what he was doing? And you didn't think he knew. Therefore, forgive him!

ALICE. Riddles! Riddles! But do you notice that there is peace in the house now? The wonderful peace of death. Wonderful as the solemn anxiety that surrounds the coming of a child into the world. I hear the silence—and on the floor I see the traces of the easy-chair that carried him away—And I feel that now my own life is ended, and I am starting on the road to dissolution! Do you know, it's queer, but those simple words of the Lieutenant—and his is a simple mind—they pursue me, but now they have become serious. My husband, my youth's beloved—yes, perhaps you laugh!—he *was* a good and noble man—nevertheless!

CURT. Nevertheless? And a brave one—as he fought for his own and his family's existence!

ALICE. What worries! What humiliations! Which he wiped out—in order to pass on!

CURT. He was one who had been passed by! And that is to say much! Alice, go in there!

ALICE. No, I cannot do it! For while we have been talking here, the image of him as he was in his younger years has come back to me—I have seen him, I see him—now, as when he was only twenty—I must have loved that man!

CURT. And hated him!

ALICE, And hated!—Peace be with him!

[*Goes toward the right door and stops in front of it, folding her hands as if to pray.*]

Curtain.

A DREAM PLAY

A REMINDER

As he did in his previous dream play, [1] so in this one the author has tried to imitate the disconnected but seemingly logical form of the dream. Anything may happen; everything is possible and probable. Time and space do not exist. On an insignificant background of reality, imagination designs and embroiders novel patterns: a medley of memories, experiences, free fancies, absurdities and improvisations.

[1] The trilogy "To Damascus."

The characters split, double, multiply, vanish, solidify, blur, clarify. But one consciousness reigns above them all—that of the dreamer; and before it there are no secrets, no incongruities, no scruples, no laws. There is neither judgment nor exoneration, but merely narration. And as the dream is mostly painful, rarely pleasant, a note of melancholy and of pity with all living things runs right through the wabbly tale. Sleep, the liberator, plays often a dismal part, but when the pain is at its worst, the awakening comes and reconciles the sufferer with reality, which, however distressing it may be, nevertheless seems happy in comparison with the torments of the dream.

PROLOGUE

The background represents cloud banks that resemble corroding slate cliffs with ruins of castles and fortresses.
The constellations of Leo, Virgo, and Libra are visible, and from their midst the planet Jupiter is shining with a strong light.

[THE DAUGHTER OF INDRA *stands on the topmost cloud.*]

THE VOICE OF INDRA. [*from above*] Where are you, daughter, where?
THE DAUGHTER. Here, father, here.
THE VOICE. You've lost your way, my child—beware, you sink—
　　How got you there?
THE DAUGHTER. I followed from ethereal heights the ray
　　Of lightning, and for car a cloud I took—
　　It sank, and now my journey downward tends.
　　O, noble father, Indra, tell what realms
　　I now draw near? The air is here so close,
　　And breathing difficult.
THE VOICE. Behind you lies the second world; the third
　　Is where you stand. From Cukra, morning star
　　You have withdrawn yourself to enter soon
　　The vapoury circle of the earth. For mark
　　The Seventh House you take. It's Libra called:
　　There stands the day-star in the balanced hour
　　When Fall gives equal weight to night and day.

THE DAUGHTER. You named the earth—is that the ponderous world
    And dark, that from the moon must take its light?
THE VOICE. It is the heaviest and densest sphere
    Of all that travel through the space.
THE DAUGHTER. And is it never brightened by the sun?
THE VOICE. Of course, the sun does reach it—now and then—
THE DAUGHTER. There is a rift, and downward goes my glance—
THE VOICE. What sees my child?
THE DAUGHTER. I see—O beautiful!—with forests green,
    With waters blue, white peaks, and yellow fields—
THE VOICE. Yes, beautiful as all that Brahma made—
    But still more beautiful it was of yore,
    In primal morn of ages. Then occurred
    Some strange mishap; the orbit was disturbed;
    Rebellion led to crime that called for check—
THE DAUGHTER. Now from below I hear some sounds arise—
    What sort of race is dwelling there?
THE VOICE. See for yourself—Of Brahma's work no ill
    I say: but what you hear, it is their speech.
THE DAUGHTER. It sounds as if—it has no happy ring!
THE VOICE. I fear me not—for even their mother-tongue
    Is named complaint. A race most hard to please,
    And thankless, are the dwellers on the earth—
THE DAUGHTER. O, say not so—for I hear cries of joy,
    Hear noise and thunder, see the lightnings flash—
    Now bells are ringing, fires are lit,
    And thousand upon thousand tongues
    Sing praise and thanks unto the heavens on high—
    Too harshly, father, you are judging them.
THE VOICE. Descend, that you may see and hear, and then
    Return and let me know if their complaints
    And wailings have some reasonable ground——
THE DAUGHTER. Well then, I go; but, father, come with me.
THE VOICE. No, there below I cannot breathe——
THE DAUGHTER. Now sinks the cloud—what sultriness—I choke!
    I am not breathing air, but smoke and steam—
    With heavy weight it drags me down,
    And I can feel already how it rolls—
    Indeed, the best of worlds is not the third——
THE VOICE. The best I cannot call it, nor the worst.
    Its name is Dust; and like them all, it rolls:
    And therefore dizzy sometimes grows the race,
    And seems to be half foolish and half mad—
    Take courage, child—a trial, that is all!
THE DAUGHTER. [*Kneeling as the cloud sinks downward*] I sink!

Curtain.

A DREAM PLAY

The background represents a forest of gigantic hollyhocks in bloom. They are white, pink, crimson, sulphureous, violet; and above their tops is seen the gilded roof of a castle, the apex of which is formed by a bud resembling a crown. At the foot of the castle walls stand a number of straw ricks, and around these stable litter is scattered. The side-scenes, which remain unchanged throughout the play, show conventionalized frescoes, suggesting at once internal decoration, architecture, and landscape.

[*Enter* THE GLAZIER *and* THE DAUGHTER.]

THE DAUGHTER. The castle is growing higher and higher above the ground. Do you see how much it has grown since last year?

THE GLAZIER. [*To himself*] I have never seen this castle before—have never heard of a castle that grew, but—[*To* THE DAUGHTER, *with firm conviction*] Yes, it has grown two yards, but that is because they have manured it—and if you notice, it has put out a wing on the sunny side.

THE DAUGHTER. Ought it not to be blooming soon, as we are already past midsummer?

THE GLAZIER. Don't you see the flower up there?

THE DAUGHTER. Yes, I see! [*Claps her hands*] Say, father, why do flowers grow out of dirt?

THE GLAZIER. [*Simply*] Because they do not feel at home in the dirt, and so they make haste to get up into the light in order to blossom and die.

THE DAUGHTER. Do you know who lives in that castle?

THE GLAZIER. I have known it, but cannot remember.

THE DAUGHTER. I believe a prisoner is kept there—and he must be waiting for me to set him free.

THE GLAZIER. And what is he to pay for it?

THE DAUGHTER. One does not bargain about one's duty. Let us go into the castle.

THE GLAZIER. Yes, let us go in.

[*They go toward the background, which opens and slowly disappears to either side.*]

[*The stage shows now a humble, bare room, containing only a table and a few chairs. On one of the chairs sits an officer, dressed in a very unusual yet modern uniform. He is tilting the chair backward and beating the table with his sabre.*]

THE DAUGHTER. [*Goes to the officer, from whose hand she gently takes the sabre*] Don't! Don't!

THE OFFICER. Oh, Agnes dear, let me keep the sabre.

THE DAUGHTER. No, you break the table. [*To* THE GLAZIER] Now you go down to the harness-room and fix that window pane. We'll meet later.

[THE GLAZIER *goes out.*]

THE DAUGHTER. You are imprisoned in your own rooms—I have come to set you free.

THE OFFICER. I have been waiting for you, but I was not sure you were willing to do it.

THE DAUGHTER. The castle is strongly built; it has seven walls, but—it can be done!—Do you want it, or do you not?

THE OFFICER. Frankly speaking, I cannot tell—for in either case I shall suffer pain. Every joy that life brings has to be paid for with twice its measure of sorrow. It is hard to stay where I am, but if I buy the sweets of freedom, then I shall have to suffer twice as much—Agnes, I'll rather endure it as it is, if I can only see you.

THE DAUGHTER. What do you see in me?

THE OFFICER. Beauty, which is the harmony of the universe—There are lines of your body which are nowhere to be found, except in the orbits of the solar system, in strings that are singing softly, or in the vibrations of light—You are a child of heaven—

THE DAUGHTER. So are you.

THE OFFICER. Why must I then keep horses, tend stable, and cart straw?

THE DAUGHTER. So that you may long to get away from here.

THE OFFICER. I am longing, but it is so hard to find one's way out.

THE DAUGHTER. But it is a duty to seek freedom in the light.

THE OFFICER. Duty? Life has never recognised any duties toward me.

THE DAUGHTER. You feel yourself wronged by life?

THE OFFICER. Yes, it has been unjust—

[*Now voices are heard from behind a partition, which a moment later is pulled away.* THE OFFICER *and* THE DAUGHTER *look in that direction and stop as if paralysed in the midst of a gesture.*]

[*At a table sits* THE MOTHER, *looking very sick. In front of her a tallow candle is burning, and every little while she trims it with a pair of snuffers. The table is piled with new-made shirts, and these she is marking with a quill and ink. To the left stands a brown-coloured wardrobe.*]

THE FATHER. [*Holds out a silk mantilla toward* THE MOTHER *and says gently*] You don't want it?

THE MOTHER. A silk mantilla for me, my dear—of what use would that be when I am going to die shortly?

THE FATHER. Do you believe what the doctor says?

THE MOTHER. Yes, I believe also what he says, but still more what the voice says in here.

THE FATHER. [*Sadly*] It is true then?—And you are thinking of your children first and last.

THE MOTHER. That has been my life and my reason for living—my joy and my sorrow—

THE FATHER. Christine, forgive me—everything!

THE MOTHER. What have I to forgive? Dearest, you forgive *me!* We have been tormenting each other. Why? That we may not know. We couldn't do anything else—However, here is the new linen for the children. See that they change twice a week—Wednesdays and Sundays—and that Louise washes them—their whole bodies—Are you going out?

THE FATHER. I have to be in the Department at eleven o'clock.

THE MOTHER. Ask Alfred to come in before you go.

THE FATHER. [*Pointing to* THE OFFICER] Why, he is standing right there, dear heart.

THE MOTHER. So my eyes are failing, too—Yes, it is turning dark. [*Trims the candle*] Come here, Alfred.

[The FATHER *goes out through the middle of the wall, nodding good-bye as he leaves.*]

[The OFFICER *goes over to* The MOTHER.]

THE MOTHER. Who is that girl?

THE OFFICER. [*Whispers*] It is Agnes.

THE MOTHER. Oh, is that Agnes?—Do you know what they say?—That she is a daughter of the god Indra who has asked leave to descend to the earth in order that she may find out what the conditions of men are—But don't say anything about it.

THE OFFICER. A child of the gods, indeed!

THE MOTHER. [*Aloud*] My Alfred, I must soon part from you and from the other children—But let me first speak a word to you that bears on all the rest of your life.

THE OFFICER. [*Sadly*] Speak, mother.

THE MOTHER. Only a word: don't quarrel with God!

THE OFFICER. What do you mean, mother?

THE MOTHER. Don't go around feeling that life has wronged you.

THE OFFICER. But when I am treated unjustly—

THE MOTHER. You are thinking of the time when you were unjustly punished for having taken a penny that later turned up?

THE OFFICER. Yes, and that one wrong gave a false twist to my whole life—

THE MOTHER. Perhaps. But please take a look into that wardrobe now—

THE OFFICER. [*Embarrassed*] You know, then? It is—

THE MOTHER. The Swiss Family Robinson—for which—

THE OFFICER. Don't say any more!

THE MOTHER. For which your brother was punished—and which you had torn and hidden away.

THE OFFICER. Just think that the old wardrobe is still standing there after twenty years— We have moved so many times, and my mother died ten years ago.

THE MOTHER. Yes, and what of it? You are always asking all sorts of questions, and in that way you spoil the better part of your life—There is Lena, now.

LENA. [*Enters*] Thank you very much, ma'am, but I can't go to the baptism.

THE MOTHER. And why not, my girl?

LENA. I have nothing to put on.

THE MOTHER. I'll let you use my mantilla here

LENA. Oh, no, ma'am, that wouldn't do!

THE MOTHER. Why not?—It is not likely that I'll go to any more parties.

THE OFFICER. And what will father say? It is a present from him—

THE MOTHER. What small minds—

THE FATHER. [*Puts his head through the wall*] Are you going to lend my present to the servant girl?

THE MOTHER. Don't talk that way! Can you not remember that I was a servant girl also? Why should you offend one who has done nothing?

THE FATHER. Why should you offend me, your husband?

THE MOTHER. Oh, this life! If you do anything nice, there is always somebody who finds it nasty. If you act kindly to one, it hurts another. Oh, this life!

[*She trims the candle so that it goes out. The stage turns dark and the partition is pushed back to its former position.*]

THE DAUGHTER. Men are to be pitied.

THE OFFICER. You think so?

THE DAUGHTER. Yes, life is hard—but love overcomes everything. You shall see for yourself.

[*They go toward the background. The background is raised and a new one revealed, showing an old, dilapidated party-wall. In the centre of it is a gate closing a passageway. This opens upon a green, sunlit space, where is seen a tremendous blue monk's-hood (aconite). To the left of the gate sits* THE PORTRESS. *Her head and shoulders are covered by a shawl, and she is crocheting at a bed-spread with a star-like pattern. To the right of the gate is a billboard, which* THE BILLPOSTER *is cleaning. Beside him stands a dipnet with a green pole. Further to the right is a door that has an air-hole shaped like a four-leaved clover. To the left of the gate stands a small linden tree with coal-black trunk and a few pale-green leaves. Near it is a small air-hole leading into a cellar.* [1]]]

[1] Though the author says nothing about it here, subsequent stage directions indicate a door and a window behind the place occupied by THE PORTRESS. Both lead into her room or lodge, which contains a telephone.

THE DAUGHTER. [*Going to* THE PORTRESS] Is the spread not done yet?

THE PORTRESS. No, dear. Twenty-six years on such a piece of work is not much.

THE DAUGHTER. And your lover never came back?

THE PORTRESS. No, but it was not his fault. He had to go—poor thing! That was thirty years ago now.

THE DAUGHTER. [*To* THE BILLPOSTER] She belonged to the ballet? Up there in the opera-house?

THE BILLPOSTER. She was number one—but when *he* went, it was as if her dancing had gone with him—and so she didn't get any more parts.

THE DAUGHTER. Everybody complains—with their eyes, at least, and often with words also—

THE BILLPOSTER. I don't complain very much—not now, since I have a dipnet and a green cauf [2]—

[2] A floating wooden box with holes in it used to hold fish.

THE DAUGHTER. And that can make you happy?

THE BILLPOSTER. Oh, I'm so happy, so—It was the dream of my youth, and now it has come true. Of course, I have grown to be fifty years—

THE DAUGHTER. Fifty years for a dipnet and a cauf—

THE BILLPOSTER. A *green* cauf—mind you, *green*—

THE DAUGHTER. [*To* THE PORTRESS] Let me have the shawl now, and I shall sit here and watch the human children. But you must stand behind me and tell me about everything.

[*She takes the shawl and sits down at the gate.*]

THE PORTRESS. This is the last day, and the house will be closed up for the season. This is the day when they learn whether their contracts are to be renewed.

THE DAUGHTER. And those that fail of engagement—

THE PORTRESS. O, Lord have mercy! I pull the shawl over my head not to see them.

THE DAUGHTER. Poor human creatures!

THE PORTRESS. Look, here comes one—She's not one of the chosen. See, how she cries.

[*The Singer enters from the right; rushes through the gate with her handkerchief to her eyes; stops for a moment in the passageway beyond the gate and leans her head against the wall; then out quickly.*]

THE DAUGHTER. Men are to be pitied!

THE PORTRESS. But look at this one. That's the way a happy person looks.

[THE OFFICER *enters through the passageway; dressed in Prince Albert coat and high hat, and carrying a bunch of roses in one hand; he is radiantly happy.*]

THE PORTRESS. He's going to marry Miss Victoria.

THE OFFICER. [*Far down on the stage, looks up and sings*] Victoria!

THE PORTRESS. The young lady will be coming in a moment.

THE OFFICER. Good! The carriage is waiting, the table is set, the wine is on ice—Oh, permit me to embrace you, ladies! [*He embraces* THE PORTRESS *and* THE DAUGHTER. *Sings*] Victoria!

A WOMAN'S VOICE FROM ABOVE. [*Sings*] I am here!

THE DAUGHTER. Do you know me?

THE OFFICER. No, I know one woman only—Victoria. Seven years I have come here to wait for her—at noon, when the sun touched the chimneys, and at night, when it was growing dark. Look at the asphalt here, and you will see the path worn by the steps of a faithful lover. Hooray! She is mine. [*Sings*] Victoria! [*There is no reply*] Well, she is dressing, I suppose. [*To* THE BILLPOSTER] There is the dipnet, I see. Everybody belonging to the opera is crazy about dipnets—or rather about fishes—because the fishes are dumb and cannot sing!—What is the price of a thing like that?

THE BILLPOSTER. It is rather expensive.

THE OFFICER. [*Sings*] Victoria! [*Shakes the linden tree*] Look, it is turning green once more. For the eighth time. [*Sings*] Victoria!—Now she is fixing her hair. [*To* THE DAUGHTER] Look here, madam, could I not go up and get my bride?

THE PORTRESS. Nobody is allowed on the stage.

THE OFFICER. Seven years I have been coming here. Seven times three hundred and sixty-five makes two thousand five hundred and fifty-five. [*Stops and pokes at the door with the four-leaved clover hole*] And I have been looking two thousand five hundred and fifty-five times at that door without discovering where it leads. And that clover leaf which is to let in light—for whom is the light meant? Is there anybody within? Does anybody live there?

THE PORTRESS. I don't know. I have never seen it opened.

THE OFFICER. It looks like a pantry door which I saw once when I was only four years old and went visiting with the maid on a Sunday afternoon. We called at several houses—on other maids—but I did not get beyond the kitchen anywhere, and I had to sit between the water barrel and the salt box. I have seen so many kitchens in my days, and the pantry was always just outside, with small round holes bored in the door, and one big hole like a clover leaf—But there cannot be any pantry in the opera-house as they have no kitchen. [*Sings*] Victoria!—Tell me, madam, could she have gone out any other way?

THE PORTRESS. No, there is no other way.

THE OFFICER. Well, then I shall see her here.

[STAGE PEOPLE *rush out and are closely watched by* THE OFFICER *as they pass.*]

THE OFFICER. Now she must soon be coming—Madam, that blue monk's-hood outside—I have seen it since I was a child. Is it the same?—I remember it from a country rectory where I stopped when I was seven years old—There are two doves, two blue doves, under the hood—but that time a bee came flying and went into the hood. Then I thought: now I have you! And I grabbed hold of the flower. But the sting of the bee went through it, and I cried—but then the rector's wife came and put damp dirt on the sting—and we had strawberries and cream for dinner—I think it is getting dark already. [*To* THE BILLPOSTER] Where are you going?

THE BILLPOSTER. Home for supper.

THE OFFICER. [*Draws his hand across his eyes*] Evening? At this time?—O, please, may I go in and telephone to the Growing Castle?

THE DAUGHTER. What do you want there?

THE OFFICER. I am going to tell the Glazier to put in double windows, for it will soon be winter, and I am feeling horribly cold. [*Goes into the gatekeeper's lodge.*]

THE DAUGHTER. Who is Miss Victoria?

THE PORTRESS. His sweetheart.

THE DAUGHTER. Right said! What she is to us and others matters nothing to him. And what she is to him, that alone is her real self.

[*It is suddenly turning dark.*]

THE PORTRESS. [*Lights a lantern*] It is growing dark early to-day.

THE DAUGHTER. To the gods a year is as a minute.

THE PORTRESS. And to men a minute may be as long as a year.

THE OFFICER. [*Enters again, looking dusty; the roses are withered*] She has not come yet?

THE PORTRESS. No.

THE OFFICER. But she will come—She will come! [*Walks up and down*] But come to think of it, perhaps I had better call off the dinner after all—as it is late? Yes, I will do that.

[*Goes back into the lodge and telephones.*]

THE PORTRESS. [*To* THE DAUGHTER] Can I have my shawl back now?

THE DAUGHTER. No, dear, be free a while. I shall attend to your duties—for I want to study men and life, and see whether things really are as bad as they say.

THE PORTRESS. But it won't do to fall asleep here—never sleep night or day—

THE DAUGHTER. No sleep at night?

THE PORTRESS. Yes, if you are able to get it, but only with the bell string tied around the wrist—for there are night watchmen on the stage, and they have to be relieved every third hour.

THE DAUGHTER. But that is torture!

THE PORTRESS. So you think, but people like us are glad enough to get such a job, and if you only knew how envied I am—

THE DAUGHTER. Envied?—Envy for the tortured?

THE PORTRESS. Yes—But I can tell you what is harder than all drudging and keeping awake nights, harder to bear than draught and cold and dampness—it is to receive the confidences of all the unhappy people up there—They all come to me. Why? Perhaps they read in the wrinkles of my face some runes that are graved by suffering and that invite confessions—In that shawl, dear, lie hidden thirty years of my own and other people's agonies.

THE DAUGHTER. It is heavy, and it burns like nettles.

THE PORTRESS. As it is your wish, you may wear it. When it grows too burdensome, call me, and I shall relieve you.

THE DAUGHTER. Good-bye. What can be done by you ought not to surpass my strength.

THE PORTRESS. We shall see!—But be kind to my poor friends, and don't grow impatient of their complaints.

[*She disappears through the passageway. Complete darkness covers the stage, and while it lasts the scene is changed so that the linden tree appears stripped of all its leaves. Soon the blue monk's-hood is withered, and when the light returns, the verdure in the open space beyond the passageway has changed into autumnal brown.*]

THE OFFICER. [*Enters when it is light again. He has gray hair and a gray beard. His clothes are shabby, his collar is soiled and wrinkled. Nothing but the bare stems remain of the bunch of roses. He walks to and fro*] To judge by all signs, Summer is gone and Fall has come. The linden shows it, and the monk's-hood also. [*Walks*] But the Fall is *my* Spring, for then the opera begins again, and then she must come. Please, madam, may I sit down a little on this chair?

THE DAUGHTER. Yes, sit down, friend—I am able to stand.

THE OFFICER. [*Sits down*] If I could only get some sleep, then I should feel better—[*He falls asleep for a few moments. Then he jumps up and walks back and forth again. Stops at last in front of the door with the clover leaf and pokes at it*] This door here will not leave me any peace—what is behind it? There must be something. [*Faint dance music is heard from above*] Oh, now the rehearsals have begun. [*The light goes out and flares up again, repeating this rhythmically as the rays of a lighthouse come and go*] What does this mean? [*Speaking in time with the blinkings of the light*] Light and dark—light and dark?

THE DAUGHTER. [*Imitating him*] Night and day—night and day! A merciful Providence wants to shorten your wait. Therefore the days are flying in hot pursuit of the nights.

[*The light shines unbrokenly once more.* THE BILLPOSTER *enters with his dipnet and his implements.*]

THE OFFICER. There is the Billposter with his dipnet. Was the fishing good?

THE BILLPOSTER. I should say so. The Summer was hot and a little long—the net turned out pretty good, but not as I had expected.

THE OFFICER. [*With emphasis*] Not as I had expected!—That is well said. Nothing ever was as I expected it to be—because the thought is more than the deed, more than the thing.

[*Walks to and fro, striking at the wall with the rose stems so that the last few leaves fall off.*]

THE BILLPOSTER. Has she not come down yet?

THE OFFICER. Not yet, but she will soon be here—Do you know what is behind that door, Billposter?

THE BILLPOSTER. No, I have never seen that door open yet.

THE OFFICER. I am going to telephone for a locksmith to come and open it. [*Goes into the lodge.*]

[THE BILLPOSTER *posts a bill and goes toward the right.*

THE DAUGHTER. What is the matter with the dipnet?

THE BILLPOSTER. Matter? Well, I don't know as there is anything the matter with it—but it just didn't turn out as I had expected, and the pleasure of it was not so much after all.

THE DAUGHTER. How did you expect it to be?

THE BILLPOSTER. How?—Well, I couldn't tell exactly—

THE DAUGHTER. I can tell you! You had expected it to be what it was not. It had to be green, but not that kind of green.

THE BILLPOSTER. You have it, madam. You understand it all—and that is why everybody goes to you with his worries. If you would only listen to me a little also—

THE DAUGHTER. Of course, I will!—Come in to me and pour out your heart. [*She goes into the lodge.*]

[THE BILLPOSTER *remains outside, speaking to her. The stage is darkened again. When the light is turned on, the tree has resumed its leaves, the monk's-hood is blooming once more, and the sun is shining on the green space beyond the passageway.*]

[*The Officer enters. Now he is old and white-haired, ragged, and wearing worn-out shoes. He carries the bare remnants of the rose stems. Walks to and fro slowly, with the gait of an aged man. Reads on the posted bill.*]

[A BALLET GIRL *comes in from the right.*]

THE OFFICER. Is Miss Victoria gone?

THE BALLET GIRL. No, she has not gone yet.

THE OFFICER. Then I shall wait. She will be coming soon, don't you think?

THE BALLET GIRL. Oh, yes, I am sure.

THE OFFICER. Don't go away now, for I have sent word to the locksmith, so you will soon see what is behind that door.

THE BALLET GIRL. Oh, it will be awfully interesting to see that door opened. That door, there, and the Growing Castle—have you heard of the Growing Castle?

THE OFFICER. Have I?—I have been a prisoner in it.

THE BALLET GIRL. No, was that you? But why do they keep such a lot of horses there?

THE OFFICER. Because it is a stable castle, don't you know.

THE BALLET GIRL. [*With confusion*] How stupid of me not to guess that!

[A MALE CHORUS SINGER *enters from the right*.]

THE OFFICER. Has Miss Victoria gone yet?

THE CHORUS SINGER. [*Earnestly*] No, she has not. She never goes away.

THE OFFICER. That is because she loves me—See here, don't go before the locksmith comes to open the door here.

THE CHORUS SINGER. No, is the door going to be opened? Well, that will be fun!—I just want to ask the Portress something.

[THE PROMPTER *enters from the right*.]

THE OFFICER. Is Miss Victoria gone yet?

The PROMPTER. Not that I know of.

THE OFFICER. Now, didn't I tell you she was waiting for me!—Don't go away, for the door is going to be opened.

The PROMPTER. Which door?

THE OFFICER. Is there more than one door?

The PROMPTER. Oh, I know—that one with the clover leaf. Well, then I have got to stay—I am only going, to have a word with the Portress.

[THE BALLET GIRL, THE CHORUS SINGER, *and* THE PROMPTER *gather beside* THE BILLPOSTER *in front of the lodge window and talk by turns to* THE DAUGHTER.]
[THE GLAZIER *enters through the gate*.]

THE OFFICER. Are you the locksmith?

THE GLAZIER. No, the locksmith had visitors, and a glazier will do just as well.

THE OFFICER. Yes, of course, of course—but did you bring your diamond along?

THE GLAZIER. Why, certainly!—A glazier without his diamond, what would that be?

THE OFFICER. Nothing at all!—Let us get to work then.

[*Claps his hands together. All gather in a ring around the door. Male members of the chorus dressed as Master Singers and Ballet Girls in costumes from the opera "Aïda" enter from the right and join the rest.*]

THE OFFICER. Locksmith—or glazier—do your duty!

THE GLAZIER *goes up to the door with the diamond in his hand.*

THE OFFICER. A moment like this will not occur twice in a man's life. For this reason, my friends, I ask you—please consider carefully—

A POLICEMAN. [*Enters*] In the name of the law, I forbid the opening of that door!

THE OFFICER. Oh, Lord! What a fuss there is as soon as anybody wants to do anything new or great. But we will take the matter into court—let us go to the Lawyer. Then we shall see whether the laws still exist or not—Come along to the Lawyer.

[*Without lowering of the curtain, the stage changes to a lawyer's office, and in this manner. The gate remains, but as a wicket in the railing running clear across the stage. The gatekeeper's lodge turns into the private enclosure of the Lawyer, and it is now entirely open to the front. The linden, leafless, becomes a hat tree. The billboard is covered with legal notices and court decisions. The door with the four-leaved clover hole forms part of a document chest.*]

[THE LAWYER, *in evening dress and white necktie, is found sitting to the left, inside the gate, and in front of him stands a desk covered with papers. His appearance indicates enormous sufferings. His face is chalk-white and full of wrinkles, and its shadows have a purple effect. He is ugly, and his features seem to reflect all the crimes and vices with which he has been forced by his profession to come into contact.*]

[*Of his two clerks, one has lost an arm, the other an eye.*]

[*The people gathered to witness "the opening of the door" remain as before, but they appear now to be waiting for an audience with the Lawyer. Judging by their attitudes, one would think they had been standing there forever.*]

[THE DAUGHTER, *still wearing the shawl, and* THE OFFICER *are near the footlights.*]

THE LAWYER. [*Goes over to* THE DAUGHTER] Tell me, sister, can I have that shawl? I shall keep it here until I have a fire in my grate, and then I shall burn it with all its miseries and sorrows.

THE DAUGHTER. Not yet, brother. I want it to hold all it possibly can, and I want it above all to take up your agonies—all the confidences you have received about crime, vice, robbery, slander, abuse—

THE LAWYER. My dear girl, for such a purpose your shawl would prove totally insufficient. Look at these walls. Does it not look as if the wall-paper itself had been soiled by every conceivable sin? Look at these documents into which I write tales of wrong. Look at myself—No smiling man ever comes here; nothing is to be seen here but angry glances, snarling lips, clenched fists—And everybody pours his anger, his envy, his suspicions, upon me. Look—my hands are black, and no washing will clean them. See how they are chapped and bleeding—I can never wear my clothes more than a few days because they smell of other people's crimes—At times I have the place fumigated with sulphur, but it does not help. I sleep nearby, and I dream of nothing but crimes—Just now I have a murder case in court—oh, I can stand that, but do you know what is worse than anything else?—That is to separate married people! Then it is as if something cried way down in the earth and up there in the sky—as if it cried treason against the primal force, against the source of all good, against love—And do you know, when reams of paper have been filled with mutual accusations, and at last a sympathetic person takes one of the two apart and asks, with a pinch of the ear or a smile, the simple question: what have you really got against your husband?—or your wife?—then he, or she, stands perplexed and cannot give the cause. Once—well, I think a lettuce salad was the principal issue; another time it was just a word—mostly it is nothing at all. But the tortures, the sufferings— these I have to bear—See how I look! Do you think I could ever win a woman's love with this countenance so like a criminal's? Do you think anybody dares to be friendly with me, who has to collect all the debts, all the money obligations, of the whole city?—It is a misery to be man!

THE DAUGHTER. Men are to be pitied!

THE LAWYER. They are. And what people are living on puzzles me. They marry on an income of two thousand, when they need four thousand. They borrow, of course—

everybody borrows. In some sort of happy-go-lucky fashion, by the skin of their teeth, they manage to pull through—and thus it continues to the end, when the estate is found to be bankrupt. Who pays for it at last no one can tell.

THE DAUGHTER. Perhaps He who feeds the birds.

THE LAWYER. Perhaps. But if He who feeds the birds would only pay a visit to this earth of His and see for Himself how the poor human creatures fare—then His heart would surely fill with compassion.

THE DAUGHTER. Men are to be pitied!

THE LAWYER. Yes, that is the truth!—[*To* THE OFFICER] What do you want?

THE OFFICER. I just wanted to ask if Miss Victoria has gone yet.

THE LAWYER. No, she has not; you can be sure of it—Why are you poking at my chest over there?

THE OFFICER. I thought the door of it looked exactly—

THE LAWYER. Not at all! Not at all!

[*All the church bells begin to ring.*]

THE OFFICER. Is there going to be a funeral?

THE LAWYER. No, it is graduation day—a number of degrees will be conferred, and I am going to be made a Doctor of Laws. Perhaps you would also like to be graduated and receive a laurel wreath?

THE OFFICER. Yes, why not. That would be a diversion, at least.

THE LAWYER. Perhaps then we may begin upon this solemn function at once—But you had better go home and change your clothes.

[THE OFFICER *goes out.*]

[*The stage is darkened and the following changes are made. The railing stays, but it encloses now the chancel of a church. The billboard displays hymn numbers. The linden hat tree becomes a candelabrum. The Lawyer's desk is turned into the desk of the presiding functionary, and the door with the clover leaf leads to the vestry.*]

[*The chorus of Master Singers become herald's with staffs, and the Ballet Girls carry laurel wreaths. The rest of the people act as spectators.*]

[*The background is raised, and the new one thus discovered represents a large church organ, with the keyboards below and the organist's mirror above.*]

[*Music is heard. At the sides stand figures symbolizing the four academic faculties: Philosophy, Theology, Medicine, and Jurisprudence.*]

[*At first the stage is empty for a few moments.*]

[HERALDS *enter from the right.*]

[BALLET GIRLS *follow with laurel wreaths carried high before them.*]

[THREE GRADUATES *appear one after another from the left, receive their wreaths from the* BALLET GIRLS, *and go out to the right.*]

[THE LAWYER *steps forward to get his wreath.*]

[THE BALLET GIRLS *turn away from him and refuse to place the wreath on his head. Then they withdraw from the stage.*]

[THE LAWYER, *shocked, leans against a column. All the others withdraw gradually until only* THE LAWYER *remains on the stage.*]

THE DAUGHTER. [*Enters, her head and shoulders covered by a white veil*] Do you see, I have washed the shawl! But why are you standing there? Did you get your wreath?

THE LAWYER. No, I was not held worthy.

THE DAUGHTER. Why? Because you have defended the poor, put in a good word for the wrong-doing, made the burden easier for the guilty, obtained a respite for the condemned? Woe upon men: they are not angels—but they are to be pitied!

THE LAWYER. Say nothing evil of men—for after all it is my task to voice their side.

THE DAUGHTER. [*Leaning against the organ*] Why do they strike their friends in the face?

THE LAWYER. They know no better.

THE DAUGHTER. Let us enlighten them. Will you try? Together with me?

THE LAWYER. They do not accept enlightenment—Oh, that our plaint might reach the gods of heaven!

THE DAUGHTER. It shall reach the throne—[*Turns toward the organ*] Do you know what I see in this mirror?—The world turned the right way!—Yes indeed, for naturally we see it upside down.

THE LAWYER. How did it come to be turned the wrong way?

THE DAUGHTER. When the copy was taken—

THE LAWYER. You have said it! The copy—I have always had the feeling that it was a spoiled copy. And when I began to recall the original images, I grew dissatisfied with everything. But men called it soreheadedness, looking at the world through the devil's eyes, and other such things.

THE DAUGHTER. It is certainly a crazy world! Look at the four faculties here. The government, to which has fallen the task of preserving society, supports all four of them. Theology, the science of God, is constantly attacked and ridiculed by philosophy, which declares itself to be the sum of all wisdom. And medicine is always challenging philosophy, while refusing entirely to count theology a science and even insisting on calling it a mere superstition. And they belong to a common Academic Council, which has been set to teach the young respect—for the university. It is a bedlam. And woe unto him who first recovers his reason!

THE LAWYER. Those who find it out first are the theologians. As a preparatory study, they take philosophy, which teaches them that theology is nonsense. Later they learn from theology that philosophy is nonsense. Madmen, I should say!

THE DAUGHTER. And then there is jurisprudence which serves all but the servants.

THE LAWYER. Justice, which, when it wants to do right, becomes the undoing of men. Equity, which so often turns into iniquity!

THE DAUGHTER. What a mess you have made of it, you man-children. Children, indeed!—Come here, and I will give you a wreath—one that is more becoming to you. [*Puts a crown of thorns on his head*] And now I will play for you.

[*She sits down at the keyboards, but instead of organ notes human voices are heard.*]

VOICES OF CHILDREN. O Lord everlasting!

[*Last note sustained.*]

VOICES OF WOMEN. Have mercy upon us!

[*Last note sustained.*]

VOICES OF MEN. [*Tenors*] Save us for Thy mercy's sake!

[*Last note sustained.*]

VOICES OF MEN. [*Basses*] Spare Thy children, O Lord, and deliver us from Thy wrath!

ALL. Have mercy upon us! Hear us! Have pity upon the mortals!—O Lord eternal, why art Thou afar?—Out of the depths we call unto Thee: Make not the burden of Thy children too heavy! Hear us! Hear us!

[*The stage turns dark.* THE DAUGHTER *rises and draws close to* THE LAWYER. *By a change of light, the organ becomes Fingal's Cave. The ground-swell of the ocean, which can be seen rising and falling between the columns of basalt, produces a deep harmony that blends the music of winds and waves.*]

THE LAWYER. Where are we, sister?

THE DAUGHTER. What do you hear?

THE LAWYER. I hear drops falling—

THE DAUGHTER. Those are the tears that men are weeping—What more do you hear?

THE LAWYER. There is sighing—and whining—and wailing——

THE DAUGHTER. Hither the plaint of the mortals has reached—and no farther. But why this never-ending wailing? Is there then nothing in life to rejoice at?

THE LAWYER. Yes, what is most sweet, and what is also most bitter—love—wife and home—the highest and the lowest!

THE DAUGHTER. May I try it?

THE LAWYER. With me?

THE DAUGHTER. With you—You know the rocks, the stumbling-stones. Let us avoid them.

THE LAWYER. I am so poor.

THE DAUGHTER. What does that matter if we only love each other? And a little beauty costs nothing.

THE LAWYER. I have dislikes which may prove your likes.

THE DAUGHTER. They can be adjusted.

THE LAWYER. And if we tire of it?

THE DAUGHTER. Then come the children and bring with them a diversion that remains for ever new.

THE LAWYER. You, you will take me, poor and ugly, scorned and rejected?

THE DAUGHTER. Yes—let us unite our destinies.

THE LAWYER. So be it then!

Curtain.

An extremely plain room inside THE LAWYER'S *office. To the right, a big double bed covered by a canopy and curtained in. Next to it, a window. To the left, an iron heater with cooking utensils on top of it.* CHRISTINE *is pasting paper strips along the cracks of the double windows. In the background, an open door to the office. Through the door are visible a number of poor clients waiting for admission.*

CHRISTINE. I paste, I paste.

THE DAUGHTER. [*Pale and emaciated, sits by the stove*] You shut out all the air. I choke!

CHRISTINE. Now there is only one little crack left.

THE DAUGHTER. Air, air—I cannot breathe!

CHRISTINE. I paste, I paste.

THE LAWYER. That's right, Christine! Heat is expensive.

THE DAUGHTER. Oh, it feels as if my lips were being glued together.

THE LAWYER. [*Standing in the doorway, with a paper in his hand*] Is the child asleep?

THE DAUGHTER. Yes, at last.

THE LAWYER. [*Gently*] All this crying scares away my clients.

THE DAUGHTER. [*Pleasantly*] What can be done about it?

THE LAWYER. Nothing.

THE DAUGHTER. We shall have to get a larger place.

THE LAWYER. We have no money for it.

THE DAUGHTER. May I open the window—this bad air is suffocating.

THE LAWYER. Then the heat escapes, and we shall be cold.

THE DAUGHTER. It is horrible!—May we clean up out there?

THE LAWYER. You have not the strength to do any cleaning, nor have I, and Christine must paste. She must put strips through the whole house, on every crack, in the ceiling, in the floor, in the walls.

THE DAUGHTER. Poverty I was prepared for, but not for dirt.

THE LAWYER. Poverty is always dirty, relatively speaking.

THE DAUGHTER. This is worse than I dreamed!

THE LAWYER. We are not the worst off by far. There is still food in the pot.

THE DAUGHTER. But what sort of food?

THE LAWYER. Cabbage is cheap, nourishing, and good to eat.

THE DAUGHTER. For those who like cabbage—to me it is repulsive.

THE LAWYER. Why didn't you say so?

THE DAUGHTER. Because I loved you, I wanted to sacrifice my own taste.

THE LAWYER. Then I must sacrifice my taste for cabbage to you—for sacrifices must be mutual.

THE DAUGHTER. What are we to eat, then? Fish? But you hate fish?

THE LAWYER. And it is expensive.

THE DAUGHTER. This is worse than I thought it!

THE LAWYER. [*Kindly*] Yes, you see how hard it is—And the child that was to become a link and a blessing—it becomes our ruin.

THE DAUGHTER. Dearest, I die in this air, in this room, with its backyard view, with its baby cries and endless hours of sleeplessness, with those people out there, and their whinings, and bickerings, and incriminations—I shall die here!

THE LAWYER. My poor little flower, that has no light and no air—

THE DAUGHTER. And you say that people exist who are still worse off?

THE LAWYER. I belong with the envied ones in this locality.

THE DAUGHTER. Everything else might be borne if I could only have some beauty in my home.

THE LAWYER. I know you are thinking of flowers—and especially of heliotropes—but a plant costs half a dollar, which will buy us six quarts of milk or a peck of potatoes.

THE DAUGHTER. I could gladly get along without food if I could only have some flowers.

THE LAWYER. There is a kind of beauty that costs nothing—but the absence of it in the home is worse than any other torture to a man with a sense for the beautiful.

THE DAUGHTER. What is it?

THE LAWYER. If I tell, you will get angry.

THE DAUGHTER. We have agreed not to get angry.

THE LAWYER. We have agreed—Everything can be overcome, Agnes, except the short, sharp accents—Do you know them? Not yet!

THE DAUGHTER. They will never be heard between us.

THE LAWYER. Not as far as it lies on me!

THE DAUGHTER. Tell me now.

THE LAWYER. Well—when I come into a room, I look first of all at the curtains—[*Goes over to the window and straightens out the curtains*] If they hang like ropes or rags, then I leave soon. And next I take a glance at the chairs—if they stand straight along the wall, then I stay. [*Puts a chair back against the wall*] Finally I look at the candles in their sticks—if they point this way and that, then the whole house is askew. [*Straightens up a candle on the chest of drawers*] This is the kind of beauty, dear heart, that costs nothing.

THE DAUGHTER. [*With bent head*] Beware of the short accents, Axel!

THE LAWYER. They were not short.

THE DAUGHTER. Yes, they were.

THE LAWYER. Well, I'll be—

THE DAUGHTER. What kind of language is that?

THE LAWYER. Pardon me, Agnes! But I have suffered as much from your lack of orderliness as you have suffered from dirt. And I have not dared to set things right myself, for when I do so, you get as angry as if I were reproaching you—ugh! Hadn't we better quit now?

THE DAUGHTER. It is very difficult to be married—it is more difficult than anything else. One has to be an angel, I think!

THE LAWYER. I think so, too.

THE DAUGHTER. I fear I shall begin to hate you after this!

THE LAWYER. Woe to us then!—But let us forestall hatred. I promise never again to speak of any untidiness—although it is torture to me!

THE DAUGHTER. And I shall eat cabbage though it means agony to me.

THE LAWYER. A life of common suffering, then! One's pleasure, the other one's pain!

THE DAUGHTER. Men are to be pitied!

THE LAWYER. You see that?

THE DAUGHTER. Yes, but for heaven's sake, let us avoid the rocks, now when we know them so well.

THE LAWYER. Let us try! Are we not decent and intelligent persons? Able to forbear and forgive?

THE DAUGHTER. Why not smile at mere trifles?

THE LAWYER. We—only we—can do so. Do you know, I read this morning—by the bye, where is the newspaper?

THE DAUGHTER. [*Embarrassed*] Which newspaper?

THE LAWYER. [*Sharply*] Do I keep more than one?

THE DAUGHTER. Smile now, and don't speak sharply—I used your paper to make the fire with—

THE LAWYER. [*Violently*] Well, I'll be damned!

THE DAUGHTER. Why don't you smile?—I burned it because it ridiculed what is holy to me.

THE LAWYER. Which is unholy to me! Yah! [*Strikes one clenched fist against the open palm of the other hand*] I smile, I smile so that my wisdom teeth show—Of course, I am to be nice, and I am to swallow my own opinions, and say yes to everything, and cringe and dissemble! [*Tidies the curtains around the bed*] That's it! Now I am going to fix things until you get angry again—Agnes, this is simply impossible!

THE DAUGHTER. Of course it is!

THE LAWYER. And yet we must endure—not for the sake of our promises, but for the sake of the child!

THE DAUGHTER. You are right—for the sake of the child. Oh, oh—we have to endure!

THE LAWYER. And now I must go out to my clients. Listen to them—how they growl with impatience to tear each other, to get each other fined and jailed—Lost souls!

THE DAUGHTER. Poor, poor people! And this pasting! [*She drops her head forward in dumb despair.*]

CHRISTINE. I paste, I paste.

[THE LAWYER *stands at the door, twisting the doorknob nervously.*]

THE DAUGHTER. How that knob squeaks! It is as if you were twisting my heart-strings—

THE LAWYER. I twist, I twist!

THE DAUGHTER. Don't!

THE LAWYER. I twist!

THE DAUGHTER. No!

THE LAWYER. I—

THE OFFICER. [*In the office, on the other side of the door, takes hold of the knob*] Will you permit me?

THE LAWYER. [*Lets go his hold*] By all means. Seeing that you have your degree!

THE OFFICER. Now all life belongs to me. Every road lies open. I have mounted Parnassus. The laurel is won. Immortality, fame, all is mine!

THE LAWYER. And what are you going to live on?

THE OFFICER. Live on?

THE LAWYER. You must have a home, clothes, food—

THE OFFICER. Oh, that will come—if you can only find somebody to love you!

THE LAWYER. You don't say so!—You don't—Paste, Christine, paste until they cannot breathe!

[*Goes out backward, nodding.*]

CHRISTINE. I paste, I paste—until they cannot breathe.

THE OFFICER. Will you come with me now?

THE DAUGHTER. At once! But where?

THE OFFICER. To Fairhaven. There it is summer; there the sun is shining; there we find youth, children, and flowers, singing and dancing, feasting and frolicking.

THE DAUGHTER. Then I will go there.

THE OFFICER. Come!

THE LAWYER. [*Enters again*] Now I go back to my first hell—this was the second and greater. The sweeter the hell, the greater—And look here, now she has been dropping hair-pins on the floor again. [*He picks up some hair-pins.*]

THE OFFICER. My! but he has discovered the pins also.

THE LAWYER. Also?—Look at this one. You see two prongs, but it is only one pin. It is two, yet only one. If I bend it open, it is a single piece. If I bend it back, there are two, but they remain one for all that. It means: these two are one. But if I break—like this!—then they become two. [*Breaks the pin and throws the pieces away.*]

THE OFFICER. All that he has seen!—But before breaking, the prongs must diverge. If they point together, then it holds.

THE LAWYER. And if they are parallel, then they will never meet—and it neither breaks nor holds.

THE OFFICER. The hair-pin is the most perfect of all created things. A straight line which equals two parallel ones.

THE LAWYER. A lock that shuts when it is open.

THE OFFICER. And thus shuts in a braid of hair that opens up when the lock shuts.

THE LAWYER. It is like this door. When I close it, then I open—the way out—for you, Agnes!

[*Withdraws and closes the door behind him.*]

THE DAUGHTER. Well then?

[*The stage changes. The bed with its curtains becomes a tent. The stove stays as it was. The background is raised.*]

[*To the right, in the foreground, are seen hills stripped of their trees by fire, and red heather growing between the blackened tree stumps. Red-painted pig-sties and outhouses. Beyond these, in the open, apparatus for mechanical gymnastics, where sick persons are being treated on machines resembling instruments of torture.*]

[*To the left, in the foreground, the quarantine station, consisting of open sheds, with ovens, furnaces, and pipe coils.*]

[*In the middle distance, a narrow strait.*]

[*The background shows a beautiful wooded shore. Flags are flying on its piers, where ride white sailboats, some with sails set and some without. Little Italian villas, pavilions, arbors, marble statues are glimpsed through the foliage along the shore.*]

[THE MASTER OF QUARANTINE, *made up like a blackamoor, is walking along the shore.*]

THE OFFICER. [*Meets him and they shake hands*] Why, Ordström! [1] Have you landed here?

[1] Means literally "wordspout."

MASTER OF QUARANTINE. Yes, here I am.

THE OFFICER. Is this Fairhaven?

MASTER OF QUARANTINE. No, that is on the other side. This is Foulstrand.

THE OFFICER. Then we have lost our way.

MASTER OF QUARANTINE. We?—Won't you introduce me?

THE OFFICER. No, that wouldn't do. [*In a lowered voice*] It is Indra's own daughter.

MASTER OF QUARANTINE. Indra's? And I was thinking of Varuna himself—Well, are you not surprised to find me black in the face?

THE OFFICER. I am past fifty, my boy, and at that age one has ceased to be surprised. I concluded at once that you were bound for some fancy ball this afternoon.

MASTER OF QUARANTINE. Right you were! And I hope both of you will come along.

THE OFFICER. Why, yes—for I must say—the place does not look very tempting. What kind of people live here anyhow?

MASTER OF QUARANTINE. Here you find the sick; over there, the healthy.

THE OFFICER. Nothing but poor folk on thin side, I suppose.

MASTER OF QUARANTINE. No, my boy, it is here you find the rich. Look at that one on the rack. He has stuffed himself with paté de foie gras and truffles and Burgundy until his feet have grown knotted.

THE OFFICER. Knotted?

MASTER OF QUARANTINE. Yes, he has a case of knotted feet. And that one who lies under the guillotine—he has swilled brandy so that his backbone has to be put through the mangle.

THE OFFICER. There is always something amiss!

MASTER OF QUARANTINE. Moreover, everybody living on this side has some kind of canker to hide. Look at the fellow coming here, for instance.

[*An old dandy is pushed on the stage in a wheel-chair. He is accompanied by a gaunt and grisly coquette in the sixties, to whom* THE FRIEND, *a man of about forty, is paying court.*]

THE OFFICER. It is the major—our schoolmate!

MASTER OF QUARANTINE. Don Juan. Can you see that he is still enamored of that old spectre beside him? He does not notice that she has grown old, or that she is ugly, faithless, cruel.

THE OFFICER. Why, that is love! And I couldn't have dreamt that a fickle fellow like him would prove capable of loving so deeply and so earnestly.

MASTER OF QUARANTINE. That is a mighty decent way of looking at it.

THE OFFICER. I have been in love with Victoria myself—in fact I am still waiting for her in the passageway—

MASTER OF QUARANTINE. Oh, you are the fellow who is waiting in the passageway?

THE OFFICER. I am the man.

MASTER OF QUARANTINE. Well, have you got that door opened yet?

THE OFFICER. No, the case is still in court—The Billposter is out with his dipnet, of course, so that the taking of evidence is always being put off—and in the meantime the Glazier has mended all the window panes in the castle, which has grown half a story higher—This has been an uncommonly good year—warm and wet—

MASTER OF QUARANTINE. But just the same you have had no heat comparing with what I have here.

THE OFFICER. How much do you have in your ovens?

MASTER OF QUARANTINE. When we fumigate cholera suspects, we run it up to one hundred and forty degrees.

THE OFFICER. Is the cholera going again?

MASTER OF QUARANTINE. Don't you know that?

THE OFFICER. Of course, I know it, but I forget so often what I know.

MASTER OF QUARANTINE. I wish often that I could forget—especially myself. That is why I go in for masquerades and carnivals and amateur theatricals.

THE OFFICER. What have you been up to then?

MASTER OF QUARANTINE. If I told, they would say that I was boasting; and if I don't tell, then they call me a hypocrite.

THE OFFICER. That is why you blackened your face?

MASTER OF QUARANTINE. Exactly—making myself a shade blacker than I am.

THE OFFICER. Who is coming there?

MASTER OF QUARANTINE. Oh, a poet who is going to have his mud bath.

[THE POET *enters with his eyes raised toward the sky and carrying a pail of mud in one hand.*]

THE OFFICER. Why, he ought to be having light baths and air baths.

MASTER OF QUARANTINE. No, he is roaming about the higher regions so much that he gets homesick for the mud—and wallowing in the mire makes the skin callous like that of a pig. Then he cannot feel the stings of the wasps.

THE OFFICER. This is a queer world, full of contradictions.

THE POET. [*Ecstatically*] Man was created by the god Phtah out of clay on a potter's wheel, or a lathe—[*sceptically*], or any damned old thing! [*Ecstatically*] Out of clay does the sculptor create his more or less immortal masterpieces—[*sceptically*], which mostly are pure rot. [*Ecstatically*] Out of clay they make those utensils which are so indispensable in the pantry and which generically are named pots and plates— [*sceptically*], but what in thunder does it matter to me what they are called anyhow? [*Ecstatically*] Such is the clay! When clay becomes fluid, it is called mud—C'est mon affaire!—[*shouts*] Lena!

[LENA *enters with a pail in her hand.*]

THE POET. Lena, show yourself to Miss Agnes—She knew you ten years ago, when you were a young, happy and, let us say, pretty girl—Behold how she looks now. Five children, drudgery, baby-cries, hunger, ill-treatment. See how beauty has perished and joy vanished in the fulfilment of duties which should have brought that inner satisfaction which makes each line in the face harmonious and fills the eye with a quiet glow.

MASTER OF QUARANTINE. [*Covering the poet's mouth with his hand*] Shut up! Shut up!

THE POET. That is what they all say. And if you keep silent, then they cry: speak! Oh, restless humanity!

THE DAUGHTER. [*Goes to* LENA] Tell me your troubles.

LENA. No, I dare not, for then they will be made worse.

THE DAUGHTER. Who could be so cruel?

LENA. I dare not tell, for if I do, I shall be spanked.

THE POET. That is just what will happen. But I will speak, even though the blackamoor knock out all my teeth—I will tell that justice is not always done—Agnes, daughter of the gods, do you hear music and dancing on the hill over there?—Well, it is Lena's sister who has come home from the city where she went astray—you understand? Now they are killing the fatted calf; but Lena, who stayed at home, has to carry slop pails and feed the pigs.

THE DAUGHTER. There is rejoicing at home because the stray has left the paths of evil, and not merely because she has come back. Bear that in mind.

THE POET. But then they should give a ball and banquet every night for the spotless worker that never strayed into paths of error—Yet they do nothing of the kind, but when Lena has a free moment, she is sent to prayer-meetings where she has to hear reproaches for not being perfect. Is this justice?

THE DAUGHTER. Your question is so difficult to answer because—There are so many unforeseen cases—

THE POET. That much the Caliph, Haroun the Just, came to understand. He was sitting on his throne, and from its height he could never make out what happened below. At last complaints penetrated to his exalted ears. And then, one fine day, he disguised himself and descended unobserved among the crowds to find out what kind of justice they were getting.

THE DAUGHTER. I hope you don't take me for Haroun the Just!

THE OFFICER. Let us talk of something else—Here come visitors.

[*A white boat, shaped like a viking ship, with a dragon for figure-head, with a pale-blue silken sail on a gilded yard, and with a rose-red standard flying from the top of a gilded mast, glides through the strait from the left.* HE *and* SHE *are seated in the stern with their arms around each other.*]

THE OFFICER. Behold perfect happiness, bliss without limits, young love's rejoicing!

[*The stage grows brighter.*]

HE. [*Stands up in the boat and sings*]
   Hail, beautiful haven,
   Where the Springs of my youth were spent,
   Where my first sweet dreams were dreamt—
   To thee I return,
   But lonely no longer!

   Ye hills and groves,
   Thou sky o'erhead,
   Thou mirroring sea,
   Give greeting to her:
   My love, my bride,
   My light and my life!

[*The flags at the landings of Fairhaven are dipped in salute; white handkerchiefs are waved from verandahs and boats, and the air is filled with tender chords from harps and violins.*]

THE POET. See the light that surrounds them! Hear how the air is ringing with music!—Eros!

THE OFFICER. It is Victoria.

MASTER OF QUARANTINE. Well, what of it?

THE OFFICER. It is his Victoria—My own is still mine. And nobody can see *her*—Now you hoist the quarantine flag, and I shall pull in the net.

[THE MASTER OF QUARANTINE *waves a yellow flag.*]

THE OFFICER. [*Pulling a rope that turns the boat toward Foulstrand*] Hold on there!

[HE *and* SHE *become aware of the hideous view and give vent to their horror.*]

MASTER OF QUARANTINE. Yes, it comes hard. But here every one must stop who hails from plague-stricken places.

THE POET. The idea of speaking in such manner, of acting in such a way, within the presence of two human beings united in love! Touch them not! Lay not hands on love! It is treason!—Woe to us! Everything beautiful must now be dragged down—dragged into the mud!

[HE *and* SHE *step ashore, looking sad and shamefaced.*]

HE. Woe to us! What have we done?

MASTER OF QUARANTINE. It is not necessary to have done anything in order to encounter life's little pricks.

SHE. So short-lived are joy and happiness!

HE. How long must we stay here?

MASTER OF QUARANTINE. Forty days and nights.

SHE. Then rather into the water!

HE. To live here—among blackened hills and pig-sties?

THE POET. Love overcomes all, even sulphur fumes and carbolic acid.

MASTER OF QUARANTINE. [*Starts afire in the stove; blue, sulphurous flames break forth*] Now I set the sulphur going. Will you please step in?

SHE. Oh, my blue dress will fade.

MASTER OF QUARANTINE. And become white. So your roses will also turn white in time.'

HE. Even your cheeks—in forty days!

SHE. [*To* THE OFFICER] That will please you.

THE OFFICER. No, it will not!—Of course, your happiness was the cause of my suffering, but—it doesn't matter—for I am graduated and have obtained a position over there—heigh-ho and alas! And in the Fall I shall be teaching school—teaching boys the same lessons I myself learned during my childhood and youth—the same lessons throughout my manhood and, finally, in my old age—the self-same lessons! What does twice two make? How many times can four be evenly divided by two?—Until I get a pension and can do nothing at all—just wait around for meals and the newspapers—until at last I am carted to the crematorium and burned to ashes—Have you nobody here who is entitled to a pension? Barring twice two makes four, it is probably the worst thing of all—to begin school all over again when one already is graduated; to ask the same questions until death comes

[*An elderly man goes by, with his hands folded behind his back.*]

THE OFFICER. There is a pensioner now, waiting for himself to die. I think he must be a captain who missed the rank of major; or an assistant judge who was not made a chief justice. Many are called but few are chosen—He is waiting for his breakfast now.

THE PENSIONER. No, for the newspaper—the morning paper.

THE OFFICER. And he is only fifty-four years old. He may spend twenty-five more years waiting for meals and newspapers—is it not dreadful?

THE PENSIONER. What is not dreadful? Tell me, tell me!

THE OFFICER. Tell that who can!—Now I shall have to teach boys that twice two makes four. And how many times four can be evenly divided by two. [*He clutches his head in despair*] And Victoria, whom I loved and therefore wished all the happiness life can give—now she has her happiness, the greatest one known to her, and for this reason I suffer—suffer, suffer!

SHE. Do you think I can be happy when I see you suffering? How can you think it? Perhaps it will soothe your pains that I am to be imprisoned here for forty days and nights? Tell me, does it soothe your pains?

THE OFFICER. Yes and no. How can I enjoy seeing you suffer? Oh!

SHE. And do you think my happiness can be founded on your torments?

THE OFFICER. We are to be pitied—all of us!

ALL. [*Raise their arms toward the sky and utter a cry of anguish that sounds like a dissonant cho*rd] Oh!

THE DAUGHTER. Everlasting One, hear them! Life is evil! Men are to be pitied!

ALL. [*As before*] Oh!

[*For a moment the stage is completely darkened, and during that moment everybody withdraws or takes up a new position. When the light is turned on again, Foulstrand is seen in the background, lying in deep shadow. The strait is in the middle distance and Fairhaven in the foreground, both steeped in light. To the right, a corner of the Casino, where dancing couples are visible through the open windows. Three servant maids are standing outside on top of an empty box, with arms around each other, staring at the dancers within. On the verandah of the Casino stands a bench, where "PLAIN" EDITH is sitting. She is bareheaded, with an abundance of tousled hair, and looks sad. In front of her is an open piano. To the left, a frame house painted yellow. Two children in light dresses are playing ball outside.*]

[*In the centre of the middle distance, a pier with white sailboats tied to it, and flag poles with hoisted flags. In the strait is anchored a naval vessel, brig-rigged, with gun ports. But the entire landscape is in winter dress, with snow on the ground and on the bare tree*s.]

[THE DAUGHTER *and* THE OFFICER *enter.*]

THE DAUGHTER. Here is peace, and happiness, and leisure. No more toil; every day a holiday; everybody dressed up in their best; dancing and music in the early morning. [*To the maids*] Why don't you go in and have a dance, girls?

THE MAIDS. We?

THE OFFICER. They are servants, don't you see!

THE DAUGHTER. Of course!—But why is Edith sitting there instead of dancing?

[EDITH *buries her face in her hands.*]

THE OFFICER. Don't question her! She has been sitting there three hours without being asked for a dance.

[*Goes into the yellow house on the left.*]

THE DAUGHTER. What a cruel form of amusement!

THE MOTHER. [*In a low-necked dress, enters from the Casino and goes up to Edith*] Why don't you go in as I told you?

EDITH. Because—I cannot throw myself at them. That I am ugly, I know, and I know that nobody wants to dance with me, but I might be spared from being reminded of it.

[*Begins to play on the piano, the Toccata Con Fuga, Op. 10, by Sebastian Bach.*]

[*The waltz music from within is heard faintly at first. Then it grows in strength, as if to compete with the Bach Toccata. EDITH prevails over it and brings it to silence. Dancers appear in the doorway to hear her play. Everybody on the stage stands still and listens reverently.*]

A NAVAL OFFICER. [*Takes ALICE, one of the dancers, around the waist and drags her toward the pier*] Come quick!

[*Edith breaks off abruptly, rises and stares at the couple with an expression of utter despair; stands as if turned to stone.*]

[*Now the front wall of the yellow house disappears, revealing three benches full of schoolboys. Among these THE OFFICER is seen, looking worried and depressed. In front of the boys stands THE TEACHER, bespectacled and holding a piece of chalk in one hand, a rattan cane in the other.*]

THE TEACHER. [*To THE OFFICER*] Well, my boy, can you tell me what twice two makes?

[THE OFFICER *remains seated while he racks his mind without finding an answer.*]

THE TEACHER. You must rise when I ask you a question.

THE OFFICER. [*Harassed, rises*] Two—twice—let me see. That makes two-two.

THE TEACHER. I see! You have not studied your lesson.

THE OFFICER. [*Ashamed*] Yes, I have, but—I know the answer, but I cannot tell it—

THE TEACHER. You want to wriggle out of it, of course. You know it, but you cannot tell.

Perhaps I may help you.

[*Pulls his hair.*]

THE OFFICER. Oh, it is dreadful, it is dreadful!

THE TEACHER. Yes, it is dreadful that such a big boy lacks all ambition—

THE OFFICER. [*Hurt*] Big boy—yes, I am big—bigger than all these others—I am full-grown, I am done with school—[*As if waking up*] I have graduated—why am I then sitting here? Have I not received my doctor's degree?

THE TEACHER. Certainly, but you are to sit here and mature, you know. You have to mature—isn't that so?

THE OFFICER. [*Feels his forehead*] Yes, that is right, one must mature—Twice two—makes two—and this I can demonstrate by analogy, which is the highest form of all reasoning. Listen!—Once one makes one; consequently twice two must make two. For what applies in one case must also apply in another.

THE TEACHER. Your conclusion is based on good logic, but your answer is wrong.

THE OFFICER. What is logical cannot be wrong. Let us test it. One divided by one gives one, so that two divided by two must give two.

THE TEACHER. Correct according to analogy. But how much does once three make?

THE OFFICER. Three, of course.

THE TEACHER. Consequently twice three must also make three.

THE OFFICER. [*Pondering*] No, that cannot be right—it cannot—or else—[*Sits down dejectedly*] No, I am not mature yet.

THE TEACHER. No, indeed, you are far from mature.

THE OFFICER. But how long am I to sit here, then?

THE TEACHER. Here—how long? Do you believe that time and space exist?—Suppose that time does exist, then you should be able to say what time is. What is time?

THE OFFICER. Time—[*Thinks*] I cannot tell, but I know what it is. Consequently I may also know what twice two is without being able to tell it. And, teacher, can you tell what time is?

THE TEACHER. Of course I can.

ALL. The Boys. Tell us then!

THE TEACHER. Time—let me see. [*Stands immovable with one finger on his nose*] While we are talking, time flies. Consequently time is something that flies while we talk.

A BOY. [*Rising*] Now you are talking, teacher, and while you are talking, I fly: consequently I am time. [*Runs out.*]

THE TEACHER. That accords completely with the laws of logic.

THE OFFICER. Then the laws of logic are silly, for Nils who ran away, cannot be time.

THE TEACHER. That is also good logic, although it is silly.

THE OFFICER. Then logic itself is silly.

THE TEACHER. So it seems. But if logic is silly, then all the world is silly—and then the devil himself wouldn't stay here to teach you more silliness. If anybody treats me to a drink, we'll go and take a bath.

THE OFFICER. That is a *posterus prius*, or the world turned upside down, for it is customary to bathe first and have the drink afterward. Old fogy!

THE TEACHER. Beware of a swelled head, doctor!

THE OFFICER. Call me captain, if you please. I am an officer, and I cannot understand why I should be sitting here to get scolded like a schoolboy—

THE TEACHER. [*With raised index finger*] We were to mature!

MASTER OF QUARANTINE. [*Enters*] The quarantine begins.

THE OFFICER. Oh, there you are. Just think of it, this fellow makes me sit among the boys although I am graduated.

MASTER OF QUARANTINE. Well, why don't you go away?

THE OFFICER. Heaven knows!—Go away? Why, that is no easy thing to do.

THE TEACHER. I guess not—just try!

THE OFFICER. [*To* MASTER OF QUARANTINE] Save me! Save me from his eye!

MASTER OF QUARANTINE. Come on. Come and help us dance—We have to dance before the plague breaks out. We must!

THE OFFICER. Is the brig leaving?

MASTER OF QUARANTINE. Yes, first of all the brig must leave—Then there will be a lot of tears shed, of course.

THE OFFICER. Always tears: when she comes and when she goes—Let us get out of here.

[*They go out.* THE TEACHER *continues his lesson in silence.*]

[THE MAIDS *that were staring through the window of the dance hall walk sadly down to the pier.* EDITH, *who has been standing like a statue at the piano, follows them.*]

THE DAUGHTER. [*To* THE OFFICER] Is there not one happy person to be found in this paradise?

THE OFFICER. Yes, there is a newly married couple. Just watch them.

[THE NEWLY MARRIED COUPLE *enter.*]

HUSBAND. [*To his* WIFE] My joy has no limits, and I could now wish to die—

WIFE. Why die?

HUSBAND. Because at the heart of happiness grows the seed of disaster. Happiness devours itself like a flame—it cannot burn forever, but must go out some time. And this presentiment of the coming end destroys joy in the very hour of its culmination.

WIFE. Let us then die together—this moment!

HUSBAND. Die? All right! For I fear happiness—that cheat! [*They go toward the water.*]

THE DAUGHTER. Life is evil! Men are to be pitied!

THE OFFICER. Look at this fellow. He is the most envied mortal in this neighbourhood.

[THE BLIND MAN *is led in.*]

THE OFFICER. He is the owner of these hundred or more Italian villas. He owns all these bays, straits, shores, forests, together with the fishes in the water, the birds in the air, the game in the woods. These thousand or more people are his tenants. The sun rises upon his sea and sets upon his land—

THE DAUGHTER. Well—is he complaining also?

THE OFFICER. Yes, and with right, for he cannot see.

MASTER OF QUARANTINE. He is blind.

THE DAUGHTER. The most envied of all!

THE OFFICER. Now he has come to see the brig depart with his son on board.

THE BLIND MAN. I cannot see, but I hear. I hear the anchor bill claw the clay bottom as when the hook is torn out of a fish and brings up the heart with it through the neck—

My son, my only child, is going to journey across the wide sea to foreign lands, and I can follow him only in my thought! Now I hear the clanking of the chain—and—there is something that snaps and cracks like clothes drying on a line—wet handkerchiefs perhaps. And I hear it blubber and snivel as when people are weeping—maybe the splashing of the wavelets among the seines—or maybe girls along the shore, deserted and disconsolate—Once I asked a child why the ocean is salt, and the child, which had a father on a long trip across the high seas, said immediately: the ocean is salt because the sailors shed so many tears into it. And why do the sailors cry so much then?—Because they are always going away, replied the child; and that is why they are always drying their handkerchiefs in the rigging—And why does man weep when he is sad? I asked at last—Because the glass in the eyes must be washed now and then, so that we can see clearly, said the child.

[*The brig has set sail and is gliding off. The girls along the shore are alternately waving their handkerchiefs and wiping off their tears with them. Then a signal is set on the foremast—a red ball in a white field, meaning "yes." In response to it Alice waves her handkerchief triumphantly.*]

THE DAUGHTER. [*To* THE OFFICER] What is the meaning of that flag?
THE OFFICER. It means "yes." It is the lieutenant's troth—red as the red blood of the arteries, set against the blue cloth of the sky.
THE DAUGHTER. And how does "no" look?
THE OFFICER. It is blue as the spoiled blood in the veins—but look, how jubilant Alice is.
THE DAUGHTER. And how Edith cries.
THE BLIND MAN. Meet and part. Part and meet. That is life. I met his mother. And then she went away from me. He was left to me; and now he goes.
THE DAUGHTER. But he will come back.
THE BLIND MAN. Who is speaking to me? I have heard that voice before—in my dreams; in my youth, when vacation began; in the early years of my marriage, when my child was born. Every time life smiled at me, I heard that voice, like a whisper of the south wind, like a chord of harps from above, like what I feel the angels' greeting must be in the Holy Night—

[THE LAWYER *enters and goes up to whisper something into* THE BLIND MAN'S *ear.*]

THE BLIND MAN. Is that so?
THE LAWYER. That's the truth. [*Goes to* THE DAUGHTER] Now you have seen most of it, but you have not yet tried the worst of it.
THE DAUGHTER. What can that be?
THE LAWYER. Repetition—recurrence. To retrace one's own tracks; to be sent back to the task once finished—come!
THE DAUGHTER. Where?
THE LAWYER. To your duties.
THE DAUGHTER. What does that mean?
THE LAWYER. Everything you dread. Everything you do not want but must. It means to forego, to give up, to do without, to lack—it means everything that is unpleasant, repulsive, painful.
THE DAUGHTER. Are there no pleasant duties?

THE LAWYER. They become pleasant when they are done.

THE DAUGHTER. When they have ceased to exist—Duty is then something unpleasant. What is pleasant then?

THE LAWYER. What is pleasant is sin.

THE DAUGHTER. Sin?

THE LAWYER. Yes, something that has to be punished. If I have had a pleasant day or night, then I suffer infernal pangs and a bad conscience the next day.

THE DAUGHTER. How strange!

THE LAWYER. I wake up in the morning with a headache; and then the repetitions begin, but so that everything becomes perverted. What the night before was pretty, agreeable, witty, is presented by memory in the morning as ugly, distasteful, stupid. Pleasure seems to decay, and all joy goes to pieces. What men call success serves always as a basis for their next failure. My own successes have brought ruin upon me. For men view the fortune of others with an instinctive dread. They regard it unjust that fate should favour any one man, and so they try to restore balance by piling rocks on the road. To have talent is to be in danger of one's life, for then one may easily starve to death!—However, you will have to return to your duties, or I shall bring suit against you, and we shall pass through every court up to the highest—one, two, three!

THE DAUGHTER. Return?—To the iron stove, and the cabbage pot, and the baby clothes—

THE LAWYER. Exactly! We have a big wash to-day, for we must wash all the handkerchiefs—

THE DAUGHTER. Oh, must I do it all over again?

THE LAWYER. All life is nothing but doing things over again. Look at the teacher in there—He received his doctor's degree yesterday, was laurelled and saluted, climbed Parnassus and was embraced by the monarch—and to-day he starts school all over again, asks how much twice two makes and will continue to do so until his death—However, you must come back to your home!

THE DAUGHTER. I shall rather die!

THE LAWYER. Die?—That is not allowed. First of all, it is a disgrace—so much so that even the dead body is subjected to insults; and secondly, one goes to hell—it is a mortal sin!

THE DAUGHTER. It is not easy to be human!

ALL. Hear!

THE DAUGHTER. I shall not go back with you to humiliation and dirt—I am longing for the heights whence I came—but first the door must be opened so that I may learn the secret—It is my will that the door be opened!

THE LAWYER. Then you must retrace your own steps, cover the road you have already travelled, suffer all annoyances, repetitions, tautologies, recopyings, that a suit will bring with it—

THE DAUGHTER. May it come then—But first I must go into the solitude and the wilderness to recover my own self. We shall meet again! [*To* THE POET] Follow me.

[*Cries of anguish are heard from a distance.* Woe! Woe! Woe!]

THE DAUGHTER. What is that?

THE LAWYER. The lost souls at Foulstrand.

THE DAUGHTER. Why do they wail more loudly than usual to-day?

THE LAWYER. Because the sun is shining here; because here we have music, dancing, youth. And it makes them feel their own sufferings more keenly.

THE DAUGHTER. We must set them free.

THE LAWYER. Try it! Once a liberator appeared, and he was nailed to a cross.

THE DAUGHTER. By whom?

THE LAWYER. By all the right-minded.

THE DAUGHTER. Who are they?

THE LAWYER. Are you not acquainted with all the right-minded? Then you must learn to know them.

THE DAUGHTER. Were they the ones that prevented your graduation?

THE LAWYER. Yes.

THE DAUGHTER. Then I know them!

Curtain.

On the shores of the Mediterranean. To the left, in the foreground, a white wall, and above it branches of an orange tree with ripe fruit on them. In the background, villas and a Casino placed on a terrace. To the right, a huge pile of coal and two wheel-barrows. In the background, to the right, a corner of blue sea.

Two coalheavers, naked to the waist, their faces, hands, and bodies blackened by coal dust, are seated on the wheelbarrows. Their expressions show intense despair.

[THE DAUGHTER *and* THE LAWYER *in the background.*]

THE DAUGHTER. This is paradise!

FIRST COAL HEAVER. This is hell!

SECOND COAL HEAVER. One hundred and twenty degrees in the shadow.

FIRST HEAVER. Let's have a bath.

SECOND HEAVER. The police won't let us. No bathing here.

FIRST HEAVER. Couldn't we pick some fruit off that tree?

SECOND HEAVER. Then the police would get after us.

FIRST HEAVER. But I cannot do a thing in this heat—I'll just chuck the job—

SECOND HEAVER. Then the police will get you for sure!—[*Pause*] And you wouldn't have anything to eat anyhow.

FIRST HEAVER. Nothing to eat? We, who work hardest, get least food; and the rich, who do nothing, get most. Might one not—without disregard of truth—assert that this is injustice?—What has the daughter of the gods to say about it?

THE DAUGHTER. I can say nothing at all—But tell me, what have you done that makes you so black and your lot so hard?

FIRST HEAVER. What have we done? We have been born of poor and perhaps not very good parents—Maybe we have been punished a couple of times.

THE DAUGHTER. Punished?

FIRST HEAVER. Yes, the unpunished hang out in the Casino up there and dine on eight courses with wine.

THE DAUGHTER. [*To* THE LAWYER] Can that be true?

THE LAWYER. On the whole, yes.

THE DAUGHTER. You mean to say that every man at some time has deserved to go to prison?

THE LAWYER. Yes.

THE DAUGHTER. You, too?

THE LAWYER. Yes.

THE DAUGHTER. Is it true that the poor cannot bathe in the sea?

THE LAWYER. Yes. Not even with their clothes on. None but those who intend to take their own lives escape being fined. And those are said to get a good drubbing at the police station.

THE DAUGHTER. But can they not go outside of the city, out into the country, and bathe there?

THE LAWYER. There is no place for them—all the land is fenced in.

THE DAUGHTER. But I mean in the free, open country.

THE LAWYER. There is no such thing—it all belongs to somebody.

THE DAUGHTER. Even the sea, the great, vast sea—

THE LAWYER. Even that! You cannot sail the sea in a boat and land anywhere without having it put down in writing and charged for. It is lovely!

THE DAUGHTER. This is not paradise.

THE LAWYER. I should say not!

THE DAUGHTER. Why don't men do something to improve their lot?

THE LAWYER. Oh, they try, of course, but all the improvers end in prison or in the madhouse—

THE DAUGHTER. Who puts them in prison?

THE LAWYER. All the right-minded, all the respectable—

THE DAUGHTER. Who sends them to the madhouse?

THE LAWYER. Their own despair when they grasp the hopelessness of their efforts.

THE DAUGHTER. Has the thought not occurred to anybody, that for secret reasons it must be as it is?

THE LAWYER. Yes, those who are well off always think so.

THE DAUGHTER. That it is all right as it is?

FIRST HEAVER. And yet we are the foundations of society. If the coal is not unloaded, then there will be no fire in the kitchen stove, in the parlour grate, or in the factory furnace; then the light will go out in streets and shops and homes; then darkness and cold will descend upon you—and, therefore, we have to sweat as in hell so that the black coals may be had—And what do you do for us in return?

THE LAWYER. [*To* THE DAUGHTER] Help them!—[*Pause*] That conditions cannot be quite the same for everybody, I understand, but why should they differ so widely?

[A GENTLEMAN *and* A LADY *pass across the stage.*]

THE LADY. Will you come and play a game with us?

THE GENTLEMAN. No, I must take a walk, so I can eat something for dinner.

FIRST HEAVER. So that he *can* eat something?

SECOND HEAVER. So that he *can*—?

[*Children enter and cry with horror when they catch sight of the grimy workers.*]

FIRST HEAVER. They cry when they see us. They cry—

SECOND HEAVER. Damn it all!—I guess we'll have to pull out the scaffolds soon and

begin to operate on this rotten body—
FIRST HEAVER. Damn it, I say, too! [*Spits.*]
THE LAWYER. [*To* THE DAUGHTER] Yes, it is all wrong. And men are not so very bad—
   but—
THE DAUGHTER. But——?
THE LAWYER. But the government—
THE DAUGHTER. [*Goes out, hiding her face in her hands*] This is not paradise.
COAL HEAVERS. No, hell, that's what it is!

Curtain.

[*Fingal's Cave. Long green waves are rolling slowly into the cave. In the foreground, a siren buoy is swaying to and fro in time with the waves, but without sounding except at the indicated moment. Music of the winds. Music of the waves.*]
[THE DAUGHTER *and* THE POET.]

THE POET. Where are you leading me?
THE DAUGHTER. Far away from the noise and lament of the man-children, to the utmost
   end of the ocean, to the cave that we name Indra's Ear because it is the place where
   the king of the heavens is said to listen to the complaints of the mortals.
THE POET. What? In this place?
THE DAUGHTER. Do you see how this cave is built like a shell? Yes, you can see it. Do
   you know that your ear, too, is built in the form of a shell? You know it, but have not
   thought of it. [*She picks up a shell from the beach*] Have you not as a child held such
   a shell to your ear and listened—and heard the ripple of your heart-blood, the
   humming of your thoughts in the brain, the snapping of a thousand little worn-out
   threads in the tissues of your body? All that you hear in this small shell. Imagine then
   what may be heard in this larger one!
THE POET. [*Listening*] I hear nothing but the whispering of the wind.
THE DAUGHTER. Then I shall interpret it for you. Listen. The wail of the winds. [*Recites
   to subdued music*:]

   Born beneath the clouds of heaven,
   Driven we were by the lightnings of Indra
   Down to the sand-covered earth.
   Straw from the harvested fields soiled our feet;
   Dust from the high-roads,
   Smoke from the cities,
   Foul-smelling breaths,
   Fumes from cellars and kitchens,
   All we endured.
   Then to the open sea we fled,
   Filling our lungs with air,
   Shaking our wings,
   And laving our feet.

Indra, Lord of the Heavens,
Hear us!
Hear our sighing!
Unclean is the earth;
Evil is life;
Neither good nor bad
Can men be deemed.
As they can, they live,
One day at a time.
Sons of dust, through dust they journey;
Born out of dust, to dust they return.
Given they were, for trudging,
Feet, not wings for flying.
Dusty they grow—
Lies the fault then with them,
Or with Thee?

THE POET. Thus I heard it once—
THE DAUGHTER. Hush! The winds are still singing. [*Recites to subdued music:*]

We, winds that wander,
We, the air's offspring,
Bear with us men's lament.

Heard us you have
During gloom-filled Fall nights,
In chimneys and pipes,
In key-holes and door cracks,
When the rain wept on the roof:
Heard us you have
In the snow-clad pine woods
Midst wintry gloom:
Heard us you have,
Crooning and moaning
In ropes and rigging
On the high-heaving sea.

It was we, the winds,
Offspring of the air,
Who learned how to grieve
Within human breasts
Through which we passed—
In sick-rooms, on battle-fields,
But mostly where the newborn
Whimpered and wailed
At the pain of living.

We, we, the winds,
We are whining and whistling:
Woe! Woe! Woe!

THE POET. It seems to me that I have already—
THE DAUGHTER. Hush! Now the waves are singing. [*Recites to subdued music:*]

We, we waves,
That are rocking the winds
To rest—
Green cradles, we waves!

Wet are we, and salty;
Leap like flames of fire—
Wet flames are we:
Burning, extinguishing;
Cleansing, replenishing;
Bearing, engendering.

We, we waves,
That are rocking the winds
To rest!

THE DAUGHTER. False waves and faithless! Everything on earth that is not burned, is drowned—by the waves. Look at this. [*Pointing to pile of debris*] See what the sea has taken and spoiled! Nothing but the figure-heads remain of the sunken ships—and the names: *Justice, Friendship, Golden Peace, Hope*—this is all that is left of *Hope*—of fickle *Hope*—Railings, tholes, bails! And lo: the life buoy—which saved itself and let distressed men perish.
THE POET. [*Searching in the pile*] Here is the name-board of the ship *Justice.* That was the one which left Fairhaven with the Blind Man's son on board. It is lost then! -And with it are gone the lover of Alice, the hopeless love of Edith.
THE DAUGHTER. The Blind Man? Fairhaven? I must have been dreaming of them. And the lover of Alice, "Plain" Edith, Foulstrand and the Quarantine, sulphur and carbolic acid, the graduation in the church, the Lawyer's office, the passageway and Victoria, the Growing Castle and the Officer—All this I have been dreaming—
THE POET. It was in one of my poems.
THE DAUGHTER. You know then what poetry is—
THE POET. I know then what dreaming is—But what is poetry?
THE DAUGHTER. Not reality, but more than reality—not dreaming, but daylight dreams—
THE POET. And the man-children think that we poets are only playing—that we invent and make believe.
THE DAUGHTER. And fortunate it is, my friend, for otherwise the world would lie fallow for lack of ministration. Everybody would be stretched on his back, staring into the sky. Nobody would be touching plough or spade, hammer or plane.
THE POET. And you say this, Indra's daughter, you who belong in part up there—
THE DAUGHTER. You do right in reproaching me. Too long have I stayed down here

taking mud baths like you—My thoughts have lost their power of flight; there is clay on their wings—mire on their feet—and I myself—[*raising her arms*] I sink, I sink—Help me, father, Lord of the Heavens! [*Silence*] I can no longer hear his answer. The ether no longer carries the sound from his lips to my ear's shell—the silvery thread has snapped—Woe is me, I am earthbound!

THE POET. Do you mean to ascend—soon?

THE DAUGHTER. As soon as I have consigned this mortal shape to the flames—for even the waters of the ocean cannot cleanse me. Why do you question me thus?

THE POET. Because I have a prayer—

THE DAUGHTER. What kind of prayer?

THE POET. A written supplication from humanity to the ruler of the universe, formulated by a dreamer.

THE DAUGHTER. To be presented by whom?

THE POET. By Indra's daughter.

THE DAUGHTER. Can you repeat what you have written?

THE POET. I can.

THE DAUGHTER. Speak it then.

THE POET. Better that you do it.

THE DAUGHTER. Where can I read it?

THE POET. In my mind—or here.

[*Hands her a roll of paper.*]

THE DAUGHTER. [*Receives the roll, but reads without looking at it*] Well, by me it shall be spoken then:

"Why must you be born in anguish?
Why, O man-child, must you always
Wring your mother's heart with torture
When you bring her joy maternal,
Highest happiness yet known?
Why to life must you awaken,
Why to light give natal greeting,
With a cry of anger and of pain?
Why not meet it smiling, man-child,
When the gift of life is counted
In itself a boon unmatched?
Why like beasts should we be coming,
We of race divine and human?
Better garment craves the spirit
Than one made of filth and blood!
Need a god his teeth be changing—"

—Silence, rash one! Is it seemly
For the work to blame its maker?
No one yet has solved life's riddle.

"Thus begins the human journey
O'er a road of thorns and thistles;
If a beaten path be offered,
It is named at once forbidden;
If a flower you covet, straightway
You are told it is another's;
If a field should bar your progress,
And you dare to break across it,
You destroy your neighbour's harvest;
Others then your own will trample,
That the measure may be evened!
Every moment of enjoyment
Brings to someone else a sorrow,
But your sorrow gladdens no one,
For from sorrow naught but sorrow springs.

"Thus you journey till you die,
And your death brings others' bread."

—Is it thus that you approach,
Son of Dust, the One Most High?

THE POET. Could the son of dust discover
    Words so pure and bright and simple
    That to heaven they might ascend—?

    Child of gods, wilt thou interpret
    Mankind's grievance in some language
    That immortals understand?
THE DAUGHTER. I will.
THE POET. [*Pointing to the buoy*] What is that floating there?—A buoy?
THE DAUGHTER. Yes.
THE POET. It looks like a lung with a windpipe.
THE DAUGHTER. It is the watchman of the seas. When danger is abroad, it sings.
THE POET. It seems to me as if the sea were rising and the waves growing larger—
THE DAUGHTER. Not unlikely.
THE POET. Woe! What do I see? A ship bearing down upon the reef.
THE DAUGHTER. What ship can that be?
THE POET. The ghost ship of the seas, I think.
THE DAUGHTER. What ship is that?
THE POET. The *Flying Dutchman.*
THE DAUGHTER. Oh, that one. Why is he punished so hard, and why does he not seek
 harbour?
THE POET. Because he had seven faithless wives.
THE DAUGHTER. And for this he should be punished?
THE POET. Yes, all the right-minded condemned him——
THE DAUGHTER. Strange world, this!—How can he then be freed from his curse?

THE POET. Freed?—Oh, they take good care that none is set free.

THE DAUGHTER. Why?

THE POET. Because—No, it is not the *Dutchman*! It is an ordinary ship in distress. Why does not the buoy cry out now? Look, how the sea is rising—how high the waves are—soon we shall be unable to get out of the cave! Now the ship's bell is ringing— Soon we shall have another figurehead. Cry out, buoy! Do your duty, watchman! [*The buoy sounds a four-voice chord of fifths and sixths, reminding one of fog horns*] The crew is signaling to us—but we are doomed ourselves.

THE DAUGHTER. Do you not wish to be set free?

THE POET. Yes, of course—of course, I wish it—but not just now, and not by water.

THE CREW. [*Sings in quartet*] Christ Kyrie!

Christ   Ky - ri - - e!

THE POET. Now they are crying aloud, and so is the sea, but no one gives ear.

THE CREW. [*As before*] Christ Kyrie!

THE DAUGHTER. Who is coming there?

THE POET. Walking on the waters? There is only one who does that—and it is not Peter, the Rock, for he sank like a stone—

[*A white light is seen shining over the water at some distance.*]

THE CREW. Christ Kyrie!

THE DAUGHTER. Can this be He?

THE POET. It is He, the crucified—

THE DAUGHTER. Why—tell me—why was He crucified?

THE POET. Because He wanted to set free—

THE DAUGHTER. Who was it—I have forgotten—that crucified Him?

THE POET. All the right-minded.

THE DAUGHTER. What a strange world!

THE POET. The sea is rising. Darkness is closing in upon us. The storm is growing—

[THE CREW *set up a wild outcry.*]

THE POET. The crew scream with horror at the sight of their Saviour—and now—they are leaping overboard for fear of the Redeemer—

[THE CREW *utter another cry.*]

THE POET. Now they are crying because they must die. Crying when they are born, and crying when they pass away!

[*The rising waves threaten to engulf the two in the cave.*]

THE DAUGHTER. If I could only be sure that it is a ship—

THE POET. Really—I don't think it is a ship—It is a two-storied house with trees in front of it—and—a telephone tower—a tower that reaches up into the skies—It is the modern Tower of Babel sending wires to the upper regions—to communicate with those above—

THE DAUGHTER. Child, the human thought needs no wires to make a way for itself—the prayers of the pious penetrate the universe. It cannot be a Tower of Babel, for if you want to assail the heavens, you must do so with prayer.

THE POET. No, it is no house—no telephone tower—don't you see?

THE DAUGHTER. What are you seeing?

THE POET. I see an open space covered with snow—a drill ground—The winter sun is shining from behind a church on a hill, and the tower is casting its long shadow on the snow—Now a troop of soldiers come marching across the grounds. They march up along the tower, up the spire. Now they have reached the cross, but I have a feeling that the first one who steps on the gilded weathercock at the top must die. Now they are near it—a corporal is leading them—ha-ha! There comes a cloud sweeping across the open space, and right in front of the sun, of course—now everything is gone—the water in the cloud put out the sun's fire!—The light of the sun created the shadow picture of the tower, but the shadow picture of the cloud swallowed the shadow picture of the tower—

[*While* THE POET *is still speaking, the stage is changed and shows once more the passageway outside the opera-house.*]

THE DAUGHTER. [*To* THE PORTRESS] Has the Lord Chancellor arrived yet?

THE PORTRESS. No.

THE DAUGHTER. And the Deans of the Faculties?

THE PORTRESS. No.

THE DAUGHTER. Call them at once, then, for the door is to be opened—

THE PORTRESS. Is it so very pressing?

THE DAUGHTER. Yes, it is. For there is a suspicion that the solution of the world-riddle may be hidden behind it. Call the Lord Chancellor, and the Deans of the Four Faculties also.

[THE PORTRESS *blows in a whistle.*]

THE DAUGHTER. And do not forget the Glazier and his diamond, for without them nothing can be done.

[STAGE PEOPLE *enter from the left as in the earlier scene.*]

THE OFFICER. [*Enters from the background, in Prince Albert and high hat, with a bunch of roses in his hand, looking radiantly happy*] Victoria!

THE PORTRESS. The young lady will be coming in a moment.

THE OFFICER. Good! The carriage is waiting, the table is set, the wine is on ice—Permit me to embrace you, madam! [*Embraces* THE PORTRESS] Victoria!

A WOMAN'S VOICE FROM ABOVE. [*Sings*] I am here!

THE OFFICER. [*Begins to walk to and fro*] Good! I am waiting.

THE POET. It seems to me that all this has happened before—

THE DAUGHTER. So it seems to me also.

THE POET. Perhaps I have dreamt it.

THE DAUGHTER. Or put it in a poem, perhaps.

THE POET. Or put it in a poem.

THE DAUGHTER. Then you know what poetry is.

THE POET. Then I know what dreaming is.

THE DAUGHTER. It seems to me that we have said all this to each other before, in some other place.

THE POET. Then you may soon figure out what reality is.

THE DAUGHTER. Or dreaming!

THE POET. Or poetry!

[*Enter the* LORD CHANCELLOR *and the* DEANS *of the* THEOLOGICAL, PHILOSOPHICAL, MEDICAL, *and* LEGAL FACULTIES.]

LORD CHANCELLOR. It is about the opening of that door, of course—What does the Dean of the Theological Faculty think of it?

DEAN OF THEOLOGY. I do not think—I believe—*Credo*—

DEAN OF PHILOSOPHY. I hold—

DEAN OF MEDICINE. I know—

DEAN OF JURISPRUDENCE. I doubt until I have evidence and witnesses.

LORD CHANCELLOR. Now they are fighting again!—Well, what does Theology believe?

THEOLOGY. I believe that this door must not be opened, because it hides dangerous truths—

PHILOSOPHY. Truth is never dangerous.

MEDICINE. What is truth?

JURISPRUDENCE. What can be proved by two witnesses.

THEOLOGY. Anything can be proved by two false witnesses—thinks the pettifogger.

PHILOSOPHY. Truth is wisdom, and wisdom, knowledge, is philosophy itself— Philosophy is the science of sciences, the knowledge of knowing, and all other sciences are its servants.

MEDICINE. Natural science is the only true science—and philosophy is no science at all. It is nothing but empty speculation.

THEOLOGY. Good!

PHILOSOPHY. [*To* THEOLOGY] Good, you say! And what are you, then? You are the arch-enemy of all knowledge; you are the very antithesis of knowledge; you are ignorance and obscuration—

MEDICINE. Good!

THEOLOGY. [*To* MEDICINE] You cry "good," you, who cannot see beyond the length of your own nose in the magnifying glass; who believes in nothing but your own unreliable senses—in your vision, for instance, which may be far-sighted, near-sighted, blind, purblind, cross-eyed, one-eyed, color-blind, red-blind, green-blind—

MEDICINE. Idiot!

THEOLOGY. Ass! [*They fight.*]

LORD CHANCELLOR. Peace! One crow does not peck out the other's eye.

PHILOSOPHY. If I had to choose between those two, Theology and Medicine, I should choose—neither!

JURISPRUDENCE. And if I had to sit in judgment on the three of you, I should find—all guilty! You cannot agree on a single point, and you never could. Let us get back to the case in court. What is the opinion of the Lord Chancellor as to this door and its opening?

LORD CHANCELLOR. Opinion? I have no opinion whatever. I am merely appointed by the government to see that you don't break each other's arms and legs in the Council—while you are educating the young! Opinion? Why, I take mighty good care to avoid everything of the kind. Once I had one or two, but they were refuted at once. Opinions are always refuted—by their opponents, of course—But perhaps we might open the door now, even with the risk of finding some dangerous truths behind it?

JURISPRUDENCE. What is truth? What is truth?

THEOLOGY. I am the truth and the life—

PHILOSOPHY. I am the science of sciences—

MEDICINE. I am the only exact science—

JURISPRUDENCE. I doubt [*They fight.*]

THE DAUGHTER. Instructors of the young, take shame!

JURISPRUDENCE. Lord Chancellor, as representative of the government, as head of the corps of instructors, you must prosecute this woman's offence. She has told all of you to take shame, which is an insult; and she has—in a sneering, ironical sense—called you instructors of the young, which is a slanderous speech.

THE DAUGHTER. Poor youth!

JURISPRUDENCE. She pities the young, which is to accuse us. Lord Chancellor, you must prosecute the offence.

THE DAUGHTER. Yes, I accuse you—you in a body—of sowing doubt and discord in the minds of the young.

JURISPRUDENCE. Listen to her—she herself is making the young question our authority, and then she charges us with sowing doubt. Is it not a criminal act, I ask all the right-minded?

ALL. RIGHT-MINDED. Yes, it is criminal.

JURISPRUDENCE. All the right-minded have condemned you. Leave in peace with your lucre, or else—

THE DAUGHTER. My lucre? Or else? What else?

JURISPRUDENCE. Else you will be stoned.

THE POET. Or crucified.

THE DAUGHTER. I leave. Follow me, and you shall learn the riddle.

THE POET. Which riddle?

THE DAUGHTER. What did he mean with "my lucre"?

THE POET. Probably nothing at all. That kind of thing we call talk. He was just talking.

THE DAUGHTER. But it was what hurt me more than anything else!

THE POET. That is why he said it, I suppose—Men are that way.

ALL. RIGHT-MINDED. Hooray! The door is open.

LORD CHANCELLOR. What was behind the door?

THE GLAZIER. I can see nothing.

LORD CHANCELLOR. He cannot see anything—of course, he cannot! Deans of the Faculties: what was behind that door?

THEOLOGY. Nothing! That is the solution of the world riddle. In the beginning God created heaven and the earth out of nothing—

PHILOSOPHY. Out of nothing comes nothing.

MEDICINE. Yes, bosh—which is nothing!

JURISPRUDENCE. I doubt. And this is a case of deception. I appeal to all the right-minded.

THE DAUGHTER. [*To* THE POET] Who are the right-minded?

THE POET. Who can tell? Frequently all the right-minded consist of a single person. To-day it is me and mine; to-morrow it is you and yours. To that position you are appointed—or rather, you appoint yourself to it.

ALL. RIGHT-MINDED. We have been deceived.

LORD CHANCELLOR. Who has deceived you?

ALL. RIGHT-MINDED. The Daughter!

LORD CHANCELLOR. Will the Daughter please tell us what she meant by having this door opened?

THE DAUGHTER. No, friends. If I did, you would not believe me.

MEDICINE. Why, then, there is nothing there.

THE DAUGHTER. You have said it—but you have not understood.

MEDICINE. It is bosh, what she says!

ALL. Bosh!

THE DAUGHTER. [*To* THE POET] They are to be pitied.

THE POET. Are you in earnest?

THE DAUGHTER. Always in earnest.

THE POET. Do you think the right-minded are to be pitied also?

THE DAUGHTER. They most of all, perhaps.

THE POET. And the four faculties, too?

THE DAUGHTER. They also, and not the least. Four heads, four minds, and one body. Who made that monster?

ALL. She has not answered!

LORD CHANCELLOR. Stone her then!

THE DAUGHTER. I have answered.

LORD CHANCELLOR. Hear—she answers.

ALL. Stone her! She answers!

THE DAUGHTER. Whether she answer or do not answer, stone her! Come, prophet, and I shall tell you the riddle—but far away from here—out in the desert, where no one can hear us, no one see us, for—

THE LAWYER. [*Enters and takes* THE DAUGHTER *by the arm*] Have you forgotten your duties?

THE DAUGHTER. Oh, heavens, no! But I have higher duties.

THE LAWYER. And your child?

THE DAUGHTER. My child—what of it?

THE LAWYER. Your child is crying for you.

THE DAUGHTER. My child! Woe, I am earth-bound! And this pain in my breast, this anguish—what is it?

THE LAWYER. Don't you know?

THE DAUGHTER. No.

THE LAWYER. It is remorse.

THE DAUGHTER. Is that remorse?

THE LAWYER. Yes, and it follows every neglected duty; every pleasure, even the most innocent, if innocent pleasures exist, which seems doubtful; and every suffering inflicted upon one's fellow-beings.

THE DAUGHTER. And there is no remedy?

THE LAWYER. Yes, but only one. It consists in doing your duty at once—

THE DAUGHTER. You look like a demon when you speak that word duty—And when, as in my case, there are two duties to be met?

THE LAWYER. Meet one first, and then the other.

THE DAUGHTER. The highest first—therefore, you look after my child, and I shall do my duty——

THE LAWYER. Your child suffers because it misses you—can you bear to know that a human being is suffering for your sake?

THE DAUGHTER. Now strife has entered my soul—it is rent in two, and the halves are being pulled in opposite directions!

THE LAWYER. Such, you know, are life's little discords.

THE DAUGHTER. Oh, how it is pulling!

THE POET. If you could only know how I have spread sorrow and ruin around me by the exercise of my calling—and note that I say *calling*, which carries with it the highest duty of all—then you would not even touch my hand.

THE DAUGHTER. What do you mean?

THE POET. I had a father who put his whole hope on me as his only son, destined to continue his enterprise. I ran away from the business college. My father grieved himself to death. My mother wanted me to be religious, and I could not do what she wanted—and she disowned me. I had a friend who assisted me through trying days of need—and that friend acted as a tyrant against those on whose behalf I was speaking and writing. And I had to strike down my friend and benefactor in order to save my soul. Since then I have had no peace. Men call me devoid of honour, infamous—and it does not help that my conscience says, "you have done right," for in the next moment it is saying, "you have done wrong." Such is life.

THE DAUGHTER. Come with me into the desert.

THE LAWYER. Your child!

THE DAUGHTER. [*Indicating all those present*] Here are my children. By themselves they are good, but if they only come together, then they quarrel and turn into demons— Farewell!

[*Outside the castle. The same scenery as in the first scene of the first act. But now the ground in front of the castle wall is covered with flowers—blue monk's-hood or aconite. On the roof of the castle, at the very top of its lantern, there is a chrysanthemum bud ready to open. The castle windows are illuminated with candles.*]

[THE DAUGHTER *and* THE POET.]

THE DAUGHTER. The hour is not distant when, with the help of the flames, I shall once more ascend to the ether. It is what you call to die, and what you approach in fear.

THE POET. Fear of the unknown.

THE DAUGHTER. Which is known to you.

THE POET. Who knows it?

THE DAUGHTER. All! Why do you not believe your prophets?

THE POET. Prophets have always been disbelieved. Why is that so? And "if God has spoken, why will men not believe then?" His convincing power ought to be irresistible.

THE DAUGHTER. Have you always doubted?

THE POET. No. I have had certainty many times. But after a while it passed away, like a dream when you wake up.

THE DAUGHTER. It is not easy to be human!

THE POET. You see and admit it?

THE DAUGHTER. I do.

THE POET. Listen! Was it not Indra that once sent his son down here to receive the complaints of mankind?

THE DAUGHTER. Thus it happened—and how was he received?

THE POET. How did he fill his mission?—to answer with another question.

THE DAUGHTER. And if I may reply with still another—was not man's position bettered by his visit to the earth? Answer truly!

THE POET. Bettered?—Yes, a little. A very little—But instead of asking questions—will you not tell the riddle?

THE DAUGHTER. Yes. But to what use? You will not believe me.

THE POET. In you I shall believe, for I know who you are.

THE DAUGHTER. Then I shall tell! In the morning of the ages, before the sun was shining, Brahma, the divine primal force, let himself be persuaded by Maya, the world-mother, to propagate himself. This meeting of the divine primal matter with the earth-matter was the fall of heaven into sin. Thus the world, existence, mankind, are nothing but a phantom, an appearance, a dream-image—

THE POET. My dream!

THE DAUGHTER. A dream of truth! But in order to free themselves from the earth-matter, the offspring of Brahma seek privation and suffering. There you have suffering as a liberator. But this craving for suffering comes into conflict with the craving for enjoyment, or love—do you now understand what love is, with its utmost joys merged into its utmost sufferings, with its mixture of what is most sweet and most bitter? Can you now grasp what woman is? Woman, through whom sin and death found their way into life?

THE POET. I understand!—And the end?

THE DAUGHTER. You know it: conflict between the pain of enjoyment and the pleasure of suffering—between the pangs of the penitent and the joys of the prodigal—

THE POET. A conflict it is then?

THE DAUGHTER. Conflict between opposites produces energy, as fire and water give the power of steam—

THE POET. But peace? Rest?

THE DAUGHTER. Hush! You must ask no more, and I can no longer answer. The altar is already adorned for the sacrifice—the flowers are standing guard—the candles are lit—there are white sheets in the windows—spruce boughs have been spread in the gateway—

THE POET. And you say this as calmly as if for you suffering did not exist!

THE DAUGHTER. You think so?—I have suffered all your sufferings, but in a hundredfold degree, for my sensations were so much more acute—

THE POET. Relate your sorrow!

THE DAUGHTER. Poet, could you tell yours so that not one word went too far? Could your word at any time approach your thought?

THE POET. No, you are right! To myself I appeared like one struck dumb, and when the mass listened admiringly to my song, I found it mere noise—for this reason, you see, I have always felt ashamed when they praised me.

THE DAUGHTER. And then you ask me—Look me straight in the eye!

THE POET. I cannot bear your glance—

THE DAUGHTER. How could you bear my word then, were I to speak in your tongue?

THE POET. But tell me at least before you go: from what did you suffer most of all down here?

THE DAUGHTER. From—*being*: to feel my vision weakened by an eye, my hearing blunted by an ear, and my thought, my bright and buoyant thought, bound in labyrinthine coils of fat. You have seen a brain—what roundabout and sneaking paths—

THE POET. Well, that is because all the right-minded think crookedly!

THE DAUGHTER. Malicious, always malicious, all of you!

THE POET. How could one possibly be otherwise?

THE DAUGHTER. First of all I now shake the dust from my feet—the dirt and the clay—

[*Takes off her shoes and puts them into the fire.*]

THE PORTRESS. [*Puts her shawl into the fire*] Perhaps I may burn my shawl at the same time? [*Goes out.*]

THE OFFICER. [*Enters*] And I my roses, of which only the thorns are left. [*Goes out.*]

THE BILLPOSTER. [*Enters*] My bills may go, but never the dipnet! [*Goes out.*]

THE GLAZIER. [*Enters*] The diamond that opened the door—good-bye! [*Goes out.*]

THE LAWYER. [*Enters*] The minutes of the great process concerning the pope's beard or the water loss in the sources of the Ganges. [*Goes out.*]

MASTER OF QUARANTINE. [*Enters*] A small contribution in shape of the black mask that made me a blackamoor against my will! [*Goes out.*]

VICTORIA. [Enters] My beauty, my sorrow! [*Goes out.*]

EDITH. [Enters] My plainness, my sorrow! [*Goes out.*]

THE BLINDMAN. [Enters; puts his hand into the fire] I give my hand for my eye. [*Goes out.*]

[DON JUAN *in his wheel chair;* SHE *and* THE FRIEND.]

DON JUAN. Hurry up! Hurry up! Life is short!

[*Leaves with the other two.*]

THE POET. I have read that when the end of life draws near, everything and everybody rushes by in continuous review—Is this the end?

THE DAUGHTER. Yes, it is my end. Farewell!

THE POET. Give us a parting word.

THE DAUGHTER. No, I cannot. Do you believe that your words can express our thoughts?

DEAN OF THEOLOGY. [*Enters in a rage*] I am cast off by God and persecuted by man; I am deserted by the government and scorned by my colleagues! How am I to believe when nobody else believes? How am I to defend a god that does not defend his own? Bosh, that's what it is!

[*Throws a book on the fire and goes out.*]

THE POET. [*Snatches the book out of the fire*] Do you know what it is? A martyrology, a calendar with a martyr for each day of the year.

THE DAUGHTER. Martyr?

THE POET. Yes, one that has been tortured and killed on account of his faith! Tell me why?—Do you think that all who are tortured suffer, and that all who are killed feel pain? Suffering is said to be salvation, and death a liberation.

CHRISTINE. [*With slips of paper*] I paste, I paste until there is nothing more to paste—

THE POET. And if heaven should split in twain, you would try to paste it together— Away!

CHRISTINE. Are there no double windows in this castle?

THE POET. Not one, I tell you.

CHRISTINE. Well, then I'll go. [*Goes out.*]

THE DAUGHTER. The parting hour has come, the end draws near.

And now farewell, thou dreaming child of man,
Thou singer, who alone knows how to live!
When from thy winged Sight above the earth
At times thou sweepest downward to the dust,
It is to touch it only, not to stay!

And as I go—how, in the parting hour,
As one must leave for e'er a friend, a place.
The heart with longing swells for what one loves,
And with regret for all wherein one failed!
O, now the pangs of life in all their force
I feel: I know at last the lot of man—
Regretfully one views what once was scorned;
For sins one never sinned remorse is felt;
To stay one craves, but equally to leave:
As if to horses tied that pull apart,
One's heart is split in twain, one's feelings rent,
By indecision, contrast, and discord.

Farewell! To all thy fellow-men make known
That where I go I shall forget them not;
And in thy name their grievance shall be placed

Before the throne. Farewell!

[*She goes into the castle. Music is heard. The background is lit up by the burning castle and reveals a wall of human faces, questioning, grieving, despairing. As the castle breaks into flames, the bud on the roof opens into a gigantic chrysanthemum flower.*]

Curtain.

THE GHOST SONATA

CHARACTERS

OLD HUMMEL
The STUDENT, *named Arkenholtz*
The MILKMAID, *an apparition*
The JANITRESS
The GHOST *of the Consul*
The DARK LADY, *daughter of the Consul and the* JANITRESS
The COLONEL
The MUMMY, *wife of the* COLONEL
The YOUNG LADY, *supposedly the* COLONEL'S *daughter, but in reality the daughter of*
    OLD HUMMEL
The DANDY, *called Baron Skansenkorge and engaged to the* DARK LADY
JOHANSSON, *in the service of* HUMMEL
BENGTSSON, *the valet of the* COLONEL
The FIANCÉE, *a white-haired old woman, formerly engaged to* HUMMEL
The COOK
A SERVANT-GIRL
BEGGARS

THE GHOST SONATA

FIRST SCENE

The stage shows the first and second stories of a modern corner house. At the left, the
    house continues into the wings; at the right, it faces on a street supposed to be
    running at right angle to the footlights.
The apartment on the ground floor ends at the corner in a round room, above which is a
    balcony belonging to the apartment on the second floor. A flagstaff is fixed to the
    balcony.
When the shades are raised in the windows of the Round Room, a statue of a young
    woman in white marble becomes visible inside, strongly illumined by sunlight. It is
    surrounded by palms. The windows on the left side of the Round Room contain a
    number of flower-pots, in which grow blue, white, and red hyacinths.
A bed quilt of blue silk and two pillows in white cases are hung over the railing of the
    balcony on the second floor. The windows at the left of the balcony are covered with
    white sheets on the inside.
A green bench stands on the sidewalk in front of the house. The right corner of the
    foreground is occupied by a drinking fountain; the corner at the left, by an
    advertising column.
The main entrance to the house is near the left wing. Through the open doorway appears
    the foot of the stairway, with steps of white marble and a banister of mahogany with
    brass trimmings. On the sidewalk, flanking the entrance, stand two laurel-trees in
    wooden tubs.
At the left of the entrance, there is a window on the ground floor, with a window-mirror

outside.
It is a bright Sunday morning.
When the curtain rises, the bells of several churches are heard ringing in the distance.
The doors of the entrance are wide open, and on the lowest step of the stairway stands
   the DARK LADY. *She does not make the slightest movement.*
The JANITRESS *is sweeping the hallway. Then she polishes the brass knobs on the doors.*
   Finally she waters the laurel-trees.
Near the advertising column, OLD HUMMEL *is reading his paper, seated in an invalid's*
   chair on wheels. His hair and beard are white, and he wears spectacles.
The MILKMAID *enters from the side street, carrying milk-bottles in a crate of wire-work.*
   She wears a light dress, brown shoes, black stockings, and a white cap.
She takes off her cap and hangs it on the fountain; wipes the perspiration from her
   forehead; drinks out of the cup; washes her hands in the basin, and arranges her
   hair, using the water in the basin as a mirror.
A steamship-bell is heard outside. Then the silence is broken fitfully by a few bass notes
   from the organ in the nearest church.
When silence reigns again, and the MILKMAID *has finished her toilet, the* STUDENT
   enters from the left, unshaved and showing plainly that he has spent a sleepless
   night. He goes straight to the fountain. A pause ensues.

STUDENT. Can I have the cup?

   [*The* MILKMAID *draws back with the cup.*]

STUDENT. Are you not almost done?

   [*The* MILKMAID *stares at him with horror.*]

HUMMEL. [*To himself*] With whom is he talking? I don't see anybody. Wonder if he's
   crazy?

   [*He continues to look at them with evident surprise.*]

STUDENT. Why do you stare at me? Do I look so terrible?—It is true that I haven't slept at
   all, and I suppose you think I have been making a night of it

   [*The* MILKMAID *remains as before.*]

STUDENT. You think I have been drinking, do you? Do I smell of liquor?

   [*The* MILKMAID *remains as before.*]

STUDENT. I haven't shaved, of course…. Oh, give me a drink of water, girl. I have earned
   it. [*Pause*] Well? Must I then tell you myself that I have spent the night dressing
   wounds and nursing the injured? You see, I was present when that house collapsed
   last night…. Now you know all about it.

   [*The* MILKMAID *rinses the cup, fills it with water, and hands it to him.*]

STUDENT. Thanks!

[*The* MILKMAID *stands immovable.*]

STUDENT. [*Hesitatingly*] Would you do me a favour? [*Pause*] My eyes are inflamed, as you can see, and my hands have touched wounds and corpses. To touch my eyes with them would be dangerous.... Will you take my handkerchief, which is clean, dip it in the fresh water, and bathe my poor eyes with it?—Will you do that?—Won't you play the good Samaritan?

[*The* MILKMAID *hesitates at first, but does finally what he has asked.*]

STUDENT. Thank you! [*He takes out his purse.*]

[*The* MILKMAID *makes a deprecatory gesture.*]

STUDENT. Pardon my absent-mindedness. I am not awake, you see....

[*The* MILKMAID *disappears.*]

HUMMEL. [*To the* STUDENT] Excuse a stranger, but I heard you mention last night's accident.... I was just reading about it in the paper....
STUDENT. Is it already in the papers?
HUMMEL. All about it. Even your portrait. They are sorry, though, that they have not been able to learn the name of the young student who did such splendid work....
STUDENT. [*Glancing at the paper*] Oh, is that me? Well!
HUMMEL. Whom were you talking to a while ago?
STUDENT. Didn't you see? [*Pause.*]
HUMMEL. Would it be impertinent—to ask—your estimable name?
STUDENT. What does it matter? I don't care for publicity. Blame is always mixed into any praise you may get. The art of belittling is so highly developed. And besides, I ask no reward....
HUMMEL. Wealthy, I suppose?
STUDENT. Not at all—on the contrary—poor as a durmouse!
HUMMEL. Look here.... It seems to me as if I recognised your voice. When I was young, I had a friend who always said "dur" instead of door. Until now he was the one person I had ever heard using that pronunciation. You are the only other one.... Could you possibly be a relative of the late Mr. Arkenholtz, the merchant?
STUDENT. He was my father.
HUMMEL. Wonderful are the ways of life.... I have seen you when you were a small child, under very trying circumstances....
STUDENT. Yes, I have been told that I was born just after my father had gone bankrupt.
HUMMEL. So you were.
STUDENT. May I ask your name?
HUMMEL. I am Mr. Hummel.
STUDENT. You are? Then I remember....
HUMMEL. Have you often heard my name mentioned at home?

STUDENT. I have.

HUMMEL. And not in a pleasant way, I suppose?

[*The* STUDENT *remains silent.*]

HUMMEL. That's what I expected.—You were told, I suppose, that I had ruined your father?—All who are ruined by ill-advised speculations think themselves ruined by those whom they couldn't fool. [*Pause*] The fact of it is, however, that your father robbed me of seventeen thousand crowns, which represented all my savings at that time.

STUDENT. It is queer how the same story can be told in quite different ways.

HUMMEL. You don't think that I am telling the truth?

STUDENT. How can I tell what to think? My father was not in the habit of lying.

HUMMEL. No, that's right, a father never lies.... But I am also a father, and for that reason....

STUDENT. What are you aiming at?

HUMMEL. I saved your father from misery, and he repaid me with the ruthless hatred that is born out of obligation.... He taught his family to speak ill of me.

STUDENT. Perhaps you made him ungrateful by poisoning your assistance with needless humiliation.

HUMMEL. All assistance is humiliating, sir.

STUDENT. And what do you ask of me now?

HUMMEL. Not the money back. But if you will render me a small service now and then, I shall consider myself well paid. I am a cripple, as you see. Some people say it is my own fault. Others lay it to my parents. I prefer to blame life itself, with its snares. To escape one of these snares is to walk headlong into another. As it is, I cannot climb stairways or ring door-bells, and for that reason I ask you: will you help me a little?

STUDENT. What can I do for you?

HUMMEL. Give my chair a push, to begin with, so that I can read the bills on that column. I wish to see what they are playing to-night.

STUDENT. [*Pushing the chair as directed*] Have you no attendant?

HUMMEL. Yes, but he is doing an errand. He'll be back soon. Are you a medical student?

STUDENT. No, I am studying philology, but I don't know what profession to choose....

HUMMEL. Well, well! Are you good at mathematics?

STUDENT. Reasonably so.

HUMMEL. That's good! Would you care to accept a position?

STUDENT. Yes, why not?

HUMMEL. Fine! [*Studying the playbills*] They are playing "The Valkyr" at the matinee.... Then the Colonel will be there with his daughter, and as he always has the end seat in the sixth row, I'll put you next to him.... Will you please go over to that telephone kiosk and order a ticket for seat eighty-two, in the sixth row?

STUDENT. Must I go to the opera in the middle of the day?

HUMMEL. Yes. Obey me, and you'll prosper. I wish to see you happy, rich, and honored. Your debut last night in the part of the brave rescuer will have made you famous by to-morrow, and then your name will be worth a great deal.

STUDENT. [*On his way out to telephone*] What a ludicrous adventure!

HUMMEL. Are you a sportsman?

STUDENT. Yes, that has been my misfortune.

HUMMEL. Then we'll turn it into good fortune.—Go and telephone now.

[*The* STUDENT *goes out.* HUMMEL *begins to read his paper again. In the meantime the* DARK LADY *has come out on the sidewalk and stands talking to the* JANITRESS. HUMMEL *is taking in their conversation, of which, however, nothing is audible to the public. After a while the* STUDENT *returns.*]

HUMMEL. Ready?

STUDENT. It's done.

HUMMEL. Have you noticed this house?

STUDENT. Yes, I have been watching it.... I happened to pass by yesterday, when the sun was making every window-pane glitter.... And thinking of all the beauty and luxury that must be found within, I said to my companion: "Wouldn't it be nice to have an apartment on the fifth floor, a beautiful young wife, two pretty little children, and an income of twenty thousand crowns?"....

HUMMEL. So you said that? Did you really? Well, well! I am very fond of this house, too....

STUDENT. Do you speculate in houses?

HUMMEL. Mm-yah! But not in the way you mean.

STUDENT. Do you know the people who live here?

HUMMEL. All of them. A man of my age knows everybody, including their parents and grandparents, and in some manner he always finds himself related to everyone else. I am just eighty—but nobody knows me—not through and through. I am very much interested in human destinies.

[*At that moment the shades are raised in the Round Room on the ground floor, and the* COLONEL *becomes visible, dressed in civilian clothes. He goes to one of the windows to study the thermometer outside. Then he turns back into the room and stops in front of the marble statue.*]

HUMMEL. There's the Colonel now, who will sit next to you at the opera this afternoon.

STUDENT. Is *he*—the Colonel? I don't understand this at all, but it's like a fairy-tale.

HUMMEL. All my life has been like a collection of fairy-tales, my dear sir. Although the tales read differently, they are all strung on a common thread, and the dominant theme recurs constantly.

STUDENT. Whom does that statue represent?

HUMMEL. His wife, of course.

STUDENT. Was she very lovely?

HUMMEL. Mm-yah—well....

STUDENT. Speak out.

HUMMEL. Oh, we can't form any judgment about people, my dear boy. And if I told you that she left him, that he beat her, that she returned to him, that she married him a second time, and that she is living there now in the shape of a mummy, worshipping her own statue—then you would think me crazy.

STUDENT. I don't understand at all.

HUMMEL. I didn't expect you would. Then there is the window with the hyacinths. That's where his daughter lives. She is out for a ride now, but she will be home in a few moments.

STUDENT. And who is the dark lady talking to the janitress?

HUMMEL. The answer is rather complicated, but it is connected with the dead man on the second floor, where you see the white sheets.

STUDENT. Who was he?

HUMMEL. A human being like you or me, but the most conspicuous thing about him was his vanity.... If you were born on a Sunday, you might soon see him come down the stairway and go out on the sidewalk to make sure that the flag of the consulate is half-masted. You see, he was a consul, and he reveled in coronets and lions and plumed hats and colored ribbons.

STUDENT. You spoke of being born on a Sunday.... So was I, I understand.

HUMMEL. No! Really?.... Oh, I should have known.... The color of your eyes shows it.... Then you can see what other people can't. Have you noticed anything of that kind?

STUDENT. Of course, I can't tell what other people see or don't see, but at times.... Oh, such things you don't talk of!

HUMMEL. I was sure of it! And you can talk to me, because I—I understand—things of that kind....

STUDENT. Yesterday, for instance.... I was drawn to that little side street where the house fell down afterward.... When I got there, I stopped in front of the house, which I had never seen before.... Then I noticed a crack in the wall.... I could hear the floor beams snapping.... I rushed forward and picked up a child that was walking in front of the house at the time.... In another moment the house came tumbling down.... I was saved, but in my arms, which I thought held the child, there was nothing at all....

HUMMEL. Well, I must say!.... Much as I have heard.... Please tell me one thing: what made you act as you did by the fountain a while ago? Why were you talking to yourself?

STUDENT. Didn't you see the Milkmaid to whom I was talking?

HUMMEL. [*Horrified*] A milkmaid?

STUDENT. Yes, the girl who handed me the cup.

HUMMEL. Oh, that's what it was.... Well, I haven't that kind of sight, but there are other things....

[*A white-haired old woman is seen at the window beside the entrance, looking into the window-mirror.*]

HUMMEL. Look at that old woman in the window. Do you see her?—Well, she was my fiancée once upon a time, sixty years ago.... I was twenty at that time.... Never mind, she does not recognise me. We see each other every day, and I hardly notice her—although once we vowed to love each other eternally.... Eternally!

STUDENT. How senseless you were in those days! We don't talk to our girls like that.

HUMMEL. Forgive us, young man! We didn't know better.—Can you see that she was young and pretty once?

STUDENT. It doesn't show.... Oh, yes, she has a beautiful way of looking at things, although I can't see her eyes clearly.

[*The* JANITRESS *comes out with a basket on her arm and begins to cover the sidewalk with chopped hemlock branches, as is usual in Sweden when a funeral is to be held.*]

HUMMEL. And the Janitress—hm! That Dark Lady is her daughter and the dead man's, and that's why her husband was made janitor.... But the Dark Lady has a lover, who is a dandy with great expectations. He is now getting a divorce from his present wife, who is giving him an apartment-house to get rid of him. This elegant lover is the son-in-law of the dead man, and you can see his bedclothes being aired on the balcony up there.... That's a bit complicated, I should say!

STUDENT. Yes, it's fearfully complicated.

HUMMEL. It certainly is, inside and outside, no matter how simple it may look.

STUDENT. But who was the dead man?

HUMMEL. So you asked me a while ago, and I answered you. If you could look around the corner, where the servants' entrance is, you would see a lot of poor people whom he used to help—when he was in the mood....

STUDENT. He was a kindly man, then?

HUMMEL. Yes—at times.

STUDENT. Not always?

HUMMEL. No-o.... People are like that!—Will you please move the chair a little, so that I get into the sunlight? I am always cold. You see, the blood congeals when you can't move about.... Death isn't far away from me, I know, but I have a few things to do before it comes.... Just take hold of my hand and feel how cold I am.

STUDENT. [*Taking his hand*] I should say so!

[*He shrinks back.*]

HUMMEL. Don't leave me! I am tired now, and lonely, but I haven't always been like this, you know. I have an endlessly long life back of—enormously long.... I have made people unhappy, and other people have made me unhappy, and one thing has to be put against the other, but before I die, I wish to see you happy.... Our destinies have become intertwined, thanks to your father—and many other things....

STUDENT. Let go my hand! You are taking all my strength! You are freezing me! What do you want of me?

HUMMEL. Patience, and you'll see, and understand.... There comes the Young Lady now....

STUDENT. The Colonel's daughter?

HUMMEL. His daughter—yes! Look at her!—Did you ever see such a masterpiece?

STUDENT. She resembles the marble statue in there.

HUMMEL. It's her mother.

STUDENT. You are right.... Never did I see such a woman of woman born!—Happy the man who may lead her to the altar and to his home!

HUMMEL. You see it, then? Her beauty is not discovered by everybody.... Then it is written in the book of life!

[*The* YOUNG LADY *enters from the left, wearing a close-fitting English riding-suit. Without looking at any one, she walks slowly to the entrance, where she stops and exchanges a few words with the* JANITRESS. *Then she disappears into the house. The* STUDENT *covers his eyes with his hand.*]

HUMMEL. Are you crying?

STUDENT. Can you meet what is hopeless with anything but despair?

HUMMEL. I have the power of opening doors and hearts, if I can only find an arm to do my will.... Serve me, and you shall also have power....

STUDENT. Is it to be a bargain? Do you want me to sell my soul?

HUMMEL. Don't sell anything!.... You see, all my life I have been used to *take*. Now I have a craving to give—to give! But no one will accept.... I am rich, very rich, but have no heirs except a scamp who is tormenting the life out of me.... Become my son! Inherit me while I am still alive! Enjoy life, and let me look on—from a distance, at least!

STUDENT. What am I to do?

HUMMEL. Go and hear "The Valkyr" first of all.

STUDENT. That's settled—but what more?

HUMMEL. This evening you shall be in the Round Room.

STUDENT. How am I to get there?

HUMMEL. Through "The Valkyr."

STUDENT. Why have you picked me to be your instrument? Did you know me before?

HUMMEL. Of course, I did! I have had my eyes on you for a long time.... Look at the balcony now, where the Maid is raising the flag at half-mast in honor of the consul.... And then she turns the bedclothes.... Do you notice that blue quilt? It was made to cover two, and now it is only covering one.... [*The* YOUNG LADY *appears at her window, having changed dress in the meantime; she waters the hyacinths*] There is my little girl now. Look at her—look! She is talking to her flowers, and she herself looks like a blue hyacinth. She slakes their thirst—with pure water only—and they transform the water into color and fragrance.... There comes the Colonel with the newspaper! He shows her the story about the house that fell down—and he points at your portrait! She is not indifferent—she reads of your deeds.... It's clouding up, I think.... I wonder if it's going to rain? Then I shall be in a nice fix, unless Johansson comes back soon.... [*The sun has disappeared, and now the stage is growing darker; the white-haired old woman closes her window*] Now my fiancée is closing her window.... She is seventy-nine—and the only mirror she uses is the window mirror, because there she sees not herself, but the world around her—and she sees it from two sides—but it has not occurred to her that she can be seen by the world, too.... A handsome old lady, after all....

[*Now the* GHOST, *wrapped in winding sheets, comes out of the entrance.*]

STUDENT. Good God, what is that I see?

HUMMEL. What *do* you see?

STUDENT. Don't *you* see?.... There, at the entrance.... The dead man?

HUMMEL. I see nothing at all, but that was what I expected. Tell me....

STUDENT. He comes out in the street.... [*Pause*] Now he turns his head to look at the flag.

HUMMEL. What did I tell you? And you may be sure that he will count the wreaths and study the visiting-cards attached to them.... And I pity anybody that is missing!

STUDENT. Now he goes around the corner....

HUMMEL. He wants to count the poor at the other entrance.... The poor are so decorative, you know.... "Followed by the blessings of many".... But he won't get any blessing from me!—Between us, he was a big rascal!

STUDENT. But charitable....

HUMMEL. A charitable rascal, who always had in mind the splendid funeral he expected to get.... When he knew that his end was near, he cheated the state out of fifty thousand crowns.... And now his daughter goes about with another woman's husband, and wonders what is in his will.... Yes, the rascal can hear every word we say, and he is welcome to it!—There comes Johansson now.

[JOHANSSON enters from the left.]

HUMMEL. Report!

[JOHANSSON *can be seen speaking, but not a word of what he says is heard.*]

HUMMEL. Not at home, you say? Oh, you are no good!—Any telegram?—Not a thing.... Go on!—Six o'clock to-night?—That's fine!—An extra, you say?—With his full name?—Arkenholtz, a student, yes.... Born.... Parents.... That's splendid!.... I think it's beginning to rain.... What did he say?—Is that so?—He won't?—Well, then he must!—Here comes the Dandy.... Push me around the corner, Johansson, so I can hear what the poor people have to say.... [*To the* STUDENT] And you had better wait for me here, Arkenholtz.... Do you understand?—[*To* JOHANSSON] Hurry up now, hurry up!

[JOHANSSON *pushes the chair into the side street and out of sight. The* STUDENT *remains on the same spot, looking at the* YOUNG LADY, *who is using a small rake to loosen up the earth in her pots. The* DANDY *enters and joins the* DARK LADY, *who has been walking back and forth on the sidewalk. He is in mourning.*]

DANDY. Well, what is there to do about it? We simply have to wait.
DARK LADY. But I can't wait!
DANDY. Is that so? Then you'll have to go to the country.
DARK LADY. I don't want to!
DANDY. Come this way, or they'll hear what we are saying.

[*They go toward the advertising column and continue their talk inaudibly.*]

JOHANSSON. [*Entering from the right; to the* STUDENT] My master asks you not to forget that other thing.
STUDENT. [*Dragging his words*] Look here.... Tell me, please.... Who *is* your master?
JOHANSSON. Oh, he's so many things, and he has been everything....
STUDENT. Is he in his right mind?
JOHANSSON. Who can tell?—All his life he has been looking for one born on Sunday, he says—which does not mean that it must be true....
STUDENT. What is he after? Is he a miser?
JOHANSSON. He wants to rule.... The whole day long he travels about in his chair like the god of thunder himself.... He looks at houses, tears them down, opens up new streets, fills the squares with buildings.... At the same time he breaks into houses, sneaks through open windows, plays havoc with human destinies, kills his enemies, and refuses to forgive anything.... Can you imagine that a cripple like him has been a Don Juan—but one who has always lost the women he loved?

STUDENT. How can you make those things go together?

JOHANSSON. He is so full of guile that he can make the women leave him when he is tired of them.... Just now he is like a horse thief practicing at a slave-market.... He steals human beings, and in all sorts of ways.... He has literally stolen me out of the hands of the law.... Hm.... yes.... I had been guilty of a slip. And no one but he knew of it. Instead of putting me in jail, he made a slave of me. All I get for my slavery is the food I eat, which might be better at that....

STUDENT. And what does he wish to do in this house here?

JOHANSSON. No, I don't want to tell! It's too complicated....

STUDENT. I think I'll run away from the whole story

[*The* YOUNG LADY *drops a bracelet out of the window so that it falls on the sidewalk.*]

JOHANSSON. Did you see the Young Lady drop her bracelet out of the window?

[*Without haste, the* STUDENT *picks up the bracelet and hands it to the* YOUNG LADY, *who thanks him rather stiffly; then he returns to* JOHANSSON.]

JOHANSSON. So you want to run away? That is more easily said than done when *he* has got you in his net.... And he fears nothing between heaven and earth.... except one thing....or one person rather....

STUDENT. Wait—I think I know!

JOHANSSON. How could you?

STUDENT. I can guess! Is it not—a little milkmaid that he fears?

JOHANSSON. He turns his head away whenever he meets a milk wagon.... And at times he talks in his sleep.... He must have been in Hamburg at one time, I think....

STUDENT. Is this man to be trusted?

JOHANSSON. You may trust him—to do anything!

STUDENT. What is he doing around the corner now?

JOHANSSON. Watching the poor.... dropping a word here and a word there.... loosening a stone at a time.... until the whole house comes tumbling down, metaphorically speaking.... You see, I am an educated man, and I used to be a book dealer.... Are you going now?

STUDENT. I find it hard to be ungrateful.... Once upon a time he saved my father, and now he asks a small service in return....

JOHANSSON. What is it?

STUDENT. To go and see "The Valkyr"....

JOHANSSON. That's beyond me.... But he is always up to new tricks.... Look at him now, talking to the policeman! He is always thick with the police. He uses them. He snares them in their own interests. He ties their hands by arousing their expectations with false promises—while all the time he is pumping them.... You'll see that he is received in the Round Room before the day is over!

STUDENT. What does he want there? What has he to do with the Colonel?

JOHANSSON. I think I can guess, but know nothing with certainty. But you'll see for yourself when you get there!

STUDENT. I'll never get there....

JOHANSSON. That depends on yourself!—Go to "The Valkyr."

STUDENT. Is that the road?

JOHANSSON. Yes, if he has said so—Look at him there—look at him in his war chariot, drawn in triumph by the Beggars, who get nothing for their pains but a hint of a great treat to be had at his funeral.

[OLD HUMMEL *appears standing in his invalid's chair, which is drawn by one of the* BEGGARS, *and followed by the rest.*]

HUMMEL. Give honor to the noble youth who, at the risk of his own, saved so many lives in yesterday's accident! Three cheers for Arkenholtz!

[*The* BEGGARS *bare their heads, but do not cheer. The* YOUNG LADY *appears at her window, waving her handkerchief. The Colonel gazes at the scene from a window in the Round Room. The* FIANCÉE *rises at her window. The* MAID *appears on the balcony and hoists the flag to the top.*]

HUMMEL. Applaud, citizens! It is Sunday, of course, but the ass in the pit and the ear in the field will absolve us. Although I was not born on a Sunday, I have the gift of prophecy and of healing, and on one occasion I brought a drowned person back to life.... That happened in Hamburg on a Sunday morning just like this....

[*The* MILKMAID *enters, seen only by the* STUDENT *and* HUMMEL. *She raises her arms with the movement of a drowning person, while gazing fixedly at* HUMMEL.]

HUMMEL. [*Sits down; then he crumbles in a heap, stricken with horror*] Get me out of here, Johansson! Quick!—Arkenholtz, don't forget "The Valkyr!"
STUDENT. What is the meaning of all this?
JOHANSSON. We'll see! We'll see!

Curtain.

SECOND SCENE

In the Round Room. An oven of white, glazed bricks occupies the centre of the background. The mantelpiece is covered by a large mirror. An ornamental clock and candelabra stand on the mantel-shelf.
At the right of the mantelpiece is a door leading into a hallway, back of which may be seen a room papered in green, with mahogany furniture. The Colonel is seated at a writing-desk, so that only his back is visible to the public.
The statue stands at the left, surrounded by palms and with draperies arranged so that it can be hidden entirely.
A door at the left of the mantelpiece opens on the Hyacinth Room, where the Young Lady is seen reading a book.

[BENGTSSON, *the valet, enters from the hallway, dressed in livery. He is followed by* JOHANSSON *in evening dress with white tie.*]

BENGTSSON. Now you'll have to do the waiting, Johansson, while I take the overclothes. Do you know how to do it?

JOHANSSON. Although I am pushing a war chariot in the daytime, as you know, I wait in private houses at night, and I have always dreamt of getting into this place.... Queer sort of people, hm?

BENGTSSON. Yes, a little out of the ordinary, one might say.

JOHANSSON. Is it a musicale, or what is it?

BENGTSSON. The usual spook supper, as we call it. They drink tea and don't say a word, or else the Colonel does all the talking. And then they munch their biscuits, all at the same time, so that it sounds like the gnawing of a lot of rats in an attic.

JOHANSSON. Why do you call it a spook supper?

BENGTSSON. Because they look like spooks.... And they have kept this up for twenty years—always the same people, saying the same things or keeping silent entirely, lest they be put to shame.

JOHANSSON. Is there not a lady in the house, too?

BENGTSSON. Yes, but she is a little cracked. She sits all the time in a closet, because her eyes can't bear the light. [*He points at a papered door*] She is in there now.

JOHANSSON. In there, you say?

BENGTSSON. I told you they were a little out of the ordinary....

JOHANSSON. How does she look?

BENGTSSON. Like a mummy.... Would you care to look at her? [*He opens the papered door*] There she is now!

JOHANSSON. Mercy!

MUMMY. [*Talking baby talk*] Why does he open the door? Haven't I told him to keep it closed?

BENGTSSON. [*In the same way*] Ta-ta-ta-ta! Polly must be nice now. Then she'll get something good. Pretty polly!

MUMMY. [*Imitating a parrot*] Pretty polly! Are you there, Jacob? Currrrr!

BENGTSSON. She thinks herself a parrot, and maybe she's right.... [*To the* MUMMY] Whistle for us, Polly.

[*The* MUMMY *whistles.*]

JOHANSSON. Much I have seen, but never the like of it!

BENGTSSON. Well, you see, a house gets mouldy when it grows old, and when people are too much together, tormenting each other all the time, they lose their reason. The lady of this house.... Shut up, Polly!.... That mummy has been living here forty years—with the same husband, the same furniture, the same relatives, the same friends.... [*He closes the papered door*] And the happenings this house has witnessed!.... Well, it's beyond me.... Look at that statue. That's the selfsame lady in her youth.

JOHANSSON. Good Lord! Can that be the Mummy?

BENGTSSON. Yes, it's enough to make you weep!—And somehow, carried away by her own imagination, perhaps, she has developed some of the traits of the talkative parrot.... She can't stand cripples or sick people, for instance.... She can't bear the sight of her own daughter, because she is sick....

JOHANSSON. Is the Young Lady sick?

BENGTSSON. Don't you know that?

JOHANSSON. No.—And the Colonel—who is he?

BENGTSSON. That remains to be seen!

JOHANSSON. [*Looking at the statue*] It's horrible to think that.... How old is she now?

BENGTSSON. Nobody knows. But at thirty-five she is said to have looked like nineteen, and that's the age she gave to the Colonel.... In this house.... Do you know what that Japanese screen by the couch is used for? They call it the Death Screen, and it is placed in front of the bed when somebody is dying, just as they do in hospitals....

JOHANSSON. This must be an awful house! And the Student was longing for it as for paradise....

BENGTSSON. What student? Oh, I know! The young chap who is coming here to-night.... The Colonel and the Young Lady met him at the opera and took a great fancy to him at once.... Hm!.... But now it's my turn to ask questions. Who's your master? The man in the invalid's chair?....

JOHANSSON. Well, well! Is he coming here, too?

BENGTSSON. He has not been invited.

JOHANSSON. He'll come without invitation—if necessary.

[OLD HUMMEL *appears in the hallway, dressed in frock coat and high hat. He uses crutches, but moves without a noise, so that he is able to listen to the two servants.*]

BENGTSSON. He's a sly old guy, isn't he?

JOHANSSON. Yes, he's a good one!

BENGTSSON. He looks like the very devil.

JOHANSSON. He's a regular wizard, I think.... because he can pass through locked doors....

HUMMEL. [*Comes forward and pinches the ear of* JOHANSSON] Look out, you scoundrel! [*To* BENGTSSON] Tell the Colonel I am here.

BENGTSSON. We expect company....

HUMMEL. I know, but my visit is as good as expected, too, although not exactly desired, perhaps....

BENGTSSON. I see! What's the name? Mr. Hummel?

HUMMEL. That's right.

[BENGTSSON *crosses the hallway to the Green Room, the door of which he closes behind him.*]

HUMMEL. [*To* JOHANSSON] Vanish!

[JOHANSSON *hesitates.*]

HUMMEL. Vanish, I say!

[JOHANSSON *disappears through the hallway.*]

HUMMEL. [*Looking around and finally stopping in front of the statue, evidently much surprised*] Amelia!—It is she!—She!

[*He takes another turn about the room, picking up various objects to look at them; then he stops in front of the mirror to arrange his wig; finally he returns to the statue.*]

MUMMY. [*In the closet*] Prrretty Polly!

HUMMEL. [*Startled*] What was that? Is there a parrot in the room? I don't see it!

MUMMY. Are you there, Jacob?

HUMMEL. The place is haunted!

MUMMY. Jacob!

HUMMEL. Now I am scared!.... So that's the kind of secrets they have been keeping in this house! [*He stops in front of a picture with his back turned to the closet*] And that's he.... He!

MUMMY. [*Comes out of the closet and pulls the wig of* HUMMEL] Currrrr! Is that Currrrr?

HUMMEL. [*Almost lifted off his feet by fright*] Good Lord in heaven!.... Who are you?

MUMMY. [*Speaking in a normal voice*] Is that you, Jacob?

HUMMEL. Yes, my name is Jacob....

MUMMY. [*Deeply moved*] And my name is Amelia!

HUMMEL. Oh, no, no, no!—Merciful heavens!...

MUMMY. How I look! That's right!—And *have* looked like that! [*Pointing to the statue*] Life is a pleasant thing, is it not?.... I live mostly in the closet, both in order to see nothing and not to be seen.... But, Jacob, what do you want here?

HUMMEL. My child.... our child....

MUMMY. There she sits.

HUMMEL. Where?

MUMMY. There—in the Hyacinth Room.

HUMMEL. [*Looking at the* YOUNG LADY] Yes, that is she! [*Pause*] And what does her father say.... I mean the Colonel.... your husband?

MUMMY. Once, when I was angry with him, I told him everything....

HUMMEL. And?....

MUMMY. He didn't believe me. All he said was: "That's what all women say when they wish to kill their husbands."—It is a dreadful crime, nevertheless. His whole life has been turned into a lie—his family tree, too. Sometimes I take a look in the peerage, and then I say to myself: "Here she is going about with a false birth certificate, just like any runaway servant-girl, and for such things people are sent to the reformatory."

HUMMEL. Well, it's quite common. I think I recall a certain incorrectness in regard to the date of your own birth....

MUMMY. It was my mother who started that.... I was not to blame for it.... And it was you, after all, who had the greater share in our guilt....

HUMMEL. No, what wrong we did was provoked by your husband when he took my fiancée away from me! I was born a man who cannot forgive until he has punished. To punish has always seemed an imperative duty to me—and so it seems still!

MUMMY. What are you looking for in this house? What do you want? How did you get in?—Does it concern my daughter? If you touch her, you must die!

HUMMEL. I mean well by her!

MUMMY. And you have to spare her father!

HUMMEL. No!

MUMMY. Then you must die.... in this very room.... back of that screen....

HUMMEL. Perhaps.... but I can't let go when I have got my teeth in a thing....

MUMMY. You wish to marry her to the Student? Why? He is nothing and has nothing.

HUMMEL. He will be rich, thanks to me.

MUMMY. Have you been invited for to-night?

HUMMEL. No, but I intend to get an invitation for your spook supper.

MUMMY. Do you know who will be here?

HUMMEL. Not quite.

MUMMY. The Baron—he who lives above us, and whose father-in-law was buried this afternoon....

HUMMEL. The man who is getting a divorce to marry the daughter of the Janitress.... The man who used to be—your lover!

MUMMY. Another guest will be your former fiancée, who was seduced by my husband....

HUMMEL. Very select company!

MUMMY. If the Lord would let us die! Oh, that we might only die!

HUMMEL. But why do you continue to associate?

MUMMY. Crime and guilt and secrets bind us together, don't you know? Our ties have snapped so that we have slipped apart innumerable times, but we are always drawn together again....

HUMMEL. I think the Colonel is coming.

MUMMY. I'll go in to Adèle, then.... [*Pause*] Consider what you do, Jacob! Spare him....

[*Pause; then she goes out.*]

COLONEL. [*Enters, haughty and reserved*] Won't you be seated, please?

[HUMMEL *seats himself with great deliberation; pause.*]

COLONEL. [*Staring at his visitor*] You wrote this letter, sir?

HUMMEL. I did.

COLONEL. Your name is Hummel?

HUMMEL. It is. [*Pause.*]

COLONEL. As I learn that you have bought up all my unpaid and overdue notes, I conclude that I am at your mercy. What do you want?

HUMMEL. Payment—in one way or another.

COLONEL. In what way?

HUMMEL. A very simple one. Let us not talk of the money. All you have to do is to admit me as a guest....

COLONEL. If a little thing like that will satisfy you....

HUMMEL. I thank you.

COLONEL. Anything more?

HUMMEL. Discharge Bengtsson.

COLONEL. Why should I do so? My devoted servant, who has been with me a lifetime, and who has the medal for long and faithful service.... Why should I discharge him?

HUMMEL. Those wonderful merits exist only in your imagination. He is not the man he seems to be.

COLONEL. *Who is?*

HUMMEL. [*Taken back*] True!—But Bengtsson must go!

COLONEL. Do you mean to order my household?

HUMMEL. I do.... as everything visible here belongs to me.... furniture, draperies, dinner ware, linen.... and other things!

COLONEL. What other things?

HUMMEL. Everything! All that is to be seen is mine! I own it!

COLONEL. Granted! But for all that, my coat of arms and my unspotted name belong to myself.

HUMMEL. No—not even that much! [*Pause*] You are not a nobleman!

COLONEL. Take care!

HUMMEL. [*Producing a document*] If you'll read this extract from the armorial, you will see that the family whose name you are using has been extinct for a century.

COLONEL. [*Reading the document*] I have heard rumours to that effect, but the name was my father's before it was mine.... [*Reading again*] That's right! Yes, you are right—I am not a nobleman! Not even that!—Then I may as well take off my signet-ring.... Oh, I remember now.... It belongs to you.... If you please!

HUMMEL. [*Accepting the ring and putting it into his pocket*] We had better continue. You are no colonel, either.

COLONEL. Am I not?

HUMMEL. No, you have simply held the title of colonel in the American volunteer service by special appointment. After the war in Cuba and the reorganization of the army, all titles of that kind were abolished....

COLONEL. Is that true?

HUMMEL. [*With a gesture toward his pocket*] Do you wish to see for yourself?

COLONEL. No, it won't be necessary.—Who are you, anyhow, and with what right are you stripping me naked in this fashion?

HUMMEL. You'll see by and by. As to stripping you naked—do you know who you are in reality?

COLONEL. How dare you?

HUMMEL. Take off that wig, and have a look at yourself in the mirror. Take out that set of false teeth and shave off your moustache, too. Let Bengtsson remove the iron stays—and perhaps a certain X Y Z, a lackey, may begin to recognise himself—the man who used to visit the maid's chamber in a certain house for a bite of something good....

[*The* COLONEL *makes a movement toward a table on which stands a bell, but is checked by* HUMMEL.]

HUMMEL. Don't touch that bell, and don't call Bengtsson! If you do, I'll have him arrested.... Now the guests are beginning to arrive.... Keep your composure, and let us continue to play our old parts for a while.

COLONEL. Who are you? Your eyes and your voice remind me of somebody....

HUMMEL. Don't try to find out! Keep silent and obey!

STUDENT. [*Enters and bows to the* COLONEL] Colonel!

COLONEL. I bid you welcome to my house, young man. Your splendid behaviour in connection with that great disaster has brought your name to everybody's lips, and I count it an honor to receive you here....

STUDENT. Being a man of humble birth, Colonel....and considering your name and position....

COLONEL. May I introduce?—Mr. Arkenholtz—Mr. Hummel. The ladies are in there, Mr. Arkenholtz—if you please—I have a few more things to talk over with Mr. HUMMEL....

[*Guided by the* COLONEL, *the* STUDENT *goes into the Hyacinth Room, where he remains visible, standing beside the* YOUNG LADY *and talking very timidly to her.*]

COLONEL. A splendid young chap—very musical—sings, and writes poetry…. If he were only a nobleman—if he belonged to our class, I don't think I should object….
HUMMEL. To what?
COLONEL. Oh, my daughter….
HUMMEL. *Your* daughter, you say?—But apropos of that, why is she always sitting in that room?
COLONEL. She has to spend all her time in the Hyacinth Room when she is not out. That is a peculiarity of hers…. Here comes Miss Betty von Holstein-Kron—a charming woman—a Secular Canoness, with just enough money of her own to suit her birth and position….
HUMMEL. [*To himself*] My fiancée!

[*The* FIANCÉE *enters. She is white-haired, and her looks indicate a slightly unbalanced mind.*]

COLONEL. Miss von Holstein-Kron—Mr. Hummel.

[*The* FIANCÉE *curtseys in old-fashioned manner and takes a seat. The* DANDY *enters and seats himself; he is in mourning and has a very mysterious look.*]

COLONEL. Baron Skansenkorge….
HUMMEL. [*Aside, without rising*] That's the jewelry thief, I think…. [*To the* COLONEL] If you bring in the Mummy, our gathering will be complete.
COLONEL. [*Going to the door of the Hyacinth Room*] Polly!
MUMMY. [*Enters*] Currrrrr!
COLONEL. How about the young people?
HUMMEL. No, not the young people! They must be spared.

[*The company is seated in a circle, no one saying a word for a while.*]

COLONEL. Shall we order the tea now?
HUMMEL. What's the use? No one cares for tea, and I can't see the need of pretending. [*Pause.*]
COLONEL. Shall we make conversation?
HUMMEL. [*Speaking slowly and with frequent pauses*] Talk of the weather, which we know all about? Ask one another's state of health, which we know just as well? I prefer silence. Then thoughts become audible, and we can see the past. Silence can hide nothing—but words can. I read the other day that the differentiation of languages had its origin in the desire among savage peoples to keep their tribal secrets hidden from outsiders. This means that every language is a code, and he who finds the universal key can understand every language in the world—which does not prevent the secret from becoming revealed without any key at times, and especially when the fact of paternity is to be proved—but, of course, legal proof is a different matter. Two false witnesses suffice to prove anything on which they agree, but you

don't bring any witnesses along on the kind of expedition I have in mind. Nature herself has planted in man a sense of modesty, which tends to hide that which should be hidden. But we slip into situations unawares, and now and then a favourable chance will reveal the most cherished secret, stripping the impostor of his mask, and exposing the villain....

[*Long pause during which everybody is subject to silent scrutiny by all the rest.*]

HUMMEL. How silent everybody is! [*Long silence*] Here, for instance, in this respectable house, this attractive home, where beauty and erudition and wealth have joined hands.... [*Long silence*] All of us sitting here now—we know who we are, don't we? I don't need to tell.... And all of you know me, although you pretend ignorance.... In the next room is my daughter—*mine*, as you know perfectly well. She has lost the desire to live without knowing why.... The fact is that she has been pining away in this air charged with crime and deceit and falsehood of every kind.... That is the reason why I have looked for a friend in whose company she may enjoy the light and heat radiated by noble deeds.... [*Long silence*] Here is my mission in this house: to tear up the weeds, to expose the crimes, to settle all accounts, so that those young people may start life with a clean slate in a home that is my gift to them. [*Long silence*] Now I grant you safe retreat. Everybody may leave in his due turn. Whoever stays will be arrested. [*Long silence*] Do you hear that clock ticking like the deathwatch hidden in a wall? Can you hear what it says?—"It's time! It's time!"— When it strikes in a few seconds, your time will be up, and then you can go, but not before. You may notice, too, that the clock shakes its fist at you before it strikes. Listen! There it is! "Better beware," it says.... And I can strike, too.... [*He raps the top of a table with one of his crutches*] Do you hear?

[*For a while everybody remains silent.*]

MUMMY. [*Goes up to the clock and stops it; then she speaks in a normal and dignified tone*] But I can stop time in its course. I can wipe out the past and undo what is done. Bribes won't do that, nor will threats—but suffering and repentance will.... [*She goes to* HUMMEL] We are miserable human creatures, and we know it. We have erred and we have sinned—we, like everybody else. We are not what we seem, but at bottom we are better than ourselves because we disapprove of our own misdeeds. And when you, Jacob Hummel, with your assumed name, propose to sit in judgment on us, you merely prove yourself worse than all the rest. You are not the one you seem to be— no more than we! You are a thief of human souls! You stole mine once upon a time by means of false promises. You killed the Consul, whom they buried this afternoon—strangling him with debts. You are now trying to steal the soul of the Student with the help of an imaginary claim against his father, who never owed you a farthing....

[*Having vainly tried to rise and say something,* HUMMEL *sinks back into his chair; as the* MUMMY *continues her speech he seems to shrink and lose volume more and* more.]

MUMMY. There is one dark spot in your life concerning which I am not certain, although

I have my suspicions.... I believe Bengtsson can throw light on it.

[*She rings the table-bell.*]

HUMMEL. No! Not Bengtsson! Not him!
MUMMY. So he *does* know? [*She rings again.*]

[*The* MILKMAID *appears in the hallway, but is only seen by* HUMMEL, *who shrinks back in horror. Then* BENGTSSON *enters, and the* MILKMAID *disappears.*]

MUMMY. Do you know this man, Bengtsson?
BENGTSSON. Oh yes, I know him, and he knows me. Life has its ups and downs, as you know. I have been in his service, and he has been in mine. For two years he came regularly to our kitchen to be fed by our cook. Because he had to be at work at a certain hour, she made the dinner far ahead of time, and we had to be satisfied with the warmed-up leavings of that beast. He drank the soup-stock, so that we got nothing but water. Like a vampire, he sucked the house of all nourishment, until we became reduced to mere skeletons—and he nearly got us into jail when we dared to call the cook a thief. Later I met that man in Hamburg, where he had another name. Then he was a money-lender, a regular leech. While there, he was accused of having lured a young girl out on the ice in order to drown her, because she had seen him commit a crime, and he was afraid of being exposed....
MUMMY. [*Making a pass with her hand over the face of* HUMMEL *as if removing a mask*] That's you! And now, give up the notes and the will!

[JOHANSSON *appears in the hallway and watches the scene with great interest, knowing that his slavery will now come to an end.*]
[HUMMEL *produces a bundle of papers and throws them on the table.*]

MUMMY. [*Stroking the back of* HUMMEL] Polly! Are you there, Jacob?
HUMMEL. [*Talking like a parrot*] Here is Jacob!—Pretty Polly! Currrr!
MUMMY. May the clock strike?
HUMMEL. [*With a clucking noise like that of a clock preparing to strike*] The clock may strike! [*Imitating a cuckoo-clock*] Cuckoo, cuckoo, cuckoo....
MUMMY. [*Opening the closet door*] Now the clock has struck! Rise and enter the closet where I have spent twenty years bewailing our evil deed. There you will find a rope that may represent the one with which you strangled the Consul as well as the one with which you meant to strangle your benefactor.... Go!

[HUMMEL *enters the closet.*]

MUMMY. [*Closes the door after him*] Put up the screen, Bengtsson.... The Death Screen!

[BENGTSSON *places the screen in front of the door.*]

MUMMY. It is finished! God have mercy on his soul!
ALL. Amen!

[*Long silence. Then the* YOUNG LADY *appears in the Hyacinth Room with the* STUDENT. *She seats herself at a harp and begins a prelude, which changes into an accompaniment to the following recitative*:]

STUDENT. [*Singing*]

"Seeing the sun, it seemed to my fancy
That I beheld the Spirit that's hidden.
Man must for ever reap what he planted:
Happy is he who has done no evil.
Wrong that was wrought in moments of anger
Never by added wrong can be righted.
Kindness shown to the man whose sorrow
Sprang from your deed, will serve you better.
Fear and guilt have their home together:
Happy indeed is the guiltless man!"

Curtain.

THIRD SCENE

A room furnished in rather bizarre fashion. The general effect of it is Oriental. Hyacinths of different colors are scattered everywhere. On the mantel-shelf of the fireplace is seen a huge, seated Buddha, in whose lap rests a bulb. From that bulb rues the stalk of a shallot (Allium Ascalonicum), spreading aloft its almost globular cluster of white, starlike flowers.
An open door in the rear wall, toward the right-hand side, leads to the Round Room, where the COLONEL *and the* MUMMY *are seated. They don't stir and don't utter a word. A part of the Death Screen is also visible.*
Another door, at the left, leads to the pantry and the kitchen.
The YOUNG LADY [*Adèle*] *and the* STUDENT *are discovered near a table. She is seated at her harp, and he stands beside her.*

YOUNG LADY. Sing to my flowers.
STUDENT. Is this the flower of your soul?
YOUNG LADY. The one and only.—Are you fond of the hyacinth?
STUDENT. I love it above all other flowers. I love its virginal shape rising straight and slender out of the bulb that rests on the water and sends its pure white rootlets down into the colorless fluid. I love the color of it, whether innocently white as snow or sweetly yellow as honey; whether youthfully pink or maturely red; but above all if blue—with the deep-eyed, faith-inspiring blue of the morning sky. I love these flowers, one and all; love them more than pearls or gold, and have loved them ever since I was a child. I have always admired them, too, because they possess every handsome quality that I lack…. And yet….
YOUNG LADY. What?
STUDENT. My love is unrequited. These beautiful blossoms hate me.
YOUNG LADY. How do you mean?
STUDENT. Their fragrance, powerful and pure as the winds of early spring, which have

passed over melting snow—it seems to confuse my senses, to make me deaf and blind, to crowd me out of the room, to bombard me with poisoned arrows that hurt my heart and set my head on fire. Do you know the legend of that flower?

YOUNG LADY. Tell me about it.

STUDENT. Let us first interpret its symbolism. The bulb is the earth, resting on the water or buried in the soil. From that the stalk rises, straight as the axis of the universe. At its upper end appear the six-pointed, starlike flowers.

YOUNG LADY. Above the earth—the stars! What lofty thought! Where did you find it? How did you discover it?

STUDENT. Let me think.... In your eyes!—It is, therefore, an image of the Cosmos. And that is the reason why Buddha is holding the earth-bulb in his lap, brooding on it with a steady gaze, in order that he may behold it spread outward and upward as it becomes transformed into a heaven.... This poor earth must turn into a heaven! That is what Buddha is waiting for!

YOUNG LADY. I see now.... Are not the snow crystals six-pointed, too, like the hyacinth-lily?

STUDENT. You are right! Thus the snow crystal is a falling star....

YOUNG LADY. And the snowdrop is a star of snow—grown out of the snow.

STUDENT. But the largest and most beautiful of all the stars in the firmament, the red and yellow Sirius, is the narcissus, with its yellow-and-red cup and its six white rays

YOUNG LADY. Have you seen the shallot bloom?

STUDENT. Indeed, I have! It hides its flowers within a ball, a globe resembling the celestial one, and strewn, like that, with white stars....

YOUNG LADY. What a tremendous thought! Whose was it?

STUDENT. Yours!

YOUNG LADY. No, yours!

STUDENT. Ours, then! We have jointly given birth to something: we are wedded....

YOUNG LADY. Not yet.

STUDENT. What more remains?

YOUNG LADY. To await the coming ordeal in patience!

STUDENT. I am ready for it. [*Pause*] Tell me! Why do your parents sit there so silently, without saying a single word?

YOUNG LADY. Because they have nothing to say to each other, and because neither one believes what the other says. This is the way my father puts it: "What is the use of talking, when you can't fool each other anyhow?"

STUDENT. That's horrible....

YOUNG LADY. Here comes the Cook.... Look! how big and fat she is!....

STUDENT. What does she want?

YOUNG LADY. Ask me about the dinner.... You see, I am looking after the house during my mother's illness.

STUDENT. Have we to bother about the kitchen, too?

YOUNG LADY. We must eat.... Look at that Cook.... I can't bear the sight of her....

STUDENT. What kind of a monster is she?

YOUNG LADY. She belongs to the Hummel family of vampires. She is eating us alive.

STUDENT. Why don't you discharge her?

YOUNG LADY. Because she won't leave. We can do nothing with her, and we have got her for the sake of our sins.... Don't you see that we are pining and wasting away?

STUDENT. Don't you get enough to eat?

YOUNG LADY. Plenty of dishes, but with all the nourishment gone from the food. She boils the life out of the beef, and drinks the stock herself, while we get nothing but fibres and water. In the same way, when we have roast, she squeezes it dry. Then she eats the gravy and drinks the juice herself. She takes the strength and savour out of everything she touches. It is as if her eyes were leeches. When she has had coffee, we get the grounds. She drinks the wine and puts water into the bottles....

STUDENT. Kick her out!

YOUNG LADY. We can't!

STUDENT. Why not?

YOUNG LADY. We don't know! But she won't leave! And nobody can do anything with her. She has taken all our strength away from us.

STUDENT. Will you let me dispose of her?

YOUNG LADY. No! It has to be as it is, I suppose.—Here she is now. She will ask me what I wish for dinner, and I tell her, and then she will make objections, and in the end she has her own way.

STUDENT. Why don't you leave it to her entirely?

YOUNG LADY. She won't let me.

STUDENT. What a strange house! It seems to be bewitched!

YOUNG LADY. It is!—Now she turned back on seeing you here.

COOK. [*Appearing suddenly in the doorway at that very moment*] Naw, that was not the reason.

[*She grins so that every tooth can be seen.*]

STUDENT. Get out of here!

COOK. When it suits me! [*Pause*] Now it does suit me!

[*She disappears.*]

YOUNG LADY. Don't lose your temper! You must practise patience. She is part of the ordeal we have to face in this house. We have a chambermaid, too, after whom we have to put everything back where it belongs.

STUDENT. Now I am sinking! *Cor in æthere!* Music!

YOUNG LADY. Wait!

STUDENT. Music!

YOUNG LADY. Patience!—This is named the Room of Ordeal.... It is beautiful to look at, but is full of imperfections....

STUDENT. Incredible! Yet such things have to be borne. It is very beautiful, although a little cold. Why don't you have a fire?

YOUNG LADY. Because the smoke comes into the room.

STUDENT. Have the chimney swept!

YOUNG LADY. It doesn't help.—Do you see that writing-table?

STUDENT. Remarkably handsome!

YOUNG LADY. But one leg is too short. Every day I put a piece of cork under that leg. Every day the chambermaid takes it away when she sweeps the room. Every day I have to cut a new piece. Both my penholder and my inkstand are covered with ink every morning, and I have to clean them after that woman—as sure as the sun rises. [*Pause*] What is the worst thing you can think of?

STUDENT. To count the wash. Ugh!

YOUNG LADY. That's what I have to do. Ugh!

STUDENT. Anything else?

YOUNG LADY. To be waked out of your sleep and have to get up and close the window—which the chambermaid has left unlatched.

STUDENT. Anything else?

YOUNG LADY. To get up on a ladder and tie on the cord which the chambermaid has torn from the window-shade.

STUDENT. Anything else?

YOUNG LADY. To sweep after her; to dust after her; to start the fire again, after she has merely thrown some wood into the fireplace! To watch the damper in the fireplace; to wipe every glass; to set the table over again; to open the wine-bottles; to see that the rooms are aired; to make over your bed; to rinse the water-bottle that is green with sediment; to buy matches and soap, which are always lacking; to wipe the chimneys and cut the wicks in order to keep the lamps from smoking.... and in order to keep them from going out when we have company, I have to fill them myself....

STUDENT. Music!

YOUNG LADY. Wait! The labour comes first—the labour of keeping the filth of life at a distance.

STUDENT. But you are wealthy, and you have two servants?

YOUNG LADY. What does that help? What would it help to have three? It is troublesome to live, and at times I get tired.... Think, then, of adding a nursery!

STUDENT. The greatest of joys....

YOUNG LADY. And the costliest.... Is life really worth so much trouble?

STUDENT. It depends on the reward you expect for your labours.... To win your hand I would face anything.

YOUNG LADY. Don't talk like that. You can never get me.

STUDENT. Why?

YOUNG LADY. You mustn't ask. [*Pause.*]

STUDENT. You dropped your bracelet out of the window....

YOUNG LADY. Yes, because my hand has grown too small.... [*Pause.*]

[*The* COOK *appears with a bottle of Japanese soy in her hand.*]

YOUNG LADY. There is the one that eats me and all the rest alive.

STUDENT. What has she in her hand?

COOK. This is my coloring bottle that has letters on it looking like scorpions. It's the soy that turns water into bouillon, and that takes the place of gravy. You can make cabbage soup out of it, or mock-turtle soup, if you prefer.

STUDENT. Out with you!

COOK. You take the sap out of us, and we out of you. We keep the blood for ourselves and leave you the water—with the coloring. It's the color that counts! Now I shall leave, but I stay just the same—as long as I please!

[*She goes out.*]

STUDENT. Why has Bengtsson got a medal?

YOUNG LADY. On account of his great merits.

STUDENT. Has he no faults?

YOUNG LADY. Yes, great ones, but faults bring you no medals, you know. [*Both smile.*]

STUDENT. You have a lot of secrets in this house....

YOUNG LADY. As in all houses.... Permit us to keep ours! [*Pause.*]

STUDENT. Do you care for frankness?

YOUNG LADY. Within reason.

STUDENT. At times I am seized with a passionate craving to say all I think.... Yet I know that the world would go to pieces if perfect frankness were the rule. [*Pause*] I attended a funeral the other day—in one of the churches—and it was very solemn and beautiful.

YOUNG LADY. That of Mr. Hummel?

STUDENT. Yes, that of my pretended benefactor. An elderly friend of the deceased acted as mace-bearer and stood at the head of the coffin. I was particularly impressed by the dignified manner and moving words of the minister. I had to cry—everybody cried.... A number of us went to a restaurant afterward, and there I learned that the man with the mace had been rather too friendly with the dead man's son....

[*The* YOUNG LADY *stares at him, trying to make out the meaning of his words.*]

STUDENT. I learned, too, that the dead man had borrowed money of his son's devoted friend.... [*Pause*] And the next day the minister was arrested for embezzling the church funds.—Nice, isn't it?

YOUNG LADY. Oh! [*Pause.*]

STUDENT. Do you know what I am thinking of you now?

YOUNG LADY. Don't tell, or I'll die!

STUDENT. I must, lest *I* die!

YOUNG LADY. It is only in the asylum you say all that you think....

STUDENT. Exactly! My father died in a madhouse....

YOUNG LADY. Was he sick?

STUDENT. No, perfectly well, and yet mad. It broke out at last, and these were the circumstances. Like all of us, he was surrounded by a circle of acquaintances whom he called friends for the sake of convenience, and they were a lot of scoundrels, of course, as most people are. He had to have some society, however, as he couldn't sit all alone. As you know, no one tells people what he thinks of them under ordinary circumstances, and my father didn't do so either. He knew that they were false, and he knew the full extent of their perfidy, but, being a wise man and well brought up, he remained always polite. One day he gave a big party.... It was in the evening, naturally, and he was tired out by a hard day's work. Then the strain of keeping his thoughts to himself while talking a lot of damned rot to his guests.... [*The* YOUNG LADY *is visibly shocked*] Well, while they were still at the table, he rapped for silence, raised his glass, and began to speak.... Then something loosed the trigger, and in a long speech he stripped the whole company naked, one by one, telling them all he knew about their treacheries. At last, when utterly tired out, he sat down on the table itself and told them all to go to hell!

YOUNG LADY. Oh!

STUDENT. I was present, and I shall never forget what happened after that. My parents had a fight, the guests rushed for the doors—and my father was taken to a madhouse, where he died! [*Pause*] To keep silent too long is like letting water stagnate so that it rots. That is what has happened in this house. There is something rotten here. And yet I thought it paradise itself when I saw you enter here the first time.... It was a Sunday morning, and I stood gazing into these rooms. Here I saw a Colonel who was no colonel. I had a generous benefactor who was a robber and had to hang himself. I saw a Mummy who was not a mummy, and a maiden—how about the maidenhood, by the by?.... Where is beauty to be found? In nature, and in my own mind when it has donned its Sunday clothes. Where do we find honor and faith? In fairy-tales and childish fancies. Where can I find anything that keeps its promise? Only in my own imagination!.... Your flowers have poisoned me and now I am squirting their poison back at you.... I asked you to become my wife in a home full of poetry, and song, and music; and then the Cook appeared.... *Sursum corda!* Try once more to strike fire and purple out of the golden harp.... Try, I ask you, I implore you on my knees.... [*As she does not move*] Then I must do it myself! [*He picks up the harp, but is unable to make its strings sound*] It has grown deaf and dumb! Only think, that the most beautiful flower of all can be so poisonous—that it can be more poisonous than any other one.... There must be a curse on all creation and on life itself.... Why did you not want to become my bride? Because the very well-spring of life within you has been sickened.... Now I can feel how that vampire in the kitchen is sucking my life juices.... She must be a Lamia, one of those that suck the blood of children. It is always in the servants' quarters that the seed-leaves of the children are nipped, if it has not already happened in the bedroom.... There are poisons that blind you, and others that open your eyes more widely. I must have been born with that second kind of poison, I fear, for I cannot regard what is ugly as beautiful, or call evil good—I cannot! They say that Jesus Christ descended into hell. It refers merely to his wanderings on this earth—his descent into that madhouse, that jail, that morgue, the earth. The madmen killed him when he wished to liberate them, but the robber was set free. It is always the robber who gets sympathy! Woe! Woe is all of us! Saviour of the World, save us—we are perishing!

[*Toward the end of the* STUDENT'S *speech, the* YOUNG LADY *has drooped more and more. She seems to be dying. At last she manages to reach a bell and rings for* BENGTSSON, *who enters shortly afterward.*]

YOUNG LADY. Bring the screen! Quick! I am dying! [BENGTSSON *fetches the screen, opens it and places it so that the* YOUNG LADY *is completely hidden behind it.*]

STUDENT. The liberator is approaching! Be welcome, thou pale and gentle one!—Sleep, you beauteous, unhappy and innocent creature, who have done nothing to deserve your own sufferings! Sleep without dreaming, and when you wake again—may you be greeted by a sun that does not burn, by a home without dust, by friends without stain, by a love without flaw!.... Thou wise and gentle Buddha, who sitst waiting there to see a heaven sprout from this earth, endow us with patience in the hour of trial, and with purity of will, so that thy hope be not put to shame!

[*The strings of the harp begin to hum softly, and a white light pours into the room.*]

STUDENT. [*Singing*]

> "Seeing the sun, it seemed to my fancy
> That I beheld the Spirit that's hidden.
> Man must for ever reap what he planted:
> Happy is he who has done no evil.
> Wrong that was wrought in moments of anger
> Never by added wrong can be righted.
> Kindness shown to the man whose sorrow
> Sprang from your deed, will serve you better.
> Fear and guilt have their home together:
> Happy indeed is the guiltless man!" [1]

[1] The lines recited by the *Student* are a paraphrase of several passages from "The Song of the Sun" in the Poetic Edda. It is characteristic of Strindberg's attitude during his final period that this Eddic poem, which apparently has occupied his mind a great deal, as he has used it a number of times in "The Bridal Crown" also, is the only one of that ancient collection which is unmistakably Christian in its colouring. It has a certain apocryphal reputation and is not regarded on a par with the other contents of the Poetic Edda.

[A faint moaning sound is heard from behind the screen.]

STUDENT. You poor little child—you child of a world of illusion, guilt, suffering, and death—a world of eternal change, disappointment, and pain—may the Lord of Heaven deal mercifully with you on your journey!

[The whole room disappears, and in its place appears Boecklin's "The Island of Death." Soft music, very quiet and pleasantly wistful, is heard from without.]

Curtain.

THE END

CPSIA information can be obtained at www.ICGtesting.com
Printed in the USA
LVOW082219190112

264584LV00004B/10/P